Praise for *Rescued by My Breath*

This is an amazing, powerful, and well-written book about a subject that I never knew existed, but that captivated me from the get-go. I learned things about breathing that I will incorporate in my own life – and that will stick with me for the rest of it. The writing is completely honest and touching, especially in the portions of the manuscript that relate to childhood abuse and challenging family dynamics.
  - Bill Worth is an editor, a writer of fiction and non-fiction, and a retired Unity minister.

This book is a touching, honest and deeply personal labor of love. Natazha, through her moving letters, bares her soul and shares her experiences, insight and - in a rather unique way – integrates wisdom across vastly different philosophical, cultural, scientific and religious traditions to share with us her own path to reintegrating herself. By sharing her own path to emotional and spiritual health she provides both an inspiration and suggests a path to healing for all of us who still have emotional wounds to heal: explore, look inside, find people worthy of your trust to share your pain with and - don't forget to breathe!
  - Igor Mitrovic, MD, Professor of Physiology, UCSF

No stranger to dysfunctional relationship (especially with my mother), books and therapy typically left me with more shame and people pleasing. In *Rescued by my Breath*, Dr. O'Connor invites us to stop poisoning ourselves with stress, unhealthy habits, and lack of boundaries with her Lifestyle Medicine practices. Medicating with our breath, we are courageous enough to trust ourselves and have fulfilling and meaningful

lives. This unique book inspires wisdom and support to forgive —
regardless of the relationship outcome.
- Dusty Meehan, CEO of Choice Digital Marketing Agency

Dr. Natazha Raine O'Connor offers us a heartfelt and intimate
tale of healing and integration in coming home to her whole self.
She writes her life story with much honesty, courage and many
interwoven insights of the importance of our breath for health,
living fully and relating. Her dedication to her personal growth
will be an inspiration to many on the path of healing.
- Mireya A. Marcet, MFT Expressive Arts Therapist and
Holotropic Breathwork Facilitator

Rescued by My Breath

By Dr. Natazha Raine O'Connor

ISBN Publisher: Sojourn Publishing, LLC
Paperback ISBN: 978-1-62747-168-8
Ebook ISBN: 978-1-62747-154-1

This book is dedicated to my Mom, who taught me to never take my breath for granted.

May we bless the distance within and between us with each exhale we take.
May we deepen our connection and affection for Source with each inhale we take.
May we be at one with ourselves with each breath we take.
May we never take our breath for granted.
May we breathe with joy and ease for the rest of our lives.

Table of Contents

Introduction

I'm incredibly grateful I grew back my exuberant belly laugh that gets everyone else in the room laughing too. That breath-based expression of sheer joy demonstrates I released my Irish brand of shame carried down for eons from one generation to the next. I now feel safe to openly love myself and shine brightly, thanks to everyone who inspired me to breathe through my pain instead of hold onto it. Taught me to hold myself together with my breath instead of hold my breath. No one, including me, could ever see that invisible shift in my respiration, but I absolutely see how it dramatically changed the trajectory of my life. Transported me from hell to heaven on the inside. Allowed me to live happily ever after with my Prince Charming, my husband Bob.

My Mom's recent death allowed me to finally bond with her and achieve the miraculous. Ironically we truly began breathing together after she stopped breathing. My mom struggled to breathe due to allergies, asthma, emphysema, lung cancer, but most of all shame. On many levels she didn't feel worthy of breathing, and I inherited her intense shame. Her respiratory struggles were both a curse and blessing. Taught me never to take my breath for granted. Made me receptive to breath-based solutions and inspired me to write a book on breathing. I failed miserably the first time I attempted to write this book in 2003; but this time, with my Mom's spiritual assistance, I succeeded. Better yet, something monumental shifted inside of me: I faced and released the seemingly insurmountable shame that has haunted my ancestors and family.

Growing up in an Irish clan on Long Island, and marrying into one in San Francisco, I have no idea why Irish Americans ever say, "Have you no shame?" To me, the Irish are burdened with excessive shame. Our culture is insidiously polluted by a sense of disgrace and self-deprecation that resembles an Eckhart Tolle cultural pain body brewed to sinister perfection during 700 years of oppression and occupation of Ireland. Please don't get me wrong: I'm not saying the

Irish have a monopoly on shame. Just as most cultures have their own style of beer, they also have their own style of shame. However, the Irish are known for drinking more than their fair share of Guinness. I'm familiar with the Irish version of disgrace and self-doubt, but suspect what I say about the relationship between breathing, shame, and boundaries holds true across most cultures.

The Irish gained their independence nearly a century ago, and my family lived by the Irish clan mentality that astonishingly saved Irish civilization. Writing this book, I became painfully aware of the menacing side of that mentality; it fosters a debilitating shame that kept my family enslaved in a poverty mindset. My own version of it ransacked my joy, sanity, sexuality, and boundaries. The Irish saved their society by adopting enmeshment and self-sacrifice as their basic bylaws. Those tenets spawn shame by inhibiting you from setting healthy boundaries, and that's a setup for shame. One must think and feel as an individual to keep out the negative, including shame, and hold in the positive, including healthy self-esteem.

Akin to a family mob mentality, enmeshment became my emotional and mental operating system. It trained me to think and feel with my family's head and heart instead of my own head and heart. Without my own unique thoughts and feelings to inform my boundaries, I became hopelessly entangled with my siblings and unable to distinguish my own feelings from others inside and outside of my home. That made me incredibly vulnerable to the whims and fancies of others.

Enmeshment reinforced childhood messages to live as a sacrificial lamb. My sole purpose was to support the group: breathe for the group instead of with the group. It's downright selfish to refuse to take a hit for the team and act on my own behalf. I was expendable; at any point I could be sacrificed for the sake of the group, to the Church or any other worthy cause. The Irish lifestyle was harsh; one child often stayed home to take care of utterly worn-out parents even before they reached old age. Irish Catholic families also sacrificed children to the Church. Their oldest sons became priests and a daughter or two entered the convent. The Church sacrifice somehow morphed into the evil sacrifice of sons and daughters to pedophiles in the Church. Thank

God, Catholics all over the world are putting an end to this wicked abomination of their religion.

Being the fifth child of an Irish Catholic family of 12 kids, growing up I yearned for some breathing space. Felt suffocated by the lack of room and permission to breathe at my own pace. Was raised in poverty by mentally ill parents. At four years old, my Mom was institutionalized for a little over a year. Growing up, I experienced my Dad suffering from depression on and off, and several bouts of catatonic depression after I left home. We lived on his humble, high school teacher salary. Not once, not twice, but at least three times, the IRS audited my parents; it just couldn't believe a family our size could live on my Dad's salary. They were convinced my parents were cheating on their taxes because folks on welfare would have received more money than us.

When I was born in July 1962, my parents moved into our Long Island home. I survived my childhood physically intact, but was emotionally and psychologically crippled. I lacked boundaries, as I had learned to hold my breath instead of hold my space. Nonetheless, I earned a full scholarship to Grinnell College, a prestigious liberal arts college and graduated with honors. In 1984 I moved to San Francisco with my college sweetheart, Bill. Back then, on paper I was sound and fit as a fiddle, but in reality was anything but sound and fit. I smoked 2 to 3 packs of cigarettes a day, a habit I began at age 11. Was well on my way to having Chronic Obstructive Pulmonary Disease (COPD) and lung cancer, just like my Mom.

I had survived my childhood traumas and poverty by splitting into Bunny and Bernadette personalities. Bunny rebelled against the clan mentality, whereas Bernadette wholeheartedly embraced it. A bitter civil war raged within me, ruining any chance of an intimate relationship or satisfying career. Bunny hated my "Bernadette" boyfriends and vice versa. Bunny chose bad boys whereas Bernadette preferred pillars of society. Lacking boundaries, I couldn't even imagine being fully present and intimate in any relationship, so I simultaneously dated "Bunny" and "Bernadette" boyfriends. All the while hated myself for lying, cheating and engaging in unsafe, promiscuous sex at the height of the AIDS and herpes epidemic. The same conflict poisoned my career and sentenced me to a life of poverty. Bunny aspired to be an actress whereas Bernadette saw herself saving the world as a public servant. Each sub-personality sabotaged the career pursuits of the other. I was diagnosed with Dissociative Identity Disorder, DID, along with depression, anxiety, and a host of debilitating phobias of rats, parking meters, enclosed parking lots, driving, and traveling alone. Breath holding sounds like a fairly benign bad habit, but in my case I held my breath with such a sinister consistency that it fueled my mental illness. Kept me insanely dissociated from my feelings.

The ugly legacy of sacrificing kids to pedophiles in the church played out in my own family. Given I was so enmeshed with my siblings, having any of them sexually abused by members of the Church left me feeling sexually assaulted, too. And, once again reinforced the message that my siblings and me were unworthy, expendable beings here to be sacrificed for the needs of others. In 1988, I openly attacked both my parents for not defending their kids from pedophiles in the church on an audiotape I titled my "Declaration Of Independence." By that point I had lived in San Francisco for four years, and had quit smoking for more than a year. I stood up for myself by lashing out against our dysfunctional family system. My mom and siblings ostracized me for trying to reform our family. Only my Dad contacted me during the five, long years that I waged my Cold War against my Mom. He provided the loving bridge back to my family in 1993. In this book, I detail the account of my breath-based reconciliation with my Mom, healing my mental illness through meditation instead of medication, and setting healthy breath-based boundaries.

Moving to my breath-based sanctuary – San Francisco in 1984 – literally saved my life, truly the most perfect place in the whole wide world to heal my emotional and psychological traumas through the often-overlooked art of breathing: meditation, aerobic exercise (running, hiking, biking, open-water swimming, rowing, snow-boarding), talk-out-your-feelings psychotherapy, Holotropic Breath Work, singing, expressive art therapy, and a tolerant social climate that gave me the breathing room I desperately needed. It was ground zero for second-hand-smoke laws that helped me stop smoking. And, my husband Bob and his clan call San Francisco their home. Bob and his relatives always have my back, enabling me to breathe more easily.

Even after years of breath-based recovery, my internalized Irish Clan mentality still wreaked havoc on my marriage. I felt an inconsolable sorrow around not having kids. Bob lives for his family. Truly means it when he says, "If you're happy, I'm happy. If you're unhappy, I'm unhappy." My heartbreak made him feel like a failure. Bob met me as a content yoga and Pilates instructor who became depressed when we learned we couldn't have kids. He began wondering if I married him only to have kids. I began wondering if he told me he wanted kids to trick me into marrying him. Unbeknownst to me at the time, my bottomless grief was linked to feeling defective for not contributing my quota of kids to the Irish cause. John Bradshaw, a pioneer in healing shame, taught if a feeling is overwhelming, then you're probably carrying someone else's feeling. On top of my own feelings, I'd been carrying an outdated Irish clan perspective about our infertility. That insight freed me to shake off "all" my grief and laugh freely again.

Writing this book helped me examine very closely another detail of our infertility odyssey. We hired Brad, a fertility specialist from New Zealand. After examining me, Brad said, "I'm not finding anything wrong with you, Natazha. But, I sense something incredibly subtle is off and it's having profound effects, even on your fertility." A decade later I'm now convinced Brad was referring to my lack of boundaries that can make any relationship, especially parenting and marriage, an absolute nightmare.

I attempted many times to set healthy boundaries all throughout my recovery, but was unsuccessful. A huge blow-up with a dishonest life coach finally got me to read *Boundaries* by Dr. Henry Cloud and Dr. John Townsend on December 16, 2016. And, listen to an audio recording of that book every day for the last two weeks of December 2016. My Mom's spirit guided me to pick up that book at her home on April 23, 2016, but I never read it until last December. Reading it transformed my life, and I gave myself the gift of healthy boundaries for Christmas 2016. Bob and other loved ones almost immediately noticed me beaming with joy even though they had no idea I had changed my invisible, very subtle, yet extremely profound boundaries.

Turns out I never had a problem setting boundaries, but rather a problem with shame and holding my breath to avoid feeling my shame-based emotions. All along, I could easily set boundaries on behalf of others. But I felt incredibly unworthy to set boundaries on my own behalf. Last summer, I released an ocean of shame with long purposeful exhales as I struggled to write this book. That's what finally empowered me to set boundaries on my own behalf. Makes sense that my breathing rescued me from my shame; Brené Brown, an expert on shame, speaks about the importance of minding your breathing in her book, *Rising Strong.*

Last summer, writing this book, I suffered from paralyzing emotional pain. Shame clobbered me each and every time I sat down to write. Who was I to abandon the clan and unleash my unique point of view on paper for the world to read? Who was I to feel worthy of publishing a book? I also struggled with these questions: *When is self-sacrifice a thinly disguised form of shame corrupting my soul with an indelible sense of unworthiness, and when is it an all-encompassing self-love that extends beyond myself to everyone and thing in the universe to a cause worth dying for? How do I know when I'm sacrificing myself for the group out of self-love versus self-loathing?*

Instead of writing my book, I spent the summer writing letters to my mom asking for her guidance. And, more often than not, I just sat and prayed to her through my breath, and sobbed as shame seeped out of my soul. Exhaled from my psyche questions to my Mom. Received her wisdom by inhaling deeply into my heart and gut. Most of the time, I never received an answer in words, but rather a sweet, serene being state that taught me to mind my breath; check my gut, heart, and brain each and every time I wanted to sacrifice myself for the group. Sometimes I'll act out of hate. Sometimes I'll act out of love. Only listening to my breath will reveal the difference.

I eventually wrote letters to my Mom clarifying my perspectives on the virtues and mechanics of breathing. Then the day came when I needed to hand in pages of my book to my writing group.

Had nothing but my letters to my Mom, so I handed in some letters. And was pleasantly surprised when my fellow writers enjoyed my letter format. That's when I decided to format my book as letters to my Mom. Reading these letters in order reveals the story about my breath-based reconciliation with my Mom. You're also invited to choose letters that pique your interest and read them in a random order.

Looking back over my life, I now realize I could have spared my loved ones and myself an inordinate amount of suffering had I learned to set boundaries sooner. Boundaries require the courage to breathe through my agony. Hold myself together by breathing instead of hold my breath to numb my pain. All my problems stemmed from or at the very least were aggravated by my lack of boundaries. I now see my dissociative identity disorder, addictions, severe breath holding, and my 3,000-mile move away from my family as poor substitutes for boundaries that I discuss in my book.

Before sending you off to read my book, I need to introduce the cast of characters I call my family. My husband Bob is a California version of Simon Cowell; straightforward and brutally honest, softened by his authentic compassion and sweet, irresistible scent. Bob always saw my light and love even when it was buried under many, many layers of shame, hurt, and doubt. His unconditional love washed away much of my emotional crud so the rest of the world could see my light and love. He grew up in a family of seven children, five boys and two girls, along with countless aunts, uncles, cousins, and family friends bestowed with the title of relatives. His family helped me update my version of Irish Clan mentality and Catholicism that includes healthy, breath-based boundaries and a deep appreciation for my Irish heritage. On top of Bob's honesty, his loving kindness restored my trust, boundaries, and faith in myself. And most importantly, our marriage enabled me to reconcile with my Mom.

Complicated doesn't even begin to describe my relationship with my Mom. It's a messy tale of us crucifying each other emotionally and psychologically, and then, seamlessly resurrecting each other despite 3,000 miles and death separating us. We mediated our miraculous reconciliation and victory over shame through many breath-based activities including: long-distance phone calls, meditation, praying together, singing lullabies, reading out loud the writings of two great Catholic mystics, John O'Donohue and Thomas Merton, plain old quietly breathing together, and me learning to "Breathe Write (Right) Now" as I wrote this book.

To me, my Mom is a mega-mom. Named for the Blessed Mother of Jesus, she gave birth to 12 kids from 1956 to 1975. She took a break from birthing babies only in 1966 when she was institutionalized after having eight kids in less than 10 years. She also mothered thousands of other children and downtrodden folks through her social-work career. My Dad, Raymond Francis Connors, taught high school in Bushwick, New York. He was a poet at heart who taught literature and reading in a socioeconomically devastated, crime-ridden neighborhood. Someday I hope to write a book in his honor. I often still wonder how my mystic mom and poet Dad managed to raise 11 kids, all of whom graduated from college.

Growing up, my siblings both saved and walloped my ass. As a child, I was enmeshed with them. Now I feel somewhat estranged from them. In 1984, the only way I could set a boundary was to move 3,000 miles away from them. That move came at the dear price of losing close proximity and connection to my siblings. Now I'm developing ways to visit them more regularly on top of all my texts and phone calls.

I invite you to read my book with the intent of transforming your relationship to your breath. Please look out for respiratory recipes to soothe and fortify yourself in times of trouble or need. May you be inspired to rescue yourself by exhaling fully instead of relying on your favorite vices.

Section One

Blessing The Space Within And Between Us

Mystical Assistance with Book Writing   March 2016

I felt heart-broken and disillusioned when in 2003 we learned we couldn't have kids. I became depressed and withdrew from my husband, Bob. For years, I had wanted to write a book on breathing, so I tried forgetting my sorrows by writing a book. That resulted in even more disappointment and heartache. Not having kids and not finishing my book were the two biggest failures in my life, one right after another, and I'm not used to failing.

I scurried back to school, a safety zone where I excelled. I earned my doctorate in Physical Therapy from University of California, San Francisco and San Francisco State University in 2011. But after graduating, I didn't feel complete. Something was still missing. Deep down inside I always felt destined to write a book on breathing that would help many people. And, the few times I received an astrology reading, my chart indicated I was a gifted writer. Plus, most of my boyfriends had asked, "Why don't you write a book? You're always writing in a journal." Some boyfriends were downright jealous of my journals. They resented me confiding much more in my journals than to them. Bob was the first guy I trusted enough to freely share my dark secrets. I began our marriage wedded to my morning pages, but eventually replaced them with our morning cuddle and bedtime chats.

Although I've always thrived on writing letters to loved ones and journal writing, book writing was a totally different story. It shoved me against my deep sense of unworthiness, my shame that goes way back to my Irish lineage. I never felt worthy of being published. I continually tortured myself with the notion that only "real" writers, unlike myself, get their books published. When my Mom's spirit blessed me with the courage to overcome my fears and shame, I finally persisted and fulfilled my promise to write and publish this book.

Dear Mom,

I so appreciate your support as I write ~~my~~, no, our book, *Rescued by My Breath.* Mystics like you work wonders through the world of spirit. And, I definitely feel uplifted by your spiritual assistance as I write a book this time. You know I failed miserably at writing a breathing book 13 years ago. I felt totally overwhelmed and depressed during the entire process. Writing book proposals. Looking for a literary agent. I felt utterly unsupported every step of the way. I just couldn't find the help I desperately needed, and actually ran into lots of competition and discouragement.

This time around is completely different. I believe your mysterious mystic magic is making all the difference. One breath at a time, I sense your presence. I ask for your help by exhaling, and receive your loving assistance by inhaling. When the going gets tough, I'm still inspired to write. I sense you orchestrating events to help me get back on the horse and this time finish our breathing book.

From your deathbed on Long Island at eighty-three years, riddled with bone cancer secondary to your lung cancer and only 30% lung capacity, you let me know in no uncertain terms that you wanted me to publish all I learned about breathing. And, share my hard-earned wisdom on how shame also robs us of the capacity to breathe easily. I feel like you really want to collaborate with me and hear what I have to say about breathing. This time around you've given me permission to include spiritual wisdom and not limit myself to just the fitness or medical aspects of breathing.

Mom, my decision to write started last November. I'll never forget Friday, November 13, 2015; the Friday the thirteenth that I learned your lung cancer had metastasized to stage four bone cancer and the horrific terrorist bombings in Paris. I sat outside the South San Francisco Hilton hotel along the San Francisco Bay on a park bench during a continuing education course lunch break. The wind blew my papers out of my hands; I ran across the sidewalk to retrieve them when my cell phone rang.

TC (my sister) had called me. The minute I heard her voice, I knew something was wrong. My neck, chest, and stomach muscles tightened up. The news took my breath away. TC reported your doctors couldn't believe you walked into their office without any assistance, and were absolutely dumbfounded you still worked. They immediately ordered you into a wheelchair. They explained you could no longer drive, walk up stairs, or work. I, too, had wondered how the hell you had worked for the last five years with only 30% lung capacity, let alone your crippling back pain.

I spent the rest of my lunch break crying. I just knew you wouldn't beat cancer for the third time. I immediately regretted not spending more time with you; I could have taught you more yoga poses and breathing practices to manage your respiratory issues. I wished I had walked with you more often and encouraged you to exercise more, another way to encourage healthy breathing habits.

The rest of last fall, I wrestled with my conflicting feelings about you: my deep fear and mistrust of you versus my deep grief and remorse for wasting opportunities to spend more time with you. On top of boosting my meditation practices and therapy, I used journal writing to process all my intense feelings. I sat in my favorite San Francisco café, Delancey Street's Crossroads café, on Christmas Eve wondering what to give myself for Christmas. I wrote in my journal, "Start writing again." And, realized I still wanted to write a book about breathing in your honor, but feared I'd fail again.

Twenty-four hours later on Christmas day, Kiki (my sister) and her family visited us. Kiki knew I had repeatedly asked you for a Virgin Mary statue from your enormous collection. I was very hurt when you said, "No." When Kiki delivered your Christmas gift she said, "Mom didn't give you a Virgin Mary Statue. Instead, she gave you a green journal with the word, WRITE, on its cover. It's a mandate from Mom for you to start writing again." A reassuring heat radiated from my heart to my belly when she said those words. I wondered, *How the hell did Mom know to send me a journal?* I silently thanked you for the perfect confirmation for me to resume writing my book on breathing. This time I'd succeed.

The last week of January, after weeks of preparation, I mustered up the courage to visit you on your deathbed. Going home to Long Island without Bob is always tough. Without him, I fear I'll regress to my wounded inner child or be re-traumatized by visiting our family home. To my surprise, I felt great providing you comfort; we genuinely connected and enjoyed each other's company. When I left on January 31st, I believed you'd live for another four-to-six months. I'd see you at least one more time at Easter. I was wrong. You took a turn for the worse on Valentine's Day: your prognosis changed from a few months to live to just a few weeks. On Thursday, February 18, I sat in my friend Lisa's kitchen talking over our homework from Brené Brown's Living Brave Semester online course on healing shame. I answered the question "What do you want to do with your life?" with "I want to write a book about breathing."

Lisa said, "That's funny. Reverend David McArthur of the Walnut Creek Unity Center just announced on Sunday that he's going to host a 'Tom Bird Write Your Book in One Weekend' Retreat from March 3 to March 6."

I hemmed and hawed, as I didn't know when you'd die. All I knew was you could die at any moment or weeks from now, so I was reluctant to sign up for a retreat. Lisa persuaded me to take Tom Bird's webinar that night to learn more about it. At that webinar, I learned Tom Bird offers a spiritual approach to writing; he encourages authors to write as fast as possible to connect with their divine author within. I also learned that I'd receive a significant discount if I signed up that night with the Walnut Creek Unity Center and could always postpone taking the retreat at that discounted rate. So, I registered for the retreat expecting you to die **after** March 6. Once again, I was wrong. You died on Thursday, February 25, perfect timing for me to attend your funeral on February 29 in New York and Tom Bird's writing retreat starting on March 3 in California.

I flew to your funeral with a renewed commitment to write my book. You boosted my commitment with what I now consider some mystic magic. When I walked through the door of Raynor's Funeral Parlor for your wake on Saturday evening, February 27, 2016, you sent a clear message from your grave: WRITE THE BREATHING BOOK. Bob and I were running late after we encountered problems with our rental car at JFK airport. We sheepishly walked into the funeral parlor trying not to make a disturbance. Gabrielle (my sister) surprised us by rushing up to greet us and handed me a large manila envelope addressed to my Mom that was postmarked January 10, 2007, nearly a decade ago.

Inside the envelope were pages from my *Hail the Exhale* book proposal and a note, *"Dear Mom, Rather than wait until I get published, I'm sharing my writing about breathing __NOW__. Each one of these pages represents a breathing lesson. I hope you get some good ideas about how to build an intimate relationship with your breath. Love, Natazha.*"

From the other side of the veil, you, my mystic mom, had managed to send yet another clear mandate for me to write a book on breathing. I thanked Gabrielle and sat down next to Bob. I asked him to hold me tight as I sobbed uncontrollably. In that moment, I felt horrible for accusing you of being a hoarder. At that moment I finally realized you never deserved that harsh label. Having 12 kids required saving lots of memorabilia and papers from your kids.

I thought. *Holy shit! How the hell did she keep track of all our correspondence? She purposely saved what I considered crap cluttering her home.* I felt flabbergasted that from your deathbed you had somehow retrieved that decade-old envelope, and more amazingly, got it delivered it to me. Once again, I heard your message loud and clear: **WRITE THE BOOK. THIS TIME YOU'LL SUCCEED.**

On Tuesday, March 1, I left Long Island grief-stricken. On the plane ride home instead of finishing the Tom Bird pre-retreat writing exercises, I meditated between bouts of crying. And, I also felt incredibly grateful for your encouraging mystic messages to write my book; the timing of your death allowed me to attend Tom Bird's writing retreat.

I showed up for the retreat shivering from grief and the wet, cold, dreary weather. Rev. David and Lisa warmed me up with openhearted welcomes. Tom Bird began the retreat, "What spirit is going to help you write this book?" I immediately started crying. I never expected him to ask that question. Of course, I thought of you and how much I missed you. I also realized you were sending yet another message with your special brand of mysticism: "You'll succeed this time. I'll help you write the book this time." That realization enabled me to dive into writing despite frequently blowing my nose and wiping away my tears.

Mom, I still regret not publishing my book while you were alive. Now after hearing Johnny's (my oldest brother) funeral speech, I believe you'd have been so proud of me, and happy for me. Growing up, I believed you were a jealous bitch. Johnny's speech at your wake jolted me. I realized the terrible price I paid for misinterpreting your shame as jealousy. You loved me so much more than I ever realized. It's late, time for me to go to bed. One last thing though, hell or high water, this time I vow to write and publish this book, even if the going gets tough and super painful as it did the last time I attempted to write this book.

Love,
Natazha

Love after Death   November 2016

Death became the boundary that finally allowed me to feel safe to love my Mom. I'm heartbroken something as innocuous as setting healthy boundaries could have spared us so much pain and anguish. Breathing through my pain instead of holding my breath to avoid my pain continues to transform my relationship with my Mom. One heartfelt breath at a time, I'm bonding with her.

Dear Mom,

You loved me so much more than I ever imagined. I'm ashamed of rejecting you. I never felt safe until you died to fully open up and receive your love.

Your death rocked my world. Living in San Francisco, we worry about "the next big one." Your death registered as a humongous earthquake in my psyche, too big to measure on the Richter scale. Many months later, I'm still feeling intense aftershocks, especially as I learn more about your undying love for me.

Now I realize what actually caused our five-year Cold War. I see much more clearly my part in our bitter feud. Last summer, I was devastated when I found out you told the other kids that I blamed you for the Uncle Mickey incident. How did you ever love me after feeling falsely accused of such a horrible act? Mom, where'd you get the super-hero forgiveness to love me after that?

I'm sorry I was just too scared to receive your love while you were alive. My deep wounds caused by the Uncle Mickey incident blocked me from expressing all my love for you. I loved you from afar except for those special occasions when I mustered up the courage to visit you in New York. I so miss our phone calls. And, still pick up the phone to call you sometimes.

I'm confused why I experience your death as an earthquake. The truth is your death actually unified me rather than tore me apart. I'm integrating my deeply divided selves: my "Bunny parts" that rebelled and hated you with the "Bernadette parts" that deeply, deeply, loved you. With your help, I officially ended my inner civil war yesterday.

While I'm not sure how you're healing me from the other side of the veil, I do know your lifelong struggle to breathe propelled me to grow beyond my wildest dreams. And, acts of devotional breathing continue to nourish and heal me now. Thanks for teaching me from afar to live happily ever after with Bob.

Love,
Natazha

Breathing through Electroshock Therapy   January 19, 2017

In 1989, I began my journey of healing my shame by reading John Bradshaw's book, *Healing the Shame that Binds You.* That book and taking a workshop with Bradshaw transformed my life. More recently, I read books and took online courses from Brené Brown, another expert on healing shame. Both Brown and Bradshaw are Texans and I wonder if Bradshaw in any way inspired Brené Brown's research on shame. I dedicate this letter to Brené Brown and to John Bradshaw, who recently died in May 2016.

The letter below is special to me. I actually wrote this letter to my Mom back in May 2016. Tom Bird, one of my editors, explicitly asked me to wait until after he read the first draft of my book on 2/28/17. Nonetheless, I felt compelled to read this letter to my brother John on 1/16/17 when he visited me from Puerto Rico on my Mom's birthday. I had repeatedly thanked John for his powerful eulogy but sensed he didn't truly understand what a miraculous healing his funeral speech gifted me. I wanted John to understand how much I appreciated his courage. He spoke his truth knowing full well that some relatives would applaud him while others would ridicule him. John became a big Brené Brown fan after I read this letter to him, and showed him my collection of Brené Brown books, expressive art journals, and online coursework.

Dear Mom,   This Letter was Written in May 2016

John's speech at your wake electrocuted me spiritually and emotionally. It felt like electroshock therapy, jolting me over and over again with lightning-bolt realizations about our relationship. I meditated, practiced yoga, and just plain breathed through my heartache and regret. But, ultimately I wrote a detailed account to integrate my new, enlightened view of you.

Even on your deathbed there was a distance between us. I'm sharing my written account to clear the air between us; to resolve our misunderstandings that started long before we stopped speaking to each other during our Cold War. I hope that somehow, somewhere, your spirit receives my message and blesses the distance between us.

<u>Three days after my Mom's Death: Sunday Afternoon, February 28, 2016</u>

I feel completely naked and adrift, even though I'm wearing a long black jacket over my gray, Ann Taylor, three-piece pants suit plus thick black stockings and boots. Bob sits next to me in a huge crowd of family, including my ten siblings and their families, loved ones, and life-long friends at Raynor's Funeral Parlor in Bayport, Long Island. Drowning in yet another wave of grief, I squeeze Bob's hand for some comfort. He gives me a reassuring hug and a tissue to wipe away the tears streaming down my face. I exhale fully only to start sobbing even harder.

Bob asks, "Do you want to leave the room?"

I say, "No, I don't want to miss any of the speeches." I soothe myself with more long, slow exhales.

My older brother John walks up to the podium, eight feet off to the side of my Mom's open casket. He looks like he's just about to walk the plank. He bows his head. Pauses before speaking very slowly, "Many of you know our Mom, Mary Connors, as the coordinator for the Saint Lawrence Community Outreach Program for the last 23 years where she championed the poor, homeless, and down-trodden. I feel it's important to tell a story of how she was institutionalized 50 years ago. I'm telling this story so you'll better understand all the obstacles she overcame." I catch myself holding my breath. I am bracing myself for the story to come: a story that I know all too well, even though I was only four years old when it happened. I'm surprised he's telling it, but trust his intentions.

John explains, "In 1966, our Mom fell into a dark depression while raising eight kids under the age of ten. Our Dad kept hoping she'd get better, and snap out of her deep despair. But after six months, she actually got much worse. So bad that they sent her to CI, short for Central Islip, the notorious "nut house" that has since been closed down. The staff at CI classified her with a severe, psychotic breakdown and put her on the 3rd floor along with all the other "lost causes" that were never expected to recover.

About a year passed. My Mom had 20 electroshock treatments, but still made no progress: so Child Protective Services arranged to put all eight of us kids into foster homes. Just days before we were supposed to go into foster care, another patient attacked our Mom with a butcher knife. At that moment her life flashed before her eyes, and our Mom snapped out of her psychosis as she realized eight little kids were waiting at home for her. Our Mom fought with all her might to throw off her attacker. And started on the painstaking path back to sanity."

As John ends his speech and takes his seat, I drift to another dimension. I realize there's a fine line between mental illness and mysticism. Now at fifty-three years old, that story takes my breath away. "Holy shit, my Mom's a mystic!" Her depression and institutionalization sound like the dark night of the soul so many mystics go through. She loved going to Church, retreats, studying and contemplating the mysteries of the Divine. Now I get her; she was a mystic who lived in the ethereal world of spirit, deeply caring about the invisible mysteries of life: love, faith, trust, healing, truth, forgiveness, compassion, and relationships (parenthood, marriage, sisterhood, and brotherhood.) She worked hard for social justice: healing society's ills where the fabric of our culture has been torn apart by invisible injustices that no pill, surgery, money alone, or electronic gadget could fix.

I stare off into space as I realize I take after her. I'm a graduate of the Berkeley Psychic Institute, Asclepion Healing Center's Hands on Healing program, many other metaphysical programs and a member of several meditation and psychic groups. I, too, have gone through a dark night of the soul and have spent my life exploring how we transform our lives through spiritual and breathing practices. Feels strange to think of myself as a mystic.

Another insight hijacks my awareness, and my mind wanders off in a completely different direction. I've heard this story many times before, what's so different? I exhale; inhale; exhale. I've never heard this story told outside our home. This time, I'm sitting in Raynor's funeral parlor in a sea of love and support from people sending us compassion instead of shame and judgment.

Their empathy blesses me with the strength to finally face the elephant in the room, the colossal mountain range of shame that my Mom faced when she returned home to Sayville. In 1967, long before the Oprahs of the world trained us to show compassion to the mentally ill, Sayville was a very parochial, conservative, small town. Back then, my Mom was stigmatized as a "nut case" and ostracized by all the other mothers on the block, except for Mrs. Krauss, a divorced, single mom raising four kids on welfare. At a time when she desperately needed help and support, my Mom got treated as an outcast.

How the hell did she do it? How did she keep going when all the odds were against her? I thought. *She must have tapped into some mystic force to pull off raising 11 healthy, college-educated kids.*

Staring into space, I wonder, *I always loved my Mom with my whole heart and soul. So why was I always so afraid to touch her, even after our reconciliation? I'm a doctor of physical therapy who is trained to heal people with my hands, and yet, I rarely touched her, even on her deathbed. Everyone else in the family calls me the "hug monster" but I very rarely hugged her.*

My eyes tear up again as another wave of grief and insight hit me hard in the gut, *Oh my God, I loved my Mommy, but her shame repulsed me. I was deathly allergic to her shame.*

Shame's been on my mind. Just two days ago I discussed a brilliant book about shame called *A Tiny Life* with my book club. And, I'm taking a four-month Brené Brown course on healing shame. Just finished reading her book, *Daring Greatly,* on the flight here. Brené's taught me that you heal shame by sharing your dark secrets with empathetic people. Thanks, John, for sharing Mom's secret with all these compassionate people. I'm now healing my shame about Mom's mental illness.

My gratitude shifts to terror, though, as I sense my head and heart wandering off in foreign, uncharted lands. I'm breathless. Feel shocked by more insights about my Mom's shame. My heart tears wide open with a more enlightened perspective of my Mom. I'm terrified of being so vulnerable and openhearted. I use all my courage and will power to fight the urge to divorce from myself and run away from these soul-piercing insights.

Thank God! My meditation practice fortifies my desire to love; I instinctively breathe through my fear instead of spacing out. Keep reminding myself, *"Exhale slowly to feel better. Exhale. Remember 'Hail the Exhale.' Dissociating just delays the pain, lets it fester and grow."* I hope nobody notices me flipping out, and struggling to stay in my body.

I feel much better after mothering myself with intentional breathing, strong enough to face more insights. I say to myself, "Did I misread my Mom's shame? She definitely felt ashamed of her mental illness, and exuded shame. But, did I totally misunderstand her? Did I misinterpret her shame about herself as her being ashamed of me? Did I misread her feeling unworthy and unlovable about herself as her saying, "Bernadette (my given birth name) you're unworthy and unlovable?"

I'm dizzy, drowning in overwhelming emotions and racing thoughts. I exhale slowly to center myself. Feel compelled to keep soul searching and question my beliefs about my Mom. Was I wrong to accuse her of being a jealous bitch? Was her "jealousy" really shame and fear of success? I remember Father Heim (a priest who was very close to my parents) lecturing my parents on their false humility and fear of success. Now I wonder if my

Mom feared success because she felt unworthy of it. As Father Heim said, "Your whole family suffered from false modesty and feeling unworthy of success." Was my Mom's shame so extreme that it caused her to feel her kids were also unworthy of success? Oh shit! She may have wanted the best for me after all. But her shame polluted her love with a pervasive undercurrent of "we're unworthy of good things."

When my Mom was institutionalized, Grandma Winnie (my Dad's mother) came to live with us. She took great care of us. And all of us kids bonded with her. I always thought my Mom was jealous of Grandma Winnie. But now I wonder if that "jealousy" was really my Mom feeling ashamed that Grandma needed to take care of us because of her mental illness.

I then flash back to my being nominated for Homecoming Queen in high school. On Homecoming Day, my Mom ignored me and kept her distance. She gave me no help with my makeup, picking out clothes, or calming my nerves. I was convinced she was jealous of me. On top of that, I hated her for sending me so many crazy, mixed messages. "Shine, make the family look good; be a Homecoming Queen and honor student." And, in the same breath, "Don't you dare stand out. Don't get too big for your britches!" I always felt like there was no way to please her. And, I desperately wanted to please her and win her approval.

Now, I see her mixed messages were fueled by raging shame, not raging jealousy. I wonder if in a perverse way she tried to protect me from success. Shame taught her: My kids and I don't deserve success. We'll be punished if we get too big for our britches and reach for the stars.

I flash back to my visit home on my way to Vienna in December 1987, just six months after I quit smoking. I was so proud of quitting, but my Mom never congratulated me. Instead she acted jealous. Now I wonder if I put her to shame by quitting nicotine; proved it was possible to quit. And here she was, still smoking. Did I misinterpret her shame about smoking as jealousy?

Seeing her behavior as motivated by shame, instead of jealousy, deeply upsets me. I made a huge mistake that I can't correct. She's dead now. I can't stay inside the funeral parlor any longer; I run outside to the far end of the parking lot to be alone. I lean against the trunk of a light blue, four-door car. My body aches from head to toe, as I'm flooded with a clear realization that misunderstanding my Mom's shame fueled our bitter five-year feud. It alienated me from the rest of the family for decades. I'm so sorry for mistaking her shame for jealousy.

It downright hurts to realize she may never have meant me any harm. Had I only known then what I know now! I crouch down behind the light blue car to hide myself as I violently weep. I went years without seeing her, my Dad, and the rest of the family, including my beloved nieces and nephews, thinking she was "jealous of me." I'm even more brokenhearted as I realize I missed my chance to help her heal her shame. At twenty-six years old, I rebelled against her with a vengeance, attacked her on my infamous "Declaration of Independence" audiotape.

I almost stop hiding behind the blue car, but my mind starts viciously interrogating me, *Why didn't you have kids?*

Without thinking about it, I automatically answer, "I was terrified I'd be crazy like my mom, and hurt my kids. Be jealous of them." My mind starts torturing me with another question, *Did I let my mom's shame or jealousy, whatever the hell it was, stop me from having kids too?* I don't want to answer that question. I just can't handle that issue right now; it's just too painful. I instinctively take several deep belly breaths. Hear my inner voice loud and clear: "Stop. Get some help. Find Bob and ask for a hug."

I slowly stand up, and lean my right side against the light blue car. Another battery of questions invades my awareness, *Why now? What the hell can I do with this insight now? She's dead and gone.* I slow down my breathing in order to slow down my thoughts. Close my eyes. Slip into heart-focused breathing. I hear a gentle, sweet voice in my head, "It's never too late. You can still love and touch your Mommy. You can still love her from afar." I walk back to the funeral parlor.

When I get inside, it takes two agonizing minutes to find Bob in the large crowd of mourners. He's not at all surprised when his hug monster wife asks for a hug. He smiles as he holds me. Breathing together consoles me; I'm no longer holding my grief and agony all by myself.

As Bob holds me, I realize today's truly my last chance to touch my Mommy. I ask Bob to visit my Mom's coffin with me. He stands beside me in the long line to see her body. I'm stone silent while waiting in line. Look down at the carpet to avoid eye contact with anyone else. I breathe deeply to connect with my Mom and myself.

I finally get a chance to kneel down beside her body. Seeing her face causes me to weep. Covered in makeup, she looks like a completely different person. My inner kids freak out seeing her this way. I breathe these words deep into my belly, *This is our mommy, even though she looks like another person.* Still scared to touch her, I caress her with an air kiss. Take another long, deliberate exhale. I check out her blue dress and hands holding a Virgin Mary medallion, a gift from one of her homeless clients. Inhale deeply, and hesitantly reach down to touch her right hand. When I finally touch her, heat radiates from my heart down my arm to my hand. I actually feel a little safer touching her now, after death, than when she was alive.

I silently say to her, "Oh how I miss you, Mom. I wish I could hug and hold you right now. I'm so sorry I never got in bed with you in January, held you when I had the chance. People were cruel and shamed you after Central Islip. I regret misinterpreting your shame as jealousy and never got too close to you. I was too scared to visit you one more time, right before you died. I could have visited you then, but didn't want to compete with the other kids for a seat by your bedside. I was afraid if I went without Bob I'd regress back to my childhood personalities of Bunny or Bernadette. Was terrified I'd get re-traumatized. I'm so sorry I didn't spend more time with you. I'm so sorry we didn't speak for 5 years and I moved 3,000 miles away from you."

Suddenly, another insight smacks me in my gut: *I carry my own mountain range of shame. That's why I react so strongly to her shame.* My neck, shoulders, and chest muscles tighten up. I'm sick to my stomach. *Shit! I'm spiraling into a full-out shame attack.* I medicate myself with several long, slow exhales, and exhale as if my life depended on it. Then I feel a warm, gentle presence, as if someone is blowing on my neck. I flash back to Sunday, January 31, 2016, the last time I saw my Mom alive and was saying goodbye to her. Remember the scene so clearly. I leaned down beside her bed. Kissed her gently on her cheek. I held her hands and kissed them, and gently put my arms around her. We looked into each other's eyes for a brief moment. Her eyes looked so sad, I couldn't stand to look at them. So I looked away as I recited a blessing that I also mailed to her a week later in a card.

May we bless the distance between us in the past.
May we bless the love between us in the present.
May we always feel connected in the future.

I exhale fully and look at my Mom's corpse for the last time, and bless my Mom with a heartfelt exhale. I stop beating myself up, and say to myself, "I truly did my best. That's all that matters." Inhale deeply to fill in with her presence before leaving the bench beside her coffin.

Mom, I still don't fully understand why John's speech impacted me so dramatically. Perhaps all my breath work, couples therapy, and especially Brené Brown's coursework primed me for those epiphanies. But I do know that day totally changed my perspective of you. I stopped thinking of you as the "jealous bitch" and began calling you "Mystic Mary."

I'm not saying you're a saint or demon when I call you a mystic. I'm just acknowledging your deep devotion to the Divine. To me, mysticism is all about the invisible, hard-to-define forces that either bless or curse our lives and are governed by our breathing. Mystic qualities can be good or bad: love or hate, trust or mistrust, connection or isolation, and so on. Most people think of mystics as being saints. I believe mystics can be saints or demons.

Here's the bottom line: I saw you in a new light after John's speech. Now I appreciate you as a mystic. I'm still revising my interpretation of you. It's downright painful to realize how emotionally stingy I was with you. I always assumed the worst about you. Bob often tells me to give him the benefit of the doubt. Now, I'm telling myself to give <u>you</u> the benefit of the doubt as I replay hundreds of childhood scenes and insert a more loving interpretation of my Mommy that assumes she was plagued by shame, not jealousy.

You know what, throughout this process, I've been incredibly grateful that you inspired me to breathe through my pain and problems. As much as I hated your violent asthma attacks, they taught me an important lesson: don't take your breath for granted. Indirectly, those breathing attacks motivated me to soothe and fortify myself in times of trouble through respiration.

I'd have flipped out if I tried to take in my epiphanies all at once. Thank God my meditation and mindful-exercise practices taught me to digest gigantic insights, one inhale and exhale at a time. And slowly, but surely, integrate the intense insights into my heart, psyche, body, and mind. Breathing breaks humongous epiphanies into manageable bite-size insights I can swallow more easily.

Having healing my own mental illness, I know one thing for sure: disconnecting from my breath always causes problems; holding my breath is the worst. Numbing doesn't solve my problems. Thinking alone can't resolve my woes; I need to breathe my way through my woes to invite all of me: my heart, mind, soul, and body to participate in the solution. All of me must participate to successfully resolve my issues. Besides, life is so much sweeter when all of me is present.

One last thing, in my early twenties my height was only 5'2". Now, my height is 5'4". I believe that feeling better about our relationship enhanced my emotional posture. And my physical posture improved as my emotional posture improved.

Love you,
Natazha

Mary the Mystic   March 2016

I still deeply regret not recognizing my Mom was a mystic when she was alive. On top of contemplating the mysteries of the Divine, my Mom modeled spectacular grace as she overcame hardship. Besides her own institutionalization, she weathered my Dad's bouts of catatonic depression, the nerve-wracking New York City teacher's strike of 1968 with nine kids to feed, the birth of 12 kids, the death of one child, and the never-ending trials and tribulations of raising 11 kids on a high-school teacher's salary. She blessed an eventful fifty-seven year marriage with a potent brand of divine love. I'm indebted to her (and my Dad) for modeling a loving marriage. I wish she were still alive to answer my questions about her deep faith. Seeing her mysticism in action taught me to rely on my respiration to reach the Divine and rescue myself in times of trouble with my breath. I followed in her mystic footprints by practicing my own brand of secular mysticism based on non-denominational meditation and respiratory techniques instead of Catholic theology.

Dear Mom,

Daddy Ray endowed you with so many terms of endearment: Own-Chick Woman, Mary Baby, The Mighty Mary, Momma Mary, Meeskite Momma, The Jungle Woman, Voluptuoso, "The Object of my Affection is in the house of Correction; she's serving 90 Days", and just plain **M-A-R-Y**, when he was mad at you. His long list of names was incomplete, though. Growing up, I muttered under my breath some other monikers for you: Jealous Bitch, Mixed Message Mary, Mean Mommy, and Mad Mary. More importantly, I posthumously add "Mary the Mystic" to that long list of nicknames.

John's funeral speech transformed my vision of you. I stopped regarding you as an insane Catholic, but rather an amazing Catholic mystic. Before your funeral, whenever I told people I came from a family of twelve kids and they'd ask, "Are you Catholic?" I always answered, "No, but my parents are insanely Catholic. I consider myself Buddhist with a very strong Catholic accent." John's speech enabled me to see that on top of being a wife for 57 years, mother of 12 kids, champion for the dregs of society, you were a mystic. You studied the mysteries of the Divine and served humanity in the same tradition of the great mystics: Thomas Merton, the Dalai Lama, and John O'Donohue, the mystical Irish poet and priest.

Mom, I apologize for making fun of you and your special brand of Catholic mysticism. I now see you devoted your life to understanding the mysterious, invisible qualities that make life so rich: love, compassion, joy, hope, community, and healing, among many others. And, how your mysticism blessed me in many ways that I took for granted. For example, I now enjoy a happy marriage because you modeled the divine qualities that sustain a successful marriage, including trust and honesty. I'm ashamed I never appreciated your mysticism while you were still alive and we could talk about it.

More importantly, your Catholic mysticism and intense battle to breathe inspired me to develop my own brand of secular mysticism based on breathing. Your respiratory woes motivated me to learn everything I could about breathing well. Your violent asthma attacks traumatized me as a kid. I felt utterly helpless and terrified loving a mommy who I expected to die at any moment. I hated you for smoking two packs of cigarettes a day when you suffered from severe respiratory disease. And was pissed and heartbroken when you developed full-blown emphysema and lung cancer that left you with only 30% lung capacity. I resented your self-abuse, one cause behind our Cold War.

You know what, though? Even in the midst of our bitter feud, deep down I dreamed of miraculously curing your allergies, asthma, emphysema, lung cancer, and most of all, shame. I longed for a healthy, happy Mommy. That yearning compelled me to explore high and low throughout the many realms of breathing: meditation, yoga, Pilates, endurance sports, fitness training, somatic psychotherapy, Holotropic breathing, expressing feelings out loud, self-expression (method acting, singing, and creative writing), open-water swimming, psychic healing, intuitive arts, acupuncture, and many more. That yearning even inspired me to work my butt off and earn a doctorate in physical therapy, a profession that uses lifestyle medicine, including breath work to heal pain and injuries and enhance posture, balance, and movement.

I thought I needed to find a how-to-breathe-well recipe to heal you. But actually, I found something much more valuable, the realization breathing is a form of secular mysticism. To me, mysticism boils down to relationships between the Divine and ourselves, and the relationships between the parts within ourselves (hearts, minds, spirit, and sub-personalities), and our relationships with others.

Breathing acts like the control buttons for all our relationships by governing the forces that affect relationships: trust, love, honesty, kindness, consciousness, and so on. I started my journey focused on the physical aspects of breathing, and tried to master pranayama techniques and achieve cardiovascular fitness. Little did I know my journey would also highlight the spiritual aspects of respiration. Thank you for leading me to understand that intentional breathing opens doors to life's greatest unseen treasures: kindness, forgiveness, joy, truth, and mercy, to name a few.

Love,
Natazha

Secular Mysticism   March 2016

John O'Donohue's writing is sweet, lyrical verbal candy. He offers soul-nourishing wisdom that goes down like a spoonful of sugar. In addition to my Mom's spirit, I also sensed his spirit mentoring me as I wrote this book. O'Donohue died unexpectedly in 2008 right after publishing *To Bless the Space Between Us.* I dedicate this letter to him and his family.

Dear Mom,

In *To Bless the Space Between Us,* O'Donohue asserted that the ancient art of blessing cures pretty much everything that ails modern society: a disconnection from self, others, and Spirit that leaves people feeling lost and isolated. He explained that the sacred art of blessing grants us access to the ethereal treasures of life, such as kindness and beauty. After reading his book, I also realized blessings can restore relationships with both others and ourselves. It connects us to others and ourselves.

While I read his book out loud to you, I wondered *can't we say mindful breathing is just like the art of blessing in that meditation also blesses the air space between us?* Meditation boils down to paying attention to our breath or being mindful of our breathing. Scientists regale it as a panacea for almost everything that ails modern society ranging from stress to chronic pain. Meditation is another gateway to the intangible, divine qualities that make life worth living. And, it helps us connect to and restore relationships with others and ourselves.

Intentional breathing or meditation heals unnecessary suffering by realigning aspects of us so we can receive life's blessings and enjoy more satisfying relationships. Respiration reigns over our hearts, minds, spirits, and bodies, and more importantly, the sacred relationship between them. To protect against the stress and rapid pace of modern culture, we go on automatic pilot to numb out. The problem with numbing is we disconnect from others and ourselves. All our relationships suffer when we dissociate. Meditation is the exact opposite of numbing. Unawareness breeds dissension with others and within ourselves. Minding our breath is how we realign and connect.

In harmonious relationships, the whole is greater than the sum of the parts. When our hearts, minds, bodies, and souls are aligned we're rewarded with the same intangibles O'Donohue ascribed to the art of blessing: love, joy, vitality, creativity, and so on. As you know Mom, those intangibles are crucial for satisfying relationships: fulfilling marriages, happy families, prosperous business partnerships, and healthy communities. Conversely, internal bickering with others and within ourselves causes stress, despair, and isolation.

Meditation positively influences our relationships so we become better people, lovers, spouses, parents, friends, employees, bosses, artists, and citizens. Mysterious, invisible forces play out over time in our daily lives, habits, and relationships. Those forces can't be fixed with pills, surgeries, electronic gadgets, or simply pouring money at the problem. Only tools like the art of blessing or breath-based meditation can heal those invisible forces.

Take marriage, for example. No one ever saved a marriage with surgery or divorce-prevention pills. Conscious breathing/meditation affects the forces required for a happy marriage: self-awareness, love, patience, empathy and willingness. Bob and I received excellent marriage counseling; however, I feel my meditation practice played a huge role in saving our marriage. Breathing in lotus pose on our living room sofa blessed me with an awareness that stopped me dead in my tracks just as I was about to verbally attack Bob. My meditation habit helped me apply what I learned in therapy.

All relationships are sacred and belong in the realm of mysticism in that mysterious, somewhat magical, forces govern relationships. We can't touch the unseen chemistry between lovers, athletes on a sports team, or children playing duck-duck-goose, but we act like mystics when we sense that chemistry and try to understand it. We also experience the Divine through loving relationships. Breathing in and of itself is often the loving connection used to build relationships because humans emote and communicate through breathing as they speak and emote (laugh, cry, shout).

When I learned you were a mystic, I began reflecting on what it meant to be a mystic and realized most mystics affiliate with a religion. O'Donohue and Thomas Merton practiced Catholicism and the Dalai Lama practices Buddhism. I now regard intentional breathing as a form of secular mysticism that requires no religious affiliation to experience a loving, divine connection with yourself, others, and Source. Scientists, not theologians, tout the virtues of mindfulness and meditation. The truth is, whether we realize it or not, everyone and thing who inhabits Earth breathes in its own fashion and thus, places Faith in the almighty, mysterious act of respiration that defines life and death.

Love,
Natazha

The Breath Tune-Up   April 2016

I tune myself up through many splendid forms of breathing. One example is singing the Beatles' song, "Let It Be." It will forever more be a tribute to my Mom. I also love using my respiration to dramatize the serenity prayer. I'm in the excellent company of Dr. Henry Cloud and Dr. John Townsend, the authors of *Boundaries.* All three of us are huge fans of this prayer. They consider it among the best boundary prayers ever written. And, of course, I tune up through meditation.

Dear Mom:

Singing is one of my favorite ways to tune into my breath and self. I guess I learned that from Daddy Ray; he sang all the time when we were little kids. For years, "This Little Light of Mine, I'm Gonna Let It Shine" has been my go-to song, along with Carole King's "You've Got A Friend."

Since your passing, I now sing or hum the Beatles' *Let It Be* to manage my grief, woes, and writing blocks. *"When I find myself in times of trouble, Mother Mary comes to me. Speaking words of wisdom. Let it be. And in my hour of darkness, she is standing right in front of me. Speaking words of wisdom. Let it be."*

I never carefully listened to those lyrics until you died. Now I realize they epitomize you: Mary, a mother of 12 kids, who spent her life dispensing simple wisdom to the downtrodden. The lyrics also epitomize how I often sense your spirit as I write. Your spirit offers me guidance as I battle my fear of success and shame. I imagine that singing sends my breath out to you somewhere in the heavens.

Reciting the serenity prayer is another trick I use to tend to my breathing. *"God, grant me the serenity to accept the things I cannot change. The courage to change the things I can, and wisdom to know the difference."* I act out that prayer through my respiration. Inhale to symbolize accepting what I can't change. Exhale to symbolize my courage. I send my breath out into the world. Intentional breathing usually grants me serenity.

It's taken me years to practice traditional meditation on my own. I settled down into a daily, first-thing-in-the-morning meditation practice after Dad's death, when I was feeling tremendous grief. For the first year, I meditated only in a traditional seated position. Now, I meditate soaking in the bathtub, hugging Bob in bed, or in various yoga poses, especially prayer or child's pose. In that pose, my back is stretched out and stomach is pressed up against my thighs so I more easily sense my belly expanding and contracting with each breath cycle. That heightens my breath awareness and connects me to Spirit. I typically feel humble, ready to receive spiritual guidance through my accentuated awareness of my breathing.

I know you did yoga and sometimes imagine you practicing yoga with me. I sense you breathing with me, both of us receiving a divine tune-up.

Love,
Natazha

Breathing is the Word of God   April 2016

I'm incredibly grateful my brother Ray finally convinced my Mom to give me the Madonna statue he bought for her when he was a teenager. Several hours before I ended my visit with my Mom on her deathbed, she looked up at Ray-Ray. He said, "I'd like for you to give the Madonna statue to Bunny (my nickname). It will help her remember you. Let her have it." That statue rests on a shelf in our living room. Every time I see it, I'm reminded of how much I love my brother Ray-Ray, my Mom, and my complicated love affair with the Roman Catholic Church.

Dear Mom:

I'm upset you thought I wasn't Catholic. Last December when I asked you for a Virgin Mary statue from your vast collection, you said, "No, you're not Catholic." I was too hurt back then to explain I'm Buddhist with a strong Catholic accent. I never really left the Church; I just stopped attending Mass.

I do cherish my Catholic upbringing and have the utmost respect for the great works of Catholic Charities and Catholic Community Outreach Programs like the one you coordinated at Saint Lawrence. I never hated the Catholic Church, just pedophiles inside the Church. It still tortures me that Sister "You-know-who" was never held accountable for molesting my sibling and other kids. But she is not the real reason I stopped going to Mass. All the other nuns were absolutely wonderful, especially Sister Kathleen and Sister Earl Mary. They loved me as their own child and taught me I was special, creative, and super bright. They consoled me when I needed it most.

I stopped going to Mass when I got stuck on Christ's crucifixion and forgot all about his resurrection. In Church, looking at the Stations of the

Cross and all the other images of Christ dying on the cross suffocated my spirit. I was turned off by the story of God sending his only son, instead of himself, to save the world. As a teenager I wondered, *if God was so almighty, then why didn't he get his own sorry ass down to Earth?* And felt the Church needed to update its logo of a dead man on a stick with more uplifting images of his glorious resurrection.

But, here's the ultimate reason I stopped attending Church. I worship with my breath instead of words. Please understand I believe breathing is the word of God. I reach the Divine through meditation and yoga rather than reciting prayers. Breathing life into my tight, neglected body parts and minding my breath connects me to Source. Sunday night yoga class reminds me of Catholic Mass. We conspire in silence until the yoga teacher gives a sermon on the class theme. Just like Mass, we follow a familiar routine that's modified according to the seasons of the year. I don't speak to my classmates or know their names. We breathe out fully to express our "Amens." Despite our anonymity and speechlessness, I feel a deep sense of community and belonging in the gently lit yoga studio that's created by the mystical power of sharing and relating through the breath.

Sunday nights, I commune with people of all ages, races, and religious backgrounds through the non-denominational, invisible act of sharing the same air. I witness how respiring with good intentions blesses the space between us, while allowing for individual differences. Sometimes I miss singing church hymns, but nonetheless, always leave my yoga "Mass" feeling renewed on all levels. I feel ready to serve humanity, the same message as my Catholic heritage. Thank you for modeling faith and an active spiritual life. I'm glad you raised me in the Catholic Church. I now practice yoga and meditation with the same devotion I learned from practicing the Catholic sacraments.

Love,
Natazha

PS: I do practice the sacrament of confession about twice a year and I'm beginning to attend Mass at Saint Patrick's Church whenever possible.

God Resides in Our Breath   June 2016

My Mom and I talked on the phone, a lovely breath-based form of communication. My Mom's sister, my Auntie Pat, is one of the few people in my life who talks on the phone. I hope our culture returns to more breath-based forms of communication, as I believe God resides in the space within and between us, which is to say our breath.

Dear Mom:

I almost called you today and still haven't deleted your contact from my cell phone. I just can't accept the fact that I can't call you anymore at 589-4002. That number is permanently emblazed on my brain. It's the only phone number I ever dialed my entire life, 53 years, to reach you. The phone company still hasn't given away your phone number, but when they do I might perform a ritual in your honor before finally deleting your contact from my phone.

Today I wanted to talk to you about prayer. You're an expert on prayer, so I wanted your opinion on why we pray in groups. Think about it: if prayer is a conversation between God and yourself, then there's actually no need to pray in a group. So why do all religions worship in groups?

I definitely need to pray privately each day through my solo yoga and meditation practice. But, I'm also compelled to attend yoga classes and my Monday night meditation group. I feel such a deep connection communing in silence with those groups. No words, we just breathe together.

You taught me God is everywhere, and I believe that more than ever. I see God residing both inside and outside our bodies, especially in the air we exchange. We build relationships one breath at a time by emoting and communicating through various acts of breathing: speaking, singing, crying, laughing, shouting, whispering, whistling, reciting prayers, changing the tone of our voice, just plain conspiring together, and so on. I now define prayer as relating to God and the "Divine" in my fellow human beings. As I said before, we build our relationships one breath at a time, even our relationship to God. Whether we're alone or in a group we share our "divinity" through exhaling and we receive each other's "divinity" through inhaling.

I recently read Thomas Merton, your hero and a dear friend of the Dalai Lama. I understand Merton integrated Catholic thought and practices with Buddhism. From the little I've read of his works, I sense he, too, regarded breathing as an important form of prayer. You extensively read Merton's works and I'd love to hear your thoughts about all of this.

Wow! I'm back to wanting to connect with you over the phone. I could always tell what was really going on with you by the quality of your voice and the sound of your breath. On bad days, it was noisy; you wheezed and coughed. On good days there was a sublime silence, and I could hear the love of God in your breath.

Love,
Your nighttime phone buddy

Altered States of Ecstasy   June 2016

Who needs drugs when you know how to get high off your breath? I hope one day our medical system teaches people to reach for their breath instead of pills. It's a great way to reach an altered state of ecstasy and ease pain without any adverse side effects like opiate-induced constipation.

Dear Mom:

I so clearly remember when I was 12 years old watching you run out of the house to attend your Pentecostal Prayer group, that group of church ladies who spoke in tongues and experienced altered states of ecstasy by channeling the Holy Spirit. At the time I thought you were crazy, acting like a "Holy Roller." I also felt neglected and resentful. Once again you were choosing someone else over me, not another sibling this time, but the Holy Ghost. Would there ever be an end to the competition for your affection? Would I ever receive your undivided attention?

Today's another one of those days I find myself breathing deeply as I allow wave after wave of inhales and exhales to wash over me. Each breath transforms my body and being as I continue to integrate John's funeral speech and reinterpret that Pentecostal prayer group as a lifeline for Mary the Mystic rather than my archenemy. I let that realization crack open my heart hardened by jealousy and resentment. I inhale the notion you absolutely needed that prayer group. Now, I understand how much you needed to explore the unconventional world of speaking in tongues.

Exhale. Inhale. Exhale as I gently touch my heart and consider, *How courageous I am to hold both my resentment, hurt, sorrow along with my love, admiration, compassion for you.* Whenever a tinge of fear creeps up in my belly, I place one hand on my belly and the other on my heart. I console myself with a deep breath into my belly. And say to myself, "I'm a big girl now. I can hold all my feelings for Mom, both the Bunny and Bernadette ones."

Whenever I integrate conflicting feelings by breathing deeply, I feel stronger, more centered, and more certain I've integrated my warring sub-personalities. And I'll never again suffer from blackouts. Today I did feel sluggish and out of it when I felt all my conflicting feelings around your Pentecostal prayer group, but then the mere act of breathing through my pain and discomfort led me to an ecstatic state. I ended up feeling super grounded and exalted all at once. Sometimes I wonder if I just channeled love or what you called the Holy Spirit.

Mom, it's not the first time I've reached an altered state through breathing. I used many breathing methods to reach an ecstatic state: Holotropic breathing, singing, hypnosis, yoga techniques like breath of fire, Wim Hoff's (breathing expert) breathing method, and aerobic exercise. I can't tell you how many times on a long run or swimming in the bay I felt other-worldly happy. I wonder how you reached your ecstatic states in that Pentecostal prayer group. Did you use your breath like so many other mystics?

Love,
Your Ecstatic Breathing Buddy

Breathing Together Bonds Us   April 2016

I dedicate this letter to my husband Bob, my "Best Breathing Buddy," as well as my hubby. He's the only person with whom I can breathe at my own unique pace while he's hugging me. He's taught me in so many precious ways how to breathe with others rather than for others.

Dear Mom,

I'm deeply disturbed that the definition of "conspire" has changed from breathing with other people to making secret plans with other people to commit an illegal or harmful act. Just think about it. For all our other basic functions, eating, sleeping, drinking, and walking, there never was specific words for doing those activities together.

I know from firsthand experience that breathing together is a sacred act that deserves a dedicated word to describe it. Breathing together helped sustain our marriage before we found an excellent couples' therapist. Prior to therapy, we too often got stuck in endless arguments. The more we talked, the worse we felt. Thank God, my inner hug monster just couldn't stand the bickering. With tears in my eyes and a soul-piercing tone of voice, I'd plead with Bob for a hug. We'd finally stop talking and let out of huge sigh of relief. Then Bob would hug me from behind, my favorite way of being held. I'd immediately calm down and so would he. Within a few minutes, we'd leave the living room to lie down on our bed for an even more intimate embrace. Full-body hugging allowed us to more easily match our breathing. And, to resolve our differences by matching our energy by synching up our respiration. We did eventually learn to use our words as well as our breath to resolve our differences.

I'm curious about how humans breathe together to match each other's energy and connect spiritually. We literally communicate our feelings and intentions through the air we exchange. Humans have created many special forms of conspiring to celebrate Spirit:

- Church choirs sing to God
- Clan members serenade their dead with Scottish bag pipes
- The Armed Forces blow bugles in unison at military ceremonies and funerals
- In the olden days, sailors sang songs to row in unison
- Yogis and monks chant in unison to commune with each other and the "Divine"
- Soldiers recite marching drills to synchronize their marching cadence and boost camaraderie
- Crowds cheer together to express team spirit
- Sleeping beside someone is a special, sweet experience in breathing together and matching energy. It's such an outstanding form of intimacy we reserve it only for those we love and trust won't take advantage of us while we're unconscious.

We also match our energy through talking out our feelings. And, all speech relies on our respiration. Oral communication, our spoken breath, is the backbone of relating. More so than writing, speaking allows us to spontaneously express our thoughts and feelings through our unique speaking voices. We modulate the tone and volume with our respiration.

Breathing also plays a role in receiving someone else's speech. Active listening is an essential skill for deep connection. It requires tuning into the speaker's body language, spoken breath, and the breath-based shifts in the speaker's pitch, quality, and pace of speech. Shifts in respiration reveal the speaker's message, undercurrents of emotion, and intentions. Active listeners express their participation primarily through silent breathing and facial expressions.

The irony is that breath-based active listening speaks a thousand words, without ever saying a word.

Love,
Natazha

Communicate versus "Infomat"   July 2016

More and more we are replacing breath-based speaking and emoting with typing and texting. Until modern times, humans expressed their feelings primarily with their mouths that are smack between their heads and hearts, the middle ground between thoughts and feelings. Today we text and type with our fingers that live off in no man's land nowhere near either our heads or hearts. As we "infomat" more and communicate less, no wonder communication is breaking down in our homes and on Capitol Hill.

Dear Mom,

Breathing is the backbone of oral communication and emoting that are crucial for healthy relationships. We exhale to speak, sing, laugh, yell, cry, scream, and so on. Holding our breath is how we shut down our feelings. We also shift our respiration to modulate the tone, volume, and pace of our voices to express ourselves. Breathing governs our one-of-a-kind voices and expression of our feelings that are so important in authentic communication.

Written words, on the other hand, are detached from our breathing. Unlike our breath-based voices, written words <u>represent</u> rather than <u>present</u> our feelings and intentions. Writing came long after speaking. Although it's great for providing facts and information, it lacks our tone of voice that so eloquently conveys intentions and emotions. Two people can write the same exact words to express different intentions and emotions. It's much easier to detect the speaker's intention when they say those same words. That makes it easier to misinterpret written messages than verbal messages.

"Infomatting" is sharing purely representational info: typed words, images, symbols, graphics, etc. It's usually not conveyed in person, but over a device like a phone, computer, or via the mail. Representational info, such as typed words, lacks the uniqueness of our handwriting and voices. Speaking and "infomatting" are completely different animals. Unlike oral communication, "infomatted" correspondence typically doesn't allow for instantaneous, back-and-forth responding. You can usually edit your authentic, first response, such as revise your email before you send it. With "infomatting," you don't share your unique self. In fact, you don't even have to participate at all; someone or thing, such as a computer, can send typed words and images on your behalf. Breath-based communication requires that you personally transmit the message, and most often, in real time by live phone call, Skype conversation, or in person.

Here's another thing: active listening is a vital ingredient for great communication. You can't actively listen to "informatted" messages that lack the tone, pitch, pace, and undercurrent of emotion of breath-based oral communication. In other words, we need breath-based communication to practice active listening.

It's pretty obvious that breath-based communication allows us to connect on a much deeper level. We share more than info; we share our uniqueness and authentically communicate that which is essential for intimate, loving, organic relationships. "Infomatting" is perfect for conveying data such as when and where a party will be held. We just need to remember however, that "infomatting" is perfect for relating info very quickly, but inappropriate for relating to each other. It can't replace vocal breath-based communication.

For millions of years we emoted and communicated through our breath and mouths that are between our hearts and heads. Both our feelings and thoughts got represented speaking from the mouth that resides in the middle ground. No wonder communication in this country is breaking down. It's easy to send a mean Tweet to someone you'll never see in person. You don't run the risk of getting punched in the face by them or one of their relatives, or suffer all the other consequences of insulting someone in your own village.

Back in the day, we aired our differences face to face. Had to see, hear, feel, touch, and taste the other person's response and reaction. Unless you're some kind a sociopath, it's much harder to speak or attack someone face to face. We automatically, unconsciously, soften our speech when the other person is right in front of you. In the past, we never tweeted with our thumbs. We used our breath and that created an entirely different experience.

It's scary how quickly our method of communication is changing. In one generation we've gone from breath-based, mouth-operated communication that's been used for thousands of years to "infomatting" with our thumbs. I'm glad in the last decade of your life we had so many phone conversations where we communicated instead of "infomatted." Your breathing often informed me if you truly understood me. And, the tone and sound of your voice conveyed more than words – they carried your love and caring across the country to me.

Love,
Natazha

The Truth about Lie Detection Technology   May 2016

I'm proud my Mom considered me incredibly honest. My harsh "Declaration of Independence" audiotape provided vocal, breath-based details that allowed my parents to hear me speaking from my heart. Even though I hurt them, my voice allowed them to know I was being sincere.

Dear Mom,

I'm sorry I was so brutally honest with you at times, but I'm really proud that you never considered me a liar. Who wants to live or work with a liar?

Trust makes or breaks relationships. In medieval times, humans formed alliances by breathing together around a fire. They looked each other in the eye, and instinctively checked each other's respiration to determine who was lying.

We still use breath to detect dishonesty. Did you know that most modern-day lie detection technology is based on respiration? The polygraph was developed for detecting lies at the end of the nineteenth century and still is the most commonly used lie-detection test. It operates under the assumption that lying can be detected by measurable physiological changes in respiration along with shifts in cardiovascular activity and perspiration.

This technology demonstrates that respiration is vital for assessing truthfulness. We build trust by breathing with each other. Breathing is a vital form of communication that reveals if we're being honest. Although they are great for conveying information, texts, emails, or typed letters supply information that lack the breath-based details needed to assess honesty and trust – the cornerstones of intimacy and connection.

Love,
Natazha

PS: I sent you and Daddy an audiotape of my Declaration of Independence instead of a letter because I wanted to communicate all my heart-felt emotion and intentions conveyed by my breath. I felt I couldn't fully express my feelings in a letter. I'm so sorry I hurt you.

A Bastion of Sharing   September 2016

In American culture I see a very disturbing trend of less sharing. It's evident in many ways. One example is the intense acrimony in our political system that thwarts our ability to share our national resources.

Dear Mom:

To be honest, growing up I often resented always having to share EVERYTHING with all my siblings. Now, I understand all intimate relationships require sharing and I'm grateful I learned the art of give-and-take. It's helped me enjoy a happy marriage.

I'm sad to see that left and right we're losing opportunities to share. Individual water bottles replaced water fountains. Private cell phones supplanted household phones. Community pay phones are now a relic. Computer screens and video games replaced the family TV and community movie theaters. Recent home building trends depict our shift away from sharing as houses now have less shared spaces: smaller living rooms, separate bathrooms for each bedroom instead of shared bathrooms, and his-and-her sinks in master bathrooms. Long gone are the days of shared bedrooms. It's assumed kids need their own bedrooms. I shock people when I tell them "I shared a small bedroom with four sisters." In response to the demand for individualized bathrooms, many colleges and retreat centers have replaced their communal bathrooms. Marriage is the ultimate act of sharing, and marriage statistics show our ancestors did a much better job at sharing with their spouses. Our roadways still require us to share, and the increasing rates of road rage are yet another telltale sign that we're incompetent in the art of give-and-take.

Breathing is one of the last bastions of sharing. Whether we realize it or not, we apportion air by inhaling and exhaling. Every day is a "Share the Air Day." To my knowledge, man has fought over everything from food, land, shelter, water rights, religious beliefs, and planes flying overhead in one's airspace; however, mankind has never battled over sharing the air we breathe. To the contrary, many times humans who hated each other have unknowingly shared by exchanging respiratory gases through their breathing. That may explain why mediators want adversarial parties to get back to the negotiating table where they will breathe together, whether they are conscious of that or not. The act of breathing in the same room becomes a basis for a common ground and an unconscious act of sharing.

Wow! I just realized all mothers completely share their bodies with their children in the womb. That's extreme sharing. Thanks for bearing me in your womb and teaching me to share.

Love,
Natazha

All Parts Clear and Present   May 2016

I feel scattered and spaced out whenever my mind and imagination run far ahead of my body and feelings. It's as if my body and feelings are the visual track of a movie whereas my mind and imagination are the soundtrack. I become disjointed whenever my soundtrack races ahead of my film. Although they're not film makers, I'm incredibly grateful to my Mom, loved ones, teachers, and therapists who taught me many splendid ways to connect to my breath to keep my visual track and sound track aligned, so I can remain more conscious and grounded, especially when I'm stressed.

Dear Mom,

The best gifts you ever gave me were a deep respect for the power of breathing and breath-based remedies. You inspired me to listen to my breath. Let it talk to me. Just as active listening speaks a thousand words, listening to my breath speaks volumes to all the different aspects of myself.

I understand the value of being present and clear after practicing the exact opposite. I survived trauma by abandoning myself, being absent and opaque. I held my breath with a sinister consistency to disconnect from myself, especially from my feelings. I hated when my classmates teased, "Bernadette's a space cadet" because I knew they were right for calling me on my habit of living outside my body, staring off into space with a glassy-eyed look.

Breathing is the universal language for thoughts, feelings, sensations, and perceptions. It affects every aspect of us so it can influence and heal every aspect of us. Tending to my breath grants a divine intervention on the neglected parts of myself, and invites them to start participating again in my life. These parts become truly clear and present when I breathe some life into them.

Although psychotherapy provided invaluable insights about my mental illness, I credit my breath-based practices (Pilates, yoga, chanting, swimming, aromatherapy, meditation, aerobic exercise) with restoring my sanity. Befriending my breath allowed me to painstakingly realign my heart, body, mind, and soul. And recover from post-traumatic stress disorder and dissociative identity disorder to receive life's rich blessings.

Before and during my visit with you on your deathbed, I worried about regressing to dissociation to manage my grief and anxiety. Breath holding was my method for overriding pain during my childhood and young adulthood. It's quite different meditating and performing yoga in San Francisco where I learned to befriend my breath than at the scene of the childhood traumas, where I learned to leave my body. That's why I spent 2½ months preparing for that visit to guarantee I'd tune into my respiration to remain whole and sane instead of spaced out.

My preparation paid off. On that visit when I communicated to you, a mom I deeply loved and admired and feared and hated, I nourished us through my breath-based practices. Each morning, I meditated in the loft above TC's living room and watched the air I exhaled transform into steam as I briskly walked the streets of Sayville on those bitterly cold winter mornings. Reading out loud to you with my spoken breath connected us on many levels. Singing lullabies soothed both of us. Your gentle snoring comforted me with pleasant proof you were still alive. Whispering sweet nothings graced our relationship. We medicated each other by breathing together with unspoken blessings exchanged through the air we exhaled.

I almost completely lost it several times, but the "Almighty Exhale" guided and protected me. I felt so rejected when you said I couldn't go with you and Luke (my youngest brother) to your oncologist appointment. Instead of running away from that pain, I ran to a Bikram yoga class where I exhaled my heartache in a room of supportive, like-minded yogis. After embracing my dense, painful feelings, they evaporated into a deep compassion for you. I wondered if you felt ashamed admitting defeat to cancer after having beaten lung and breast cancer. And, I sensed how heart broken you felt saying goodbye to your 11 children, our extended clan, plus the Saint Lawrence parish community.

Then grief and relief tore me apart when you announced, "No more chemo." Part of me wanted you to continue chemo so we'd have more time together; another part saw the wisdom in ending your agony. I'm proud I held myself together with my breath instead of held my breath. Inhaled and exhaled deeply into the pit in my stomach caused by the emotional schism of wanting you to both discontinue and continue chemo. We helped each other resolve our conflicting feelings by breathing together: Exhaled. Inhaled. Exhaled. Inhaled. Punctuated by loud sighs.

You smiled slightly as you acknowledged my heartfelt acceptance of your decision when I spontaneously began singing "Too-ra-loo-ra-loo-ral, Too-ra-loo-ra-li, Too-ra-loo-ra-loo-ral, hush now, don't you cry! Too-ra-loo-ra-loo-ral, Too-ra-loo-ra-li, Too-ra-loo-ra-loo-ral, that's an Irish lullaby." Once again, I had used singing to hold myself together. Singing unifies me whenever my body, mind, heart, and soul wander away from each other. I become present and clear again as these facets united by working together on a common goal: my mind remembers the lyrics, my heart infuses my voice with emotion, my body contracts my respiratory muscles to forcefully expel air from my lungs, and my psyche paints pictures to embellish the song with deeper meaning. Singing or chanting silently in my head also does the trick.

I'm grateful my breath sponsored a loving goodbye with all of me clear and present. And, continues to sponsor my communication with you now.

Love,
Natazha

Defining Life and Death   April 2016

I missed my Mom's last physical breath, but I'm grateful that I still feel her spirit around me now as I write and meditate.

Dear Mom,

I regret missing your last breath on February 25th. When I kissed you goodbye on January 31st, I was convinced you'd live for several more months and I'd see you at least one more time at Easter. On the plane flight home I began planning which books I'd read to you.

I was wrong. Just before Valentine's Day, your health took a turn for the worse. Your doctors expected you to die in only a few weeks. Bob's Mom also died of cancer. She lived eight years longer than her doctors predicted, so Bob strongly advised against us buying airline tickets before you died, otherwise we could wind up waiting around longer than we could afford to attend your funeral.

Mom, I'm sorry I told Ray-Ray (my brother) that I'd fly home by Thursday 2/25. He says he told you I'd come home on 2/25, and believes you died on Thursday 2/25 after waiting for me. I'm sorry if I disappointed you by breaking my promise and didn't show up on 2/25.

Please understand I wanted to be there. But, by the weekend of February 20th all the other kids were back in Sayville vying for space around your deathbed. I was terrified to compete with 10 other grief-stricken siblings for a seat by your cramped bedside. I needed Bob by my side to keep me in present time and grounded under those circumstances. I was terrified of regressing back to childhood rivalries, numbing out, and splitting back into Bunny or Bernadette mode without Bob's support.

Mom, I loved seeing you in private in January, when I could express my love for you without being in somebody else's way. I loved sharing simple pleasures with you: reading out loud the works of John O'Donohue and Thomas Merton; staring out the windows at the brightly lit snow; humming lullabies; watching water drip from icicles on the gutters; listening to kids playing tag next door; watching the Catholic Network TV Channel; singing lullabies; and communicating silently by matching our breathing. All those simple pleasures were acts of intentional breathing. I feel blessed we breathed together last January, and that's the last breath of yours I want to remember.

It's so ironic, as a kid I was terrified you'd die from a violent asthma attack and I'd be there for your last breath. And now, I feel so guilty and disappointed I missed your last breath.

I'm quite aware that breathing defines life and death. In other words, our breathing proves our spirit resides in our body. That's why our words for breathing all share the same Latin root word as spirit, *spirare.* Respire *(re + spirare)* means breathe in and out or breathe again. Inspire *(in + spirare)* means blow into or breathe upon, and figuratively to infuse with spirit, excite, or inflame. Its derivations, inspired and inspiration have meanings ranging from filled with spirit, uplifted, communicated by divine or supernatural powers, and under the immediate influence of a god. Expire *(ex + spirare)* means to breathe out, blow out, breathe one's last breath, and literally expire, die, and cease. Conspire *(con + spirare)* means to breathe together and blow together musical instruments, as in to sound in unison. Conspiracy took on the meaning of a secret plan by a group to do something unlawful or harmful much later, after the 1400s.

The Bible makes many references about God breathing life into humans. For example, "And the Lord God formed man of the dust of the ground, and breathed into his nostrils the breath of life; and man became a living soul." (Genesis ii.7). Wind often symbolizes the presence of Spirit or God in the Bible. Humans blow out air to create wind. It makes perfect sense that we use the ritual of blowing out candles to celebrate one more year of life.

Mom, I missed your last physical breath. And yet, I do feel your spirit breathing with me now and providing me lots of love and support to write our book.

Love,
Natazha

Breathing, Our Second Mother   April 2016

My sister, Evangeline, inspired this letter. She died three days after her birth on June 15, 1969. Born with a hole in her heart, she never converted to breathing on her own. I still vividly remember the day she died when I was 7 years old. My Dad came into our bedroom to wake us up for school. I immediately asked him, "How's the baby?" I expected him to say she's fine, but instead he bowed his head and said, "She died." I also remember my 2nd grade teacher, Sister Kathleen, consoling me. That entire week she hugged me, and let me sit on her lap whenever she played her flute for our class. But, most of all I still wonder about Evangeline. I believe we would have been super close. As her older sister, I'd have been a second mother to her. I still hold a special place in my heart for her.

Dear Mom,

My favorite part of visiting you last January on your deathbed was reading out loud John O'Donohue's book *To Bless the Space between Us*. Finding that book was a sweet experience. Reading it out loud to you was even sweeter.

When Kiki visited me in San Francisco last Christmas, we went to Stinson Beach. It's the same beach near Muir Woods you and Daddy loved when you visited us for our wedding. While Kiki threw a football on the Stinson Beach with Luke and Peter (Kiki's son and husband) I wandered off and found a bookstore two blocks away. The moment I saw *To Bless the Space between Us* in the bookstore window, I instantly knew it was the perfect gift for you.

However, on the flight to New York, I began fretting about the possibility that you and Daddy loved O'Donohue's writings so much that you may already have that book. That's why I felt exhilarated when you smiled brightly as I handed you *To Bless the Space between Us.* It was the only O'Donohue book you didn't already own. Being a mystic, I see why you loved his books, especially *Anam Cara* about Celtic spirituality and mysticism.

Anyway, I just loved playing our John O'Donohue game; I'd flip open the pages of *To Bless the Space between Us* for you to pick a blessing for me to read out loud. No matter how I arranged the book, half the time you chose the blessing entitled, "In Praise of Water." Since your death, I've read that blessing many times to commemorate our precious last time together. I'm a water person who loves to swim, row, run along the beach and watch the San Francisco Bay from our living room window. So of course I love reading "In Praise of Water" that depicts the many virtues of water: its humility to take the shape of whatever otherness holds it and its courage to continue belief and always fall toward the unseen ocean.

Those last two lines of that blessing are "Blessed be water, Our first Mother." Those two lines changed my view of motherhood. I started to regard breathing as my second mother. Of course both water and you are my First Mother. You gave birth to me plus my eleven siblings. And, you're named after the Blessed Mother, Mary. You also mothered countless other children and thousands of clients seeking food, shelter, and comfort at the Saint Lawrence Community Outreach Program.

Having so many kids, I think you'll be able to understand O'Donohue's claim that water is our First Mother and why I consider breathing as my second mother. You know babies develop in amniotic fluid, much like water. The amniotic fluid hugs and nourishes babies like a good Mother. Babies can't breathe, as their lungs are filled with amniotic fluid; their moms breathe for them by exchanging gases through the placenta and umbilical cord.

Evangeline's death serves as a painful reminder of the miraculous transition babies make when they begin breathing on their own. A baby takes its first breath when it cries for the first time after birth. That moment marks the baby breathing on its own and mothering itself through its own breathing. The baby officially checks out of its First Mother's womb and officially registers with its Second Mother, its own breathing. From there on out, the baby's breathing exchanges gases required for all its life processes. And, the baby expresses its needs through acts of breathing: screaming, crying, cooing, and so on. A baby grows into an adult who mothers herself with her breath: heart-focused exhales to console her grieving heart, sobbing to release sorrows, belly laughs to share joy, and purposeful exhales to calm herself down when she's scared and terribly cold swimming in the frigid San Francisco Bay without a wetsuit.

Mom, there's another reason why I agree with O'Donohue's claim that water is our First Mother. When I underwent all that psychotherapy to heal split-personality disorder, my therapist advised taking hot baths with Epsom salts. I also added aromatherapy oils to seduce me into a soothing, meditative state. I just love being fully embraced by the warm, maternal bathwater.

About 25 years ago, I lived in an apartment with a deep claw bathtub that allowed me to reenact being in the womb submerged in warm water. I'd roll over on my side. Fold my body into the fetal position. Push my back against one side of the bathtub while my feet pushed against the other side. The warm water hugged my entire body except for the side of my face sticking out of water so I could breathe. I still perform that ritual in our shallow modern bathtub, even though it's much harder to do. I feel your loving maternal presence every time I venture back to the womb. When you breathed for me, because I couldn't breathe for myself. You'll never know how much I wanted to return the favor. So often, when I heard you struggling to breathe over the phone, I wanted to breathe for you, my First Mother.

Love,
Natazha

Section Two

Start with the Exhale To Heal and Forgive

It's Never Too Late to Say I'm Sorry   July 2016

During the 1980s, two family factions emerged in my parent's home. The younger kids who lived all year long at home called themselves "the lifers." And they nicknamed the older kids who went away to college or graduate school and lived at home only during school vacations, "the loafers." I remember several lively arguments where "the lifers" shouted, "It's just not fair. You 'loafers' come home and boss us around. We live here year round. You're only 'loafers' who have no right to tell us what to do." When I left my parent's home on Long Island in July 1984, I stepped out of the family system. Declared myself as an independent, neither "lifer" nor "loafer." Writing this apology letter to my Mom incidentally healed my shame and regret around leaving her on harsh terms. I finally forgave myself. And I actually felt like a "lifer" again.

Dear Mom:

I broke your heart the day I left home for good. I was the first girl to leave the nest, and on terms that tortured you, "living in sin." It killed you to see me leave with a guy you felt didn't love me. Back then I thought you didn't love me either. I felt you were a hypocrite, pointing out Bill didn't say, "I love you" out loud to me. I couldn't remember the last time you said, "I love you" to me. And, I felt you had no right to ask me to stay home where I felt unwanted and neglected. I was just another mouth to feed. One more kid demanding your attention, one more problem to solve.

Now I regret what I call my "Surprise Attack." I gave you and Daddy less than three days to process and respond to my announcement: "I'm moving to San Francisco with my college sweetheart, Bill." I gave you no chance to talk it out with me. Bill arrived two days later. And I didn't soften the blow by telling you all my reasons for leaving New York. Long before 1984, my heart and soul ran away to California after reading John Steinbeck's books as a kid. I fell in love with the Golden State reading *East of Eden, Of Mice and Men,* and *Cannery Row.* You know how much I loved Emerson and Thoreau, the forefathers to the Haight-Ashbury hippies. I longed to join "my people" on the hills of San Francisco. Roam in a much gentler, breath-based culture. Truth is I didn't run away only from you and the family. I also ran from New York culture.

I also never told you about my pathetic attempts to find work in San Francisco. During my last semester at Grinnell College, I applied for jobs I was completely unqualified to do. I came home after graduation fully aware New York wasn't my scene. I fooled you by going on so many job interviews in New York City. My last one was with a creepy publisher, who tried to seduce me into sleeping with him. Strangely enough that awful interview left me exhilarated, absolutely clear I just didn't belong on the streets of the Big Apple or the highways of Long Island.

Riding back home on the LIRR train, I sat in my seat and closed my eyes to shut out all the chaos. I breathed in and out from the core of my being. I connected to my deep desire to live in San Francisco, and with all my heart and soul, pleaded to the Universe: "I need to live in San Francisco. Please, please, somehow, some way, let me live in San Francisco." Exhaled over and over again my desire to the Powers that be.

The very next day, out of the blue Bill called me. We left Grinnell on confused terms. We didn't want to break up, but we didn't want to commit to each other either. I never expected to hear from him. But he knew how much I wanted to live in San Francisco. He told me that he got a job interview with DEC Computers in San Francisco. He asked me to live with him in California. We could drive to San Francisco, but we needed to leave New York in less than a week for his job interview.

Three days later, Bill arrived many hours later than expected, on a very dark night punctuated by howling rains and wind. As you know, late June is hurricane season. He drove from Iowa to Long Island in a storm that was never declared a hurricane, but sure as hell acted like one. The little kids, aka the lifers, insisted on surprising him. They made sure all the lights were turned off in the house. Only the front porch was lit when his car pulled up in the driveway. He rang the front door bell, and when he finally came through the front door, exhausted, bugged-eye, and skeletal thin, the lifers screamed at the top of their lungs, "Surprise." They all at once turned on all the lights and threw confetti and balloons at him. Bill was frightened by all that unexpected commotion. He could barely speak for the first 10 minutes, and didn't make a good first impression on you.

Bill stayed two nights. He barely spoke the first night, leaving us with very little time to speak in private on the second evening. Daddy Ray was fine with me going on this adventure. Years before we talked about my Steinbeck-inspired love affair with California. He thought I could always come home if things didn't work out. For you it was a completely different story.

I saw you crouched in a corner of the kitchen over by the china cabinet and coffee grinder on the wall. You were holding back your tears and trying to compose yourself. And, figure out what to say. Suddenly you blurted out, "What will the neighbors say? What will they think?"

I retorted in a firm defiant voice, "I don't care what they have to say. It's none of their business."

My tone stung you. You retreated. Daddy Ray got up and held your hand, but didn't say anything. His comfort helped you persevere, and make another protest, "How can you live with a man who can't even say he loves you out loud?"

You stung me. We stared at each other in complete silence until Daddy changed the subject, "Does anyone want more coffee?" My bull-getting-ready-to-charge breathing spoke volumes. With or without your blessing, I was moving to California. I gave you no choice, and very reluctantly, you finally gave your consent. Early the next morning, with the sun shining on our faces, we stood on the brick front steps. I kissed Daddy Ray first. He held me tight for a few seconds and promised to visit me in San Francisco. He fulfilled that promise two years later in 1986.

I stopped to look at you before our final hug. Daddy stood beside you, providing silent support. You looked so tormented, so wounded. I'm ashamed I took so much perverse pleasure in seeing you so hurt. It was my "sick" way of sensing you actually cared about me. We shared a moment of silence and acknowledged, "I don't get you and you don't get me." In that moment, I felt so justified torturing you. I felt justified saying goodbye without acknowledging all the sacrifices you made for me. I felt justified leaving out details that could have softened my goodbye, and left you believing this move was a "fuck-you." I thought to myself: "You never had enough time for me when I was growing up; you were always too busy with the other kids. Now it's my turn to choose someone else over you. Put someone else ahead of you."

When we finally hugged, you suddenly pulled out of our embrace. You took my cheeks in your hands, looked directly into my eyes, and exclaimed, "I love you. Call us anytime if you ever get into any trouble." You took me off guard. My Bernadette parts immediately wanted to say, "I love you too." My Bunny parts, poisoned by resentment, trauma, and misunderstanding, almost choked when you said, "I love you." You sensed my ambivalence, and yet accepted my awkward, reluctant response.

For decades, I routinely replayed our good-bye scene on the front steps. Leaving New York was absolutely the right choice. Moving to San Francisco saved my life. But I truly regret seeking revenge. I never gave you a chance to clear up our misunderstandings. To this day, I regret intentionally inflicting pain on you, rather than airing my resentments. We could have consoled each other instead of continuing to wound each other.

This incident bothers me so much more than my miscommunication about the Uncle Mickey incident. I'm not exactly sure what I said on my Declaration of Independence audiotape, but I do know, I didn't act from malice. I spoke from a raw, honest, intense place. But when I left New York, I purposely hurt you. I replay that scene often because I need to apologize to you. Exonerate myself. I pray somewhere, somehow, your spirit hears my apology: "I am so sorry. Please forgive me. If I could do it all over again, I'd comfort and console you instead of deliberately hurting you."

Love,
The Bunny part of Natazha

Putting You to Shame   April 2016

I see my December 1987 visit to my parents in an entirely different light after listening to my brother John's funeral speech. I now view my Mom's behavior with more compassion; she was motivated by shame not jealousy.

Dear Mom,

Even before visiting you in December 1987 on my way to Vienna, I felt damned if I did and damned if I didn't go home. Visiting home triggered traumas that left me depressed and anxious for months, but I suffered from loneliness and homesickness if I stayed away. However, that visit was the last straw for me. I felt utterly crushed by your reaction to me quitting smoking, and experienced you as a jealous bitch. I had miraculously quit smoking after 14 years of smoking two or three packs a day. I felt incredibly proud for accomplishing the impossible. No one ever expected me to quit, especially me. I still cherish Gabrielle's "Congratulations on quitting smoking" card. As a sixteen year old, she totally understood what a big deal this meant to me. Her card highlighted your lack of support.

On the third day, I told you how great I felt about quitting. In a snide tone, you said, "My, my, you're taking care of yourself. Next you'll be taking vitamins." Dead silence. No congratulations. Then you demanded me to empty the dishwasher. I froze. Without a peep, I emptied it, and deliberately held back my tears until you left the room. Your words pierced through the core of my being. I thought, *I'm not imagining her cold-shoulder treatment. She only talks to me to ask me to do something for her. Of all people, she knows how hard it is to quit smoking. I started smoking by stealing her cigarettes. She's not happy for me, she's jealous.* I then withdrew from you, and you seemed happy when I kept my distance. I wondered *why do I subject myself to her abuse? How could anyone resent their daughter's victory over cigarettes?* As a kid I pleased you by being a perfect little girl. I did as much as possible to help including laundry, lunches, cooking, and cleaning. I got straight A's and a full scholarship to Grinnell College. For once I needed sincere congratulations for winning the biggest battle of my life, my fatal addiction to cigarettes. Instead I felt ridiculed by you. I became convinced you were a jealous bitch who didn't have my best interest at heart.

On December 22 before flying out to Vienna, I wished you, Dad, and the rest of the family a Merry Christmas. I never told you how upset I was with you: I just stopped talking to you. Living in Vienna was the perfect excuse to cut off contact and ignited our five-year rift. I vacillated between guilt and remorse for divorcing from you, but felt utterly justified hating you for treating me like a servant and not truly loving me.

After John's funeral I saw that visit in a completely different light. My quitting cigarettes threatened you. It served as a painful reminder that you were killing yourself by smoking. You actually felt ashamed of not being able to quit. I now see how I put you to shame by making it perfectly clear if I could quit than anyone could quit smoking. Today, I see how terrible you must have felt. You weren't jealous, but rather ashamed.

Love,
Natazha

Start with the Exhale to Heal and Forgive   May 2016

The most important lesson I learned in psychotherapy was how to process and express my feelings through my breath. Holding my breath was my go-to method for repressing my feelings. And, exhaling fully was a simple, always accessible tool that cured my breath holding.

Dear Mom,

I was terrified to see you after five years of feuding, and all the other kids who were upset with me, too. Besides Dad, only John and TC spoke to me during our Cold War. Going home also meant dealing with all my other siblings who had ostracized me.

In the last year of our feud, I wanted to see you but didn't know how to revive our relationship after so much deadly silence. I had no idea where to begin. I had spent years in therapy terrified to go home, but also aching to go home. That conflict tortured me. Being out of touch with the family made me feel lost and disconnected. I often dreamed about 52 Hampton Street. Every cell in my body was exhausted after years of lonely, self-imposed exile. Daddy told me you wanted to see me, but I wasn't convinced. He had said it, not you.

An insight about the "Almighty Exhale" gave me the courage to visit you. I realized exhaling is how I could set emotional boundaries to feel safe around you and the rest of the family. I also realized I hold grudges by holding my breath. I forgive and heal when I exhale freely. I saw how breathing rules my emotional life. It was the control buttons that I had been searching for. I could use my breathing to process my feelings instead of spacing out without any boundaries. I came to this realization after a painful therapy session that took place in my therapist's Nob Hill office back in November 1992. Now, I want to tell you the whole story including how much I hated you back then because it highlights how much I've grown and truly love you now.

My Psychotherapist's San Francisco Nob Hill Office in November 1992

I explode at her. Huffing and puffing, I almost stand up and march out of her office, but manage to keep sitting on my therapist's couch. I just can't believe after two years of weekly therapy sessions, she was giving me this useless, bullshit irritating advice, "You need to get some emotional boundaries."

I look at her, roll my eyes, and in a snide voice shout, "What the fuck do you think I'm here for? If I knew what emotional boundaries were, don't you think I'd use them? Don't you get it! That's why I'm in therapy. You know I'm number five of a crazy family of 11 kids. My mentally ill parents never had emotional boundaries. Teach me emotional boundaries: B-R-E-A-K I-T D-O-W-N for me. BREAK DOWN EMOTIONAL BOUNDARIES."

Silence. My therapist looks deeply disturbed, and seems at a loss for words. I clench my fists, butt, and thighs. Sigh loudly several times, my way of demanding her to say something. We continue to sit in silence. "I understand that you're very upset. Next time, we will address emotional boundaries." She looks at the clock beside her chair. "We're out of time." Pause. "I hope to see you next week. Get some rest. You did some good work today. Take good care of yourself."

I feel grateful to escape and get some fresh air. I just hate feeling so frustrated, but she always reassures me frustration is a normal part of the process. I gather my stuff and walk super-fast out of the room without looking at her. I run down the red-carpeted flight of stairs onto Sacramento Street. Walk aimlessly for about six-to-eight blocks until I find a huge oak tree with a wrap-around, iron bench at its base between two buildings. It's just the resting spot I need, private enough for me to close my eyes and breathe.

I start crying. I feel so hopeless. It's five years since I've gone home to Long Island. As much as I hate my Mom, I miss her. I miss my Dad, and siblings too. How the hell can I go home to see them without emotional boundaries? That's why when I do go home, I get emotionally drunk. It takes weeks to undo the trauma that gets triggered.

After a minute or so of intentional breathing, I remember the advice my teachers from the San Francisco Zen Center gave me: Focus on exhaling. Make the exhale slightly longer than your inhale. I drop my shoulders and relax my butt, thighs and chest muscles. Relax more and more with each out-breath. I start calming down, feeling clear-headed and suddenly realize: *Just thinking about my Mom makes me hold my breath. I despise her so much I don't even want to share any air with her. I just want to seal myself off from her. The depth of my hate shocks me, but I also see a way to develop emotional boundaries. I need to start with my breath and explore my breath holding.*

The next day, I observe my respiration in all sorts of situations: office meetings, acting class, phone calls, riding the bus, and yoga class. I learn that I hold my breath pretty much all day long. I especially do it to avoid pain, when I engage with people I dislike, to dissociate from challenging situations, but most of all, after breathing in. I inhale like I'm sucking in as much nicotine as possible from a cigarette, then hold my breath, end with a half-assed exhale. *The exhale is a waste of time, you don't get any nicotine,* I think. *Shit! I still breathe like I'm smoking, even though I quit five years ago.*

I cringe as I acknowledge I don't conspire with the people in my daily life, not just my Mom: loved ones, fellow bus riders, friends, people in line with me at the grocery store, men at bars making advances, busy bodies, and co-workers. I run breath experiments on other people, too. Similar results. I watch them stop breathing to minimize contact with their enemies. I amuse myself at office meetings by seeing foes halt their breathing and tighten their shoulder muscles in each other's presence.

My observations expose my reward for holding my breath: It allows me to leave my body and escape "undesirable" sensations and feelings, especially conflicting feelings between Bunny and Bernadette. My stomach turns upside down as I realize emotional boundaries require breathing through my discomfort and staying present with "undesirable" feelings. Oh my God! I've done the exact opposite by withdrawing from my breath all my life. Refusing to exhale and experience what's happening. No wonder I can't set emotional boundaries.

Simply imagining myself breathing through tough times scares the hell out of me. I feel myself numbing out and the all-too-familiar sensation of my eyes glazing over. I'm just about to completely space out when I let out a sigh. And that humble exhale brings me back to my body. Instead of checking out, I acknowledge that I'm having a flashback. I'm about six years old, hiding under my bed sheets and blanket. I nearly suffocate under my blankets to escape from my sisters fighting over underwear. Back to present time. Tears start pouring down my face. I commit to the present moment with another long, pronounced exhale, followed by sobbing and more tears.

I gently smile as I realize, *I just did it; I actually breathed through a painful memory.* Feeling proud of my accomplishment, I exhale fully. That humble exhale sends me back to a memory of when I was about four years old. My mom is in the upstairs hallway screaming at my Dad who is in the bathroom. My mom runs into the bathroom and throws a glass coffee pot into the bathtub where my Dad's bathing. He runs out of the bathtub to get away from the broken glass. I see the terror in his eyes as he runs out of the bathroom naked. I run as fast as I can down the stairs to the kitchen pantry. I sneak into my favorite hiding spot and squeeze myself into a milk crate at the bottom of the pantry. I put my thumb in my mouth and seal off my breath by sucking on it. I'm once again just about to drift off to a never-never land when I'm rescued by an honest, heartfelt exhale. Tears start running down my face. Sob. Sigh. Sob. I let it go, and giggle as I realize I just breathed through a terrifying memory. Sobbing, crying, sighing — they all count as exhaling, and I'm doing it. I'm breathing through and processing these memories one breath at a time.

I'm finally willing to accept I must stop running away from my feelings. I'm not sure what it means to feel my feelings. But, I'm very clear that breathing is an essential ingredient for feeling my emotions. And I emote by exhaling: cry, laugh, shout, gasp, sigh, speak, sing, cheer, and whistle. The common advice, "Take a deep breath" backfires on me. I tend to hold my breath after a deep inhale, and actually need to cue my breathing out. After a full exhale, I automatically inhale, but after an inhale, I often hold my breath, stop breathing. Just as my Zen Buddhist teachers taught me, I need to "Focus on the exhale."

I congratulate myself for breaking down the nebulous concept of emotional boundaries into a simple, concrete action, "Exhale." Breathing out helps me to stop holding my breath, be present with my feelings, and choose how I express them. Breaking my breath-holding habit promises to be the biggest obstacle on my journey toward maintaining emotional boundaries.

Mom, I hope that story didn't offend you. I just wanted you to know how hard I worked to reconcile our relationship. In the months after that super painful therapy session, I still panicked whenever I imagined going home to see you. But I'm so happy that I finally made the journey to see you. And, at long last, we talked to each other.

Love,
Natazha

Reconnected by Exhaling   August 2016

More than ever before I now consider my reconciliation with my Mom a miracle. This summer, my siblings shared stories about my Mom that made me realize she forgave me for much more than I ever imagined. In this letter I describe the encounter that ended our five-year Cold War and exemplifies the power of the "Almighty Exhale."

Dear Mom:

It was super hard for me to reconnect with you after five years of silence. I was terrified the first time we saw each other again. I was still struggling with emotional boundaries. Here's my account of our reunion in your kitchen in February 1993.

I sit all alone on the bench adjacent to my parent's twelve-foot kitchen table that can sit 14 people. The same kitchen clock from my childhood ticks in the background, announcing this is not a dream: I am in fact back home in Sayville. Anxious, disoriented, and excited, I feel so much emotion that I steadily blow air out of my mouth to remain in my body.

My Dad just ran upstairs to get my Mom. The encounter I've both dreaded and desired is only seconds away. I hear my parents' footsteps as they climb down the stairs. My Dad enters the kitchen first, my Mom trailing behind him. "Do you want a cup of tea?" My Dad asks.

"No, I'm okay." I respond.

My mom sits at the opposite end of the table, a safe distance from me. Silence. She looks down to avoid my eyes. My Dad excuses himself to go to the bathroom to give us some privacy. I look at my Mom and say nothing; however, I exhale my commitment to rebuilding our relationship. She doesn't look at me, but stares at the refrigerator across the room. I stick to my plan. Exhale. Focus on exhaling. My Mom senses my deep, slow breathing, and at one point looks at me, but quickly diverts her gaze toward the windows. She still struggles to breathe, wheezing slightly.

My Dad returns from the bathroom and quietly sits down. I'm overwhelmed by the silence. I expected so much more. We sit there without talking for about another five minutes. I calm myself with long, slow out-breaths. Despite connecting with my breath, I still feel overwhelmed and believe I have failed. I look up at my Mom and attempt to say good-bye with my words, but instead use my breath to proclaim I'm leaving with a long, pronounced exhale.

I do manage to say good-bye to my Dad, and promise to come back tomorrow to take them to lunch at the new café on Main Street at 12:30. As I stand in the kitchen doorway, we all breathe together for a few moments. I sense my Dad feels this quiet act of conspiring was a perfect first step toward reconciliation. The serene silence speaks volumes about our progress: We are, in fact, peacefully cohabitating in the same space. And that's a big first step for us.

Nevertheless, I walk back to my sister TC's, house feeling like an utter failure. I had envisioned us talking and hugging on this first encounter.

Looking back at it now, I was crazy to think that we'd go from five years of bitter silence to speaking on the first visit. That's like going from five years of sitting on the sofa to running a marathon on your first run. Now I agree with Dad, and consider our conspiring a perfect first step toward forgiveness. I know that it worked because the next day, I met you and Dad at Café Joelle. We chatted and even hugged each other at the end of our lunch.

More than ever, I now understand that I can't think my way to an emotional boundary. I must express it with my body and respiration. Breathing is the gateway to my body and feelings. The simplest way to honor my breath is to exhale. And, when I'm not suffocating myself, I'm better able to set emotional boundaries and maintain healthy relationships. It's how I continued to build our relationship ever since our February 1993 kitchen table encounter.

Love,
Natazha

Healing Trauma Through Meditation, Not Medication September 2016

My therapists told me, "There's no easy way to heal from trauma." I'm so grateful they encouraged me to breathe through my intense, painful feelings to love and heal myself. They taught me to breathe in order to "feel" my emotions. I hope sharing my experience inspires others to feel and heal through the almighty act of respiration.

Dear Mom,

You'll never know how hard our Cold War was on me. I didn't stop talking to you out of pure hate. I was actually trying to protect you. I felt so enraged that I was terrified of what I'd do to you if I saw you. Underneath my rage was soul-shattering hurt, and beneath the hurt was incredible love for you and the rest of the family. I missed you, Daddy Ray, and everyone else terribly during my five-year absence. The holidays were the worst. We always had at least 13 people, usually more, sitting around our dining table. It felt strange celebrating with only Bill or whomever else I was dating at the time.

It still hurts just thinking about those lonely five years. I was haunted by shame, rage, sorrow, confusion, and terror back then. I felt like such a failure compared to the other kids. I couldn't even tolerate a visit to Sayville, let alone live there. The others didn't seem to have any childhood traumas like me. In confidence, I only recently learned that some of them were traumatized. I got treated for depression and anxiety, and now they're addressing trauma. It breaks my heart that you and

Daddy tried so hard, and yet we got traumatized anyway.

It also breaks my heart, even after we reconciled, that we never discussed what happened. I never explained why I sent my "Declaration of Independence." I never shared that 30 years ago, long before it was well known or understood, I got diagnosed with post-traumatic stress disorder and dissociative identity disorder. On top of anxiety and depression my therapists recognized I was first and foremost traumatized. I feel blessed they skipped the latest and greatest anti-depressant and anti-anxiety drugs. Instead they prescribed simple breath-based practices: meditation, self-hypnosis, exercise, expressive arts therapy, and sage advice to slow down and catch my breath. Stop holding my breath.

I'm no longer ashamed of my mental illness. I can now talk openly about it. After decades of awesome help, including basic breathing techniques, I now realize I was like a Vietnam vet; Sayville was my Vietnam. In order to heal, I needed to leave Sayville to stop being retriggered and integrate my shattered soul. Living in San Francisco granted me the breathing room to rescue myself with my breath. By changing my respiration I became more self-compassionate and restored my sanity. As a child, I saved my life by holding my breath to dissociate from life-threatening traumas. As an adult I learned to stop holding my breath by exhaling fully. And that enabled me to re-inhabit my body so I could enjoy a full-capacity life. I'm incredibly grateful for my happy marriage, private Physical

Therapy practice, and excellent health. Those treasures are the rewards of healing from trauma by restoring my innate breathing pattern.

Love,
Natazha

The Fine Line between Psychic and Psychotic   September 2016

Meditation and aerobic exercise ground me so I can use my psychic abilities as gifts instead of feeling overwhelmed and handicapped by them.

Dear Mom:

I'm beginning to see my five-year break from you, the family, and Sayville as an act of self-love. Staying away permitted me to heal traumas affecting the whole family. And it set the stage for the rest of the family to heal.

As I said earlier, I missed you, Daddy Ray, and all the other kids terribly. Dad talked to me during our Cold War. I still marvel at how well he managed to honor both of us during our phone calls. He reminded me that you loved me, and acted as the bridge that eventually brought us back together. He repeatedly said, "It's funny you're healing from sexual abuse; your Mom is now in therapy healing from her own sexual abuse." Dad never directly talked about my accusations of sexual abuse I made on my "Declaration of Independence" audiotape. But he did imply you acknowledged them when you got help for yourself. I strongly believe in family systems. When one person heals, everyone in the family heals. Both of us healed our sexual abuse wounds after I sent my explosive "Declaration of Independence."

I still regret we never talked openly about what fueled our bitter feud. We never totally cleared the air between us. Until I heard John's funeral speech, I felt too ashamed of my mental illness to talk about it. His speech transformed my consciousness and relationship with you. I realized I'm definitely my Mother's daughter.

Mom, you're a mystic, and I take after you. I'm always in some metaphysical program. Now, I'm in a metaphysical writing program and several other meditation groups. We never talked about how my Berkeley Psychic Institute (BPI) training helped me forgive you and regard my sensitivity as a gift, rather than a liability. We're both psychic and I wished we had talked about it. Many of us "mentally ill" people never learned to use our sensitivity to our advantage. We are often misunderstood in a culture that doesn't value sensitivity. Dr. Elaine Aaron in *The Highly Sensitive Person* does a great job of explaining how being sensitive is a gift, not a defect.

Psychic people are misunderstood and sometimes mislabeled as psychotic for many reasons. Our culture is emotionally and spiritually illiterate. Also, our medical system doesn't address the spiritual realm. That makes me wonder if you were erroneously mislabeled as psychotic when you were really a psychic working on an intense spiritual mission. I believe during your institutionalization you were in part working on healing Irish shame.

I want you to know that I struggled at BPI. I felt conflicted. Part of me thought it was hocus pocus, but I'm grateful the part of me that knew my life depended on learning how to use my intuition and psychic abilities won out. For several years I read the aura of whoever sat in front of me. Felt weird giving psychic readings, but kept reading auras anyway. My reward was receiving an insight that spawned my reconciliation with you.

At BPI, we learned how to check for beings that could take on many different forms. I interpreted these spiritual beings as "belief clusters" or ancestral ghosts we inherited from our ancestors or other people around us. For example, they can be unresolved, centuries-old shame that has been passed down from one generation to the next. Many of these beings or ghosts are completely out of context and literally drive us nuts.

Sometimes I'd see an aura cluttered with beings or "belief clusters." Instead of seeing one being I'd see the person's spirit plus other objects or beings. Slowly but surely I learned to trust what I saw and reported whatever I saw, no matter how weird I thought it was. That actually helped me relearn to trust my own instincts.

In 1992, I gave an aura reading that cracked open my cold, shutdown heart. And I started to forgive you. I read a victim of sexual abuse who carried many intense shame beings in her space. Other people call these belief clusters demonic beings that drive people mad. She inherited them from the maternal side of her family. Looking at her space, I realized I hated your mental illness and shame beings with all my might and yet I loved your loving true essence, your innate spirit, with all my heart and soul. That was the first time I realized you didn't hurt me, but your mental illness or shame beings deeply wounded me. In that moment, I found a way to reconcile with you and yet still acknowledge the abuse. You didn't abuse me per se. It was your beings that abused me. Dad was right; you always loved me. The beings on your maternal side, Nanny's side of the family, hurt me. I just needed to embrace you and protect myself from those evil beings.

I thought a lot about this psychic reading after hearing John's funeral speech. His speech reminded me that your mental illness, not your loving essence, was what abused me. And, you fought with every fiber of your being to leave Central Islip so you could love and mother me. John's speech made the notion of "shame beings" real to me again.

BPI was a crazy place, but nonetheless, I'm grateful that giving psychic readings enabled me to recognize your lovely beautiful essence. That psychic reading was the first step in forgiving you. I exhaled thousands of times to digest the significance of that reading to feel safe enough to see you in person. And, just as I had to meditate and write to absorb all the electrifying insights I gained from John's funeral speech, I meditated and wrote in my journal for months to integrate the life-altering insights from that psychic reading.

Mom, please understand I always loved you. I despised the shame beings that have haunted our lineage for centuries, but I never hated your loving essence. And, as I write *Rescued by My Breath*, I'm finally making peace with those shame beings, and releasing them from my own space. I'm so grateful you're helping me to stop passing down shame to the next generation.

Love,
Natazha

The Science Behind the Almighty Exhale   April 2016

My professional training reinforced what I already learned about exhalation. Stress cues us to over-exaggerate our inhalation and fire up the part of the nervous system that's responsible for our flight-or-fight response and stressing out. Interestingly enough, research shows exhaling twice as long as you inhale induces the relaxation response necessary to combat stress.

Dear Mom,

After years of smoking and incessantly holding my breath, I had horrible breathing habits and often caught myself out of breath. I instinctively knew that I needed to rehabilitate my breathing habits, and began this process by breaking down my breathing into its two main phases: inhalation and exhalation. I quickly discovered that I had been neglecting to exhale fully. I needed to concentrate on the "Almighty Exhale" to release my pent-up emotions, frustrations, worries, and unexpressed impulses ransacking my being.

In my PT training, I learned more about why exhaling helps us heal and forgive. The chart below depicts how breathing interfaces with the autonomic nervous system (ANS). The ANS is a special part of the nervous system that controls many of our responses that happen automatically, without us thinking about it. Some examples are our hearts pumping blood, sweating, and digesting our food.

The ANS is comprised of the sympathetic nervous system (SNS) and parasympathetic nervous system (PNS). The SNS controls our flight-and-fight response. The PNS enables us to rest and digest. Ideally, the SNS and PNS are in balance.

Together with the endocrine system, the ANS controls our response to stress. And guess what, breathing strongly influences this stress-response system. It's one way breathing directly affects how we manage stress, including shame and other people testing our boundaries.

The chart below shows exhaling is linked to the PNS. And the PNS enables us to recover from stress by stimulating us to heal, forgive, rest, digest, and replenish our energy. So it makes sense that research shows exhaling twice as long as you inhale induces the relaxation response that helps us recuperate from our busy lives.

PNS - Parasympathetic Nervous System	SNS – Sympathetic Nervous System
Linked to Exhaling and Relaxation	Linked to Inhaling and Stress
Recover from stress, rest and digest Slow down and relax Make and restore energy	Become alert and stressed Speed up and ready to fight Spend energy; can't renew energy
Enhances functions not essential to survival: healing, recovering from exertion, digesting food, replenish energy, forgiving, creating art	Shuts down functions unessential for survival: digestion, healing, renewing energy, creating art, etc.

Most of us suffer from stress due to our busy, over-stimulated lifestyles. And, stress is no small matter. In many ways, it's the number one killer of Americans. The research of neuroscientists Bruce

McEwen and Robert Sapolsky, among others, reveals that stress causes or greatly contributes to many of our fatal diseases. Illnesses ranging from heart disease, cancer, type II diabetes, strokes, asthma and many other medical conditions. Moreover, we've become an SNS-dominant nation and that keeps us chronically stressed out. Hailing the "Almighty Exhale" taps into our body's built-in mechanism to reduce stress, the PNS. It's another good reason to "Hail the Almighty Exhale" whenever you can.

I believe you and Daddy Ray actually died from the stress of raising us kids. Both of you had type II diabetes, which is linked to stress. Plus Dad died of stress-related heart disease. You smoked to manage your stress. Smoking is linked to your lung and fatal bone cancer. I regret not taking more time to help you relax and rejuvenate yourself. That regret inspires me to share my expertise about medicating ourselves through our breathing to combat the effects of stress.

Hail the Exhale,
Natazha

Chronic Obstructive Pulmonary Disease Often Goes Undiagnosed

October 2016

Dr. Valerie Schneider is the only person I know who loves talking about breathing as much as I do. She is a pulmonologist who wants more people aware of Chronic Obstructive Pulmonary Disease (COPD.) All too often it goes undiagnosed until it's too late to be effectively treated.

Dear Mom:

You of all people understand that with most respiratory disease people fight to get air out of their lungs. Hyperventilation is the most common symptom of COPD and all respiratory disease. COPD is the third leading cause of death in America. It is also the most common form of respiratory illness that represents an umbrella term for several irreversible, progressive lung diseases: emphysema, chronic bronchitis, and non-reversible asthma. For my entire life you pretty much suffered from every form of COPD and struggled to exhale fully.

Your severe COPD went undiagnosed until Auntie Pat saved your life by calling for an ambulance on Christmas Day 1987. It bothers me COPD so often goes undiagnosed. The Centers for Disease Control and Prevention estimate 15 million Americans suffer from it; however, the American Lung Association and many other experts estimate over 24 million Americans have it.

Why is COPD under-diagnosed? Shortness of breath (SOB) is an inability to exhale fully. Most people and doctors don't take it seriously. They erroneously believe SOB is a normal aspect of aging. Truth is, no one, not even a ninety-year old, should suffer from SOB. Breathlessness indicates deconditioning, pulmonary disease, or heart disease, but not ordinary aging.

Just like heart palpitations, SOB necessitates a visit to your doctor. The fact that COPD is correlated with aging confuses people: correlation does not equal causation. In other words, normal aging does not cause COPD. Longer exposure to air pollution increases your chances of developing COPD. And guess what? Living longer increases your chances of being exposed to air pollution, including cigarette smoke. Living longer increases the chances of you being exposed to cigarette smoke and it affords you more years to smoke. Make no mistake – smoking is the number one cause of COPD.

To add to the confusion about aging and breathlessness, aging also correlates with, but does not cause, some other obstacles to exhaling. As they grow older, many Americans gain weight, especially belly fat. This weight gain prevents the diaphragm from moving properly and hinders their ability to exhale fully. Poor posture with aging also hinders your ability to exhale. Lastly, we lose elasticity in our lung tissue with aging and that also slightly diminishes our ability to exhale.

I remember teaching you a classic COPD breath technique called pursed-lip breathing. I told you it's like silent whistling and joked that "Whistle while you work really does work." You told me you couldn't whistle. That saddened me because whistling is a really fun way to exhale. Ironically, I also cherish that moment. It was a rare tender moment with you. I just loved learning about one of your idiosyncrasies and knowing a secret about you.

Love,
Natazha

Take a Deep Breath Out   May 2016

Do yourself a favor. Cue your exhale instead of your inhale. Why? Exhaling triggers you to inhale and continue breathing. However, inhaling does not automatically cue you to exhale.

Dear Mom,

I stopped saying, "Take a deep breath in" to my yoga and Pilates students several decades ago. All too often, they'd over-inflate their lungs with a dramatic inhale, then hold their breath, and neglect to exhale. Now, I say, "Luxuriate in your exhale. Take a deep breath out."

Try this breath holding experiment. Inhale as much air as possible. Plug your nose. Time how long you can hold your breath. Now exhale as much air as possible, as in blowing out 16 birthday candles. Plug your nose. Time how long you hold your breath. Did you notice you could hold your breath much longer after inhaling than exhaling? That's why "Take a deep breath out" is a more appropriate phrase than "Take a deep breath in."

I pretty much never say, "Inhale." And yet, no student has ever died. Without any cueing, they all automatically inhale. Stress triggers us to over-emphasize inhalation and hyperventilate. We're hard-wired to suck in air when we feel scared, rushed, pressured, overwhelmed, or misunderstood. Our consumer culture also trains us to over-consume air, another way of saying hyperventilate. We really need to cue the "Almighty Exhale."

Breathing out deserves the nickname the "Almighty Exhale." A whole-hearted exhale rewards us on all levels: physical, emotional, intellectual, and spiritual. In Chinese medicine, they instruct patients to place a gentle emphasis on exhalation, and call this breathing technique "Buddha's Breath." Yogis and spiritual leaders, including the Buddha, intuitively knew of the benefits of exhaling and for centuries taught us to "Hail the Exhale" via chanting and singing that emphasize the out-breath. "Buddha's Breath" benefits us by stimulating the parasympathetic nervous system (PNS) that's responsible for the relaxation response necessary to combat stress in our modern lives. The PNS enables us to relax, love, digest, heal, and recover from stress. In other words, the "Almighty Exhale" tunes us into many delicious intangibles: creativity, love, and self-expression, to name a few.

It takes a leap of faith to fully let go and fully exhale. Over the years I've developed several techniques for seducing students to breathe out fully. One example is the "Sharing Breath." To do it you imagine you're sharing some divine quality like joy, beauty, or humor with loved ones anywhere in the world by exhaling. My students automatically improve their posture and breathe more deeply by taking deep breaths out.

I use "Sharing Breath" to send you love and tenderness I didn't express to you when you were alive.

Love,
Natazha

The Inhale Bias   June 2016

A poor relationship with our breath is one of many reasons why we become inhale-dominant breathers.

Dear Mom:

We demonstrate our bias for inhaling through our language and behavior. The word for inhalation, *inspiration,* denotes both breathing in and feeling uplifted. The word for exhalation, *expiration,* denotes breathing out and dying. Inhaling gets associated with enthusiasm and angels whereas exhaling gets associated with death and the expiration date on moldy cheese.

Hyperventilation displays our tendency to favor inhalation. It means overinflating your lungs, the most common symptom being respiratory disease and stress. You gulp air down too fast to adequately exhale. Think about it. There's no equivalent word for excessive exhalation. You don't injure yourself by exhaling too long. In fact, you emote, express feelings and create art through prolonged exhales: talk, sing, cheer, chant, play wind instruments, laugh, sob, shriek, and so on.

As an ex-smoker, I'm painfully aware how our addictions train us to overindulge our in-breath. With smoking, you're rewarded with a rush of nicotine by inhaling, but not exhaling. The same is true for most vices. Whether you snort, eat, or drink your drug of choice, you satiate your cravings by inhaling, not exhaling. Bill Clinton's infamous remark about his pot smoking illustrates my point: "But, I didn't inhale."

The often-used phrase, "Take a deep breath" also demonstrates how we play respiratory favorites. That phrase elicits a big, dramatic inhale from most people. They over-inflate their lungs, typically hold their breath and skip the out-breath. Breathing this way causes us to use our secondary respiratory muscles in the neck and shoulders instead of the deeper, primary respiratory muscles found in the core, the diaphragm and abdominal muscles. Ironically that inhale-dominant response results in shallow, not deep, breathing. A full exhale triggers us to breathe more deeply.

Here's yet another way to look at our inhale bias. Fully exhaling creates a vacuum in our lungs. Since Nature abhors a vacuum, we automatically inhale to fill that void. Exhaling cues us to inhale, but the converse is not true. Inhaling does not automatically cue us to exhale. In fact, many of us hold our breath after an exaggerated in-breath and neglect to exhale consciously.

I want to add just one more thing. We apologize for yawning, an elongated exhale. It's regarded as a rude expression of boredom, but it's actually our attempt to stay awake because we want to hear what's being said. It helps us reset our autonomic nervous system. What's so rude about that? I get riled up about what I perceive as a prejudice against exhaling. I believe that bias creates so many problems in the world. Exhaling is the backbone of emotional literacy and I feel emotional illiteracy is the cause behind so much misery in the world.

Love,
Natazha

BrEAThing Affects Your Weight   June 2016

I'll always think of my Mom as thin. When I was a child she looked slender to me even when she was pregnant. She did, however, gain weight after taking prednisone for her COPD. She once asked me about losing weight. I never gave her an answer when she was alive. That's why I wrote this letter to her.

Dear Mom,

I have long suspected our breathing affects our weight. I don't have any hard core research studies to prove my hunch. However, I want to share some anecdotal evidence that supports my assertion.

People lose weight, both emotional and physical, by changing their breathing. You can shift your respiration in a variety of ways. Meditate regularly. Change your environment by living at much higher altitude or scuba diving in deep water. Using a continuous positive air pressure device, a CPAP machine, is a surefire way to change your breathing.

Many sleep-apnea patients lose weight once they start using a CPAP machine. These patients stop breathing during their sleep and wake up all throughout the night. It causes them to sleep poorly. The CPAP device keeps their airways open so they can't stop breathing. By changing only these patients' breathing, the CPAP device often triggers weight loss. You may argue that the person sheds pounds once they sleep well. But, I'd argue the CPAP machine helps them both slim down and sleep better by changing only their respiration. It is anecdotal proof that changing your breathing simultaneously addresses several problems, including poor sleeping and obesity.

You also lose weight when conditions force you to work harder to breathe, for example climbing Mount

Everest at 29,000 feet above sea level. At one point, I dreamed of summiting Mount Everest and I actually interviewed several mountaineers who reached its peak. They all advised the same thing: "Gain as much weight as you possibly can. The weight just pours off of you in the Himalayas."

Scientists believe we lose weight at higher altitudes because there's less oxygen in the air, forcing us to work harder to inhale the same amount of oxygen. And here's one more thing to consider. Colorado consistently ranks as America's number one "skinny" state. It routinely has the lowest percentage of obese citizens of any other state in the USA. And guess what? Colorado has the highest mean elevation of any state in America. Its capital city, Denver, is known as the mile-high city. It's a city where people have to breathe harder to receive the same amount of oxygen as someone at sea level.

Exercise also changes how you breathe. You need to breathe more efficiently to meet your muscles' increased demand for oxygen. Research shows how you breathe during exercise dictates whether or not you lose fat. Sustained aerobic exercise has been proven to cause weight loss. Aerobic exercise means exercising with oxygen. The father of aerobic exercise, Dr. Kenneth Cooper, advises people to use the talk test – that's actually a breath test – to see if they're exercising aerobically. During exercise, you should be able to talk in short sentences. If you can't, you're working too hard and need to slow down. If you can sing, you aren't working hard enough, and need to pick up the pace.

It makes total sense to me that how you breathe during exercise can affect weight loss. Here's my rationale. We know the need for oxygen increases as we move faster and harder. Unable-to-talk breathing indicates you're not keeping up with this oxygen demand and are incurring a bigger post-exercise oxygen deficit. Experiencing a post-exercise oxygen deficit may explain why some exercise doesn't help you slim down. Beta-oxidation needed for burning fat requires much more oxygen than metabolizing carbohydrates. When there's less oxygen available, your body is more likely to crave carbohydrates that require less oxygen than protein and fats to be metabolized. When you eat more carbohydrates after exercising, those carbs get stored as extra fat. Thus, you gain fat and weight instead of losing it.

I watched this phenomenon play out when I coached San Francisco's Team in Training Marathon Run teams for five years. Each season a significant number of participants gained weight when they increased their running. I suspect these runners breathed in an unable-to-talk manner as they ran and acquired a post-exercise oxygen deficit. It compelled them to overeat carbohydrates after running, and those extra carbs turned into extra fat.

Meditation also shifts our breathing. Research shows meditation can help people lose weight. Scientists believe meditation induces weight loss by reducing stress that makes some people over-eat. Also, being more mindful makes you more likely to notice what you're eating and how much you're eating. That enables you to make wiser food choices.

Lastly, I don't think it's a mere coincidence that the word brEAThing contains the word EAT. You can think of brEAThing as the ultimate form of eating. We consume the essential elements of carbon dioxide and oxygen by brEAThing. Every physiological process in the human body requires either oxygen or carbon dioxide. We can skip food for days, but can survive only minutes without brEAThing. We endlessly debate over the perfect diet, but everyone agrees we need oxygen and carbon dioxide to live. Given that oxygen and carbon dioxide are required for all our physiological processes, it just makes sense that our breathing affects gaining and losing weight.

Love,
Natazha

How to Hail the Exhale

April 2016

It was incredibly kind of my sister Gabrielle to throw me a surprise 50th birthday party. My favorite part was the spring-green tee shirts with "Hail the Exhale" written across the front. I coined that phrase to celebrate breaking my seemingly innocuous, but nonetheless lethal, habit of holding my breath via consciously exhaling. Most of us hold our breath after inhaling. That's why any cue to exhale is also a cue to stop holding our breath. I worked hard to stop short-shrifting myself with half-assed exhales and hope this list inspires you to "Hail the Exhale."

Dear Mom:

Learning to fully exhale gave me a new lease on life. I began expressing my feelings more freely and released long-repressed grief, shame, and terror. I felt so much better after releasing emotional baggage that I wrote this list of glorious ways to stop waiting to exhale.

Howl at the moon. Chuckle. Whistle while you work. Giggle with glee. Shout to let it all out. Chirp like a bird saluting the sunrise. Blow a whistle. Yawn for refreshment. Sob. Chant your favorite mantra. When in doubt, breathe out. Roar like a lion. Sing an aria. Speak your truth to get "it" off your chest. Cry. Go caroling at Christmas time. Yell at idiots on TV. Cheer for your playmates and coworkers. Hum a lovely melody. Blow off people who tell you to take a deep breath. Sing the blues. Play a sonnet on a flute. Proclaim a sexual orgasm with your breath. Sound the trumpets. Laugh until your belly aches. Bark. Leave a trail of bubbles as you swim underwater. Ha! Ha! Ha! Share your life's story. Join a choir. Scream at the top of your lungs. Tell a joke. Stop holding your breath. Mock the mockingbird. Meow. Play "Home on the Range" on a harmonica. Coo with delight. Blow off steam. Gasp in horror. Seduce your lover with the saxophone. Grunt while lifting heavy objects. Punctuate sex with wild moaning. Talk to plants. Beat your chest and roar like Tarzan. Quack. Whisper sweet nothings. Hoot and holler for your favorite team. Give a speech. Blow out all your birthday candles on the first try. Shriek. Perform a Gregorian chant. Recite poetry. Sneeze. Make steam by blowing out air on a cold winter night. Blow soap bubbles. Lullaby your loved ones. Breathe out hard to push your baby from the womb. Sing along with the radio. Cough. Gush with excitement. Let the air flow for better Mo Jo. Chat with close friends. Yodel. Kiai (a Japanese term used for the short yell uttered when performing an attacking move) to declare your strength in a karate class. Ahh! Take a sigh of relief. Life begins with an exhale and ends on an inhale. Hail the Exhale, right now.

I try to inspire my students to try some of these delicious ways to "Hail the Exhale." And I'm sorry that I didn't spend more time helping you "Hail the Exhale."

Love,
Natazha

When in Doubt, Breathe Out   June 2016

I dedicate this letter to my students who teach me something every time I'm supposedly "teaching" them.

Dear Mom,

One of my students reminds me so much of you. She's a good mom to her two lovely daughters. She gave a generous donation to the Saint Lawrence Outreach Program when you died. At 80, she's still running all over San Francisco and the world with her St. Dominick's Church group. She's also a Eucharistic minister, prayer professional, and strongly believes in the power of the Holy Spirit. You're also a big believer in the power of the Holy Ghost and share her incredible faith in God's love for all of us.

The biggest reason she reminds me of you is her severely compromised posture. She's a tiny Asian woman who began looking like a question mark with her head drooping down and ribs trailing behind instead of leading the way for the rest of her body. She began physical therapy because she kept falling, due to her severely stooped posture that took her off balance.

She began training with me after her doctor told her she had severe degenerative kyphosis (poor, stooped posture) and he could do nothing for her. Surgery can't fix that condition. Posture is all about how your muscles relate to each other, which is controlled by breathing habits. No surgery or pill can fix this type of muscle imbalance.

After two Cesarean births and growing up in a culture where women were told it's undignified and unladylike to exercise, she had terribly weak abdominal muscles. Those muscles are critical for exhaling fully and good posture. Just like you, she's extremely hardworking and persistent. She came to my Better Balance, Breathing and Posture class twice a week and took a weekly private lesson. More importantly, she practiced what I taught her outside the classroom in her daily life.

She's a great example of slow and steady progress. One breath at a time, she learned to breathe and move differently. Doing so improved her posture. Her family was the first to notice her improved posture, even when she couldn't see it. However, she did notice that she stopped falling, walked faster, and was stronger. Now she hikes up San Francisco's famous Lyon Street stairs that are a true uphill battle.

It took a year before my client acknowledged her progress. In the meantime, she often felt frustrated and said, "I just can't feel my abs. They're so weak." I kept advising, "Don't focus on the problem. Focus on the solution: exhale. When in doubt, breathe out. That's how you strengthen your abs." I gave her the breathing tip that I once gave you. "Imagine you're blowing out birthday candles to exhale fully." I also taught her the martial arts breathing technique called *Kiai.* The silent forceful exhale helped her engage her core muscles.

She made my day when she returned from a church trip to Cuba. Smiling brightly, she said. "Now I know why you're always saying 'Exhale.' The first few days were miserable. I just couldn't keep up with the group, and kept trailing far behind. I was working so hard I couldn't enjoy any of the sights. I prayed to the Holy Spirit and that's when I remembered you always saying, 'Exhale. When in doubt, breathe out.' I figured I had nothing to lose, so I finally tried exhaling. And it worked! I focused on exhaling. I could feel my abdominal muscles working harder, and began walking faster. I kept up with the group. From then on, I had a great time."

Mom, exhaling works because we contract our diaphragm and abdominal muscles to exhale fully. Breathing out is the power phase of breathing. With inhaling, we expand and slightly relax our core muscles. My student is a great example of how posture is affected by breathing habits. All along she had made progress. She got stronger and improved her balance. But I noticed her posture improved the most when she wholeheartedly applied my advice, "Exhale. Just remember to exhale."

We breathe all the time. Therefore, changing our breathing creates profound effects, including alleviating conditions that doctors say there's nothing they can do for it.

Love,
Natazha

Touching You With My Exhale   August 2016

I still miss my Mom. Although I connect to her through writing and breathing with her spirit, I still ache to touch her with my hands, and not just my breath.

Dear Mom,

The physical therapist and "hug monster" in me still regrets not touching you more during my final visit. I miss you so much and wish we had cuddled in bed last January. Whenever I'm haunted by that regret, I remind myself, "Your bone cancer made being touched downright painful for you. Besides, you weren't a feely, touchy person. I touched you on your terms, a mystic's terms, through the breath that reigns over spirit."

I feel better once I acknowledge how we embraced through the almighty exhale. You could no longer read on your own. Reading out loud the writings of your two favorite Catholic mystics, Thomas Merton and John O'Donohue, was a perfect way to touch "Mary the Mystic." I used my respiration to modulate the tone, volume, cadence and pitch of my reading voice to caress your body and soul. You seemed to appreciate me dramatizing their writings by changing my breathing.

Noreen and Luke (Natazha's siblings) warned me your sleep was usually agitated. They advised doing everything possible to help you sleep well. So I did what moms have always done, consoled and nourished their babies by singing lullabies and whispering sweet nothings. I lulled you to fitful sleep with a breath-based maternal medicine.

When your energy was high, we talked and even laughed a little. We swapped stories about Daddy. Talking about your decision to stop chemotherapy seemed to take a weight off your chest. You breathed more easily. Silent at first, we eventually shared a sigh of relief as we acknowledged the bitter truth: you felt chemotherapy wasn't worth it. You wanted to die with dignity.

You were so exhausted and tortured by pain that conspiring was the only form of connection you could easily tolerate. You just hated being bedbound and unable to explore the world. Without uttering a word, we shared what you could still take in of life. We conversed by inhaling and exhaling about the lovely happenings outside your bedroom windows: tiny birds standing up to winter; howling winds blowing snow through the air; and trees half dressed in sparkling snow and ice.

While you slept, I meditated and blessed you. I exhaled comfort and grace to you in the hopes of making your journey to the other side more peaceful. Now that you're dead and I can't call you anymore, I sit on our living room sofa and meditate. As I meditate, I imagine our spirits exhaling to touch each other.

Love you,
Natazha

Section Three

Held By My Breath
Instead Of Hold
My Breath

Holding Your Breath Suffocates Your Soul   September 2016

It's very common for incest survivors to legally change their names. When I changed my breathing habits, I no longer breathed like either rambunctious Bunny or saintly Bernadette. I also stopped holding my breath in anticipation of more traumas to come. I celebrated the integration of my personality by legally changing my name to Natazha Raine O'Connor.

Dear Mom,

I can't believe we never talked about why I legally changed my name from Bernadette Connors to Natazha Raine O'Connor. I officially changed it during our Cold War on 4/17/92. When we finally broke our silence in 1993, I struggled in your presence to simply stay present and breathe with ease. We weren't ready to tackle such a heavy topic right off the bat. Even though I had 23 years from 1993 to 2016, I never set the record straight. I knew you believed I threw away my chosen name, Bernadette, to hurt you. Nothing could be further from the truth. I suffered from Dissociative Identity Disorder (DID), what some people call multiple personality disorder. I felt too ashamed to tell you about how healing my mental illness inspired me to change my name. I did appreciate you naming me after Saint Bernadette. It was a very appropriate name as I am a clairvoyant and a talented healer like St. Bernadette. I travelled to Lourdes three times to visit Saint Bernadette's shrine that is famous as a site where people receive miraculous healings.

I also regret not telling you about Bob's connection to Saint Bernadette. He and Saint Bernadette share the same birthday, January 7. And back in the 1930s, Bob's paternal grandmother,

Grandma Bernie, went to Lourdes. She had developed debilitating, "incurable" tinnitus after her twelve-year old son was killed in a trolley-car accident. In the 1930s travelling to Lourdes was an expensive expedition. She took a train from San Francisco to New York City, then an ocean liner to Britain, another boat to Normandy, and finally a train to Lourdes, in the French and Spanish border in the Pyrenees Mountains. Her pilgrimage was well worth the trouble and expense because her tinnitus was cured.

John's funeral speech reminded me that you, too, suffered from mental illness and healed yourself. Now, I think you'd have understood my struggles with DID. I so wish I confided more in you when you were alive. We missed an opportunity to grow by sharing our stories. I used breath-based therapies to become whole again. I wonder if that path would have worked for you, too.

Mom, I stopped calling myself Bernadette and my other aliases – Bunny, Melanie, Connors, Bones, and Marie – in order to hit a reset button. I was no longer rebellious Bunny who rebelled from our family or self-sacrificing Bernadette who was enmeshed with our family. Each name represented only a fragment of me. Breathing differently allowed me to live from a deeper, more authentic place that housed all my love and hate for you and our family.

Mom, let's clear the air between us. Let's talk about why I split into Bunny and Bernadette. You and Dad did your absolute best to love and protect us, but despite your best efforts I often felt terrified and abused. I held my breath to numb myself from the trauma of being raised in poverty, by mentally ill parents with 11 kids. And I blamed myself for our family's woes.

All things considered, breath holding sounds like a fairly benign bad habit, but it's not. Slowly but surely that habit suffocated my soul. I never breathed fully to allow myself to feel or express my own individual feelings. It actually caused incredible psychological damage. I suffocated myself in such a sinister, insidious manner that I was completely unaware how I was destroying my emotional and spiritual health in addition to trashing my lungs and body. I'm terrified you'll take what I'm saying the wrong way. Both you and Daddy quite literally went insane several times after you completely spent yourselves on us kids. That's probably why I never talked to you about this stuff when you were alive. Regardless, I need to get this crap off my chest. I hope you take what I say as a tribute to you, not as an indictment.

Here it goes. On top of the Uncle Mickey incident, I felt traumatized growing up in our household. I blamed myself for our family's problems, and couldn't process the never-ending chaos and unmet needs. It felt like a war zone. Kids were always fighting over food, clothes, and your attention. To escape the drama, I held my breath with a vicious tenacity. I successfully numbed all my feelings, including love and joy as well as shame, heartache, and terror. Divorcing myself from my breath essentially took me out of my body without any drugs. This is how my so-called innocuous habit fueled my Dissociative Identity Disorder (DID). When I refused to exhale, I not only spaced out, I also unconsciously switched sub-personalities.

Doing so ensured my entire self was never fully present.

I'm sure it seemed normal to you that I used two names growing up, Bunny and Bernadette. Almost all us kids had an assortment of names. Ray-Ray got a new nickname almost every week. You didn't know about my other aliases, Connors, Melanie, Bones, and Marie. Furthermore, you didn't know Bunny and Bernadette represented two warring sub-personalities. Around four years old, when you were institutionalized for that agonizing year, I split into Bunny and Bernadette. I did it to protect myself from ever again being abandoned by someone I loved with my whole heart and soul. Words can't describe how crushed I felt when you, my mommy, left for CI.

Splitting gave me a reprieve from the pain created by your absence. It literally saved my life by divorcing me from the trauma of living with seven other siblings under 10 years old without our Mom. We didn't understand why our mommy left and took it out on each other by constantly fighting. I've finally forgiven myself for splitting. I now understand splitting was my salvation. If only part of me showed up, then my absent parts were spared the heartache of rejection and the terror of living in a family that I feared was about to fall apart at any moment. I basically vowed never to be entirely clear and present. That's the exact opposite of the Buddhist traditions and meditation practices that I follow today.

At four years old, I couldn't process both my deep love and hate for you. Bernadette loved you with all her might and did everything possible to please you; Bunny hated you for "abandoning" us and coming back a "different" person. As Bernadette, I loved being

Mommy's little helper. In Bunny mode, I rebelled by chain-smoking, drinking, and having promiscuous, unprotected sex during the height of the AIDS and herpes epidemic in New York and San Francisco. I'm glad you never found out about all my sexual escapades when I worked on Fire Island during college. I still wonder what mystical power protected me when I acted so recklessly.

A bitter civil war that raged inside of me ruined any chance of an intimate relationship or satisfying career. Bunny hated my "Bernadette" boyfriends, and vice versa. Bunny chose wild, drug and alcohol addicts, whereas Bernadette preferred pillars of society. Since I couldn't be fully present and intimate in any relationship, I simultaneously dated "Bunny" and "Bernadette" boyfriends. All the while I hated myself for lying and cheating. The same conflict poisoned my career. Bunny aspired to become an actress whereas Bernadette saw herself as a public servant saving the world. Each sub-personality sabotaged the other's career pursuits.

My recovery from mental illness truly began when I quit smoking and changed how I breathed. Nicotine is an incredibly potent drug; it stifled my consciousness, squelched my feelings, and that kept me unaware of my split personality. Additionally, smoking trained me to hold my breath and promoted the dissociation driving my mental illness.

Mom, you're probably wondering how smoking trained me to hold my breath. Here's how. I changed my breathing pattern to ingest more nicotine. I received nicotine only when I inhaled. On the other hand, I received no nicotine when I exhaled. Smoking rewarded me for exaggerating my inhalation and short-shrifting my exhalation. To suck in as much nicotine as possible, I learned to inhale super long.

And then hold my breath to allow my body to absorb that nicotine. I'd then barely exhale because I wasn't receiving any nicotine as I breathed out. Mom, can you see how that's a set-up for holding my breath?

Trust me, changing my breathing habits was much harder than managing my nicotine withdrawal. Learning to breathe in a more balanced fashion required me to love and mother myself. Instead of dissociating, I had to pay attention to my breathing. With tremendous patience, I trained myself to stop holding my breath, but instead breathe out fully. And exhaling fully allowed me to become aware of and express my feelings. That helped me stop spacing out and numbing my feelings. And it's how I ultimately integrated my personality to become whole again.

Going back to the topic of my name change, I chose to call myself Natazha Raine O'Connor when I began breathing from deep inside of myself. I no longer operated as either Bunny or Bernadette. My new breathing style freed me to live from a more authentic place that embodied Bernadette and Bunny plus much more of myself. I finally felt safe to have only one boyfriend. I felt strong enough to consciously house all my love and hate for you.

I chose my new name for its sound and meaning. **Natazha** is a derivative of the Greek name Anastasia that means resurrection or rebirth. **Raine** represents my love of water and sounds like reign, as in I rule my world now. Originally I was going to spell it Rayne in honor of Daddy Ray, Ray-Ray, Doc Ray, B-Ray, and my godfather Uncle Ray. But, ultimately went with the Irish spelling. **O'Connor** symbolizes changing the beginning and ending of my story by changing the beginning and ending of my surname, Connors. Also, Grandma Winnie told me originally our surname was O'Connor until an ancestor changed it to Connors after fighting with his brother.

One last thing Mom: when I married Bob I never intended to change my last name to Bernie. I loved my name, Natazha Raine O'Connor. However, about a year into our marriage, I realized Bernie is a nickname for Bernadette. That's when I decided to honor you naming me after Saint Bernadette and made Natazha Bernie my legal name. I've chosen however to publish *Rescued by My Breath* under Natazha Raine O'Connor because it's my integration name, and this book is about how I released an ocean of shame and integrated myself through devotional breathing.

Love,
Natazha

Exhaling Emotional Crud Healed
My Poverty Mentality   September 2016

Poverty left many invisible scars that took decades for me to heal. These scars include the inability to separate my feelings from the "mob mentality" of my family and feeling unworthy of setting boundaries. Even though I never had COPD like my Mom, I felt so unworthy of having my needs met that on some level I even felt unworthy of breathing.

Dear Mom,

Your institutionalization wasn't the sole cause of my DID. I lived outside my body for many other reasons. Conflicting feedback and treatment from the other kids tore me apart. The younger kids looked up to me. They appreciated my help, whereas the older kids looked down on me. They resented me for stealing your attention and took their resentments out on me. Those contradictory messages made me feel schizophrenic. *"Was I a good or bad guy? Should I be proud or ashamed of myself? Did I deserve to be beaten up?"* I wanted to love my siblings and trust what they said. I absolutely hated rejecting their conflicting opinions of me. It made me feel like I was rejecting them. I avoided feeling like I was rejecting them by sucking my thumb and holding my breath. And those breathing habits fueled my DID.

Growing up poor fostered a poverty mentality that also fed my DID. You locked the refrigerator, pantry and phone. Our family routinely didn't get our basic needs met. Those experiences taught me it's selfish to satisfy my needs. Being hungry sent me a clear message: I was unworthy of having my basic needs met. When I saw one kid get your attention at the expense of another kid, that message was reinforced. I began to believe I'd always have to sacrifice one part of myself for another part. I could meet my intellectual, or spiritual, or physical or emotional needs, but never satisfy all my needs simultaneously. This belief system definitely fueled my inner civil war. I was convinced my sub-personalities of Bunny and Bernadette had to fiercely compete with each other rather than cooperate with each other. I truly believed either my spiritual/intellectual Bernadette side or my physical/emotional Bunny side could be expressed, but I could never simultaneously fulfill both their needs.

Much of my therapy was learning to have all of me show up, and just trust all my needs could be met. The simple act of breathing is so subtle, and yet it affects all of me, including my warring sub-personalities as well as my heart, body, mind, and soul. That's why it makes total sense that in order to heal the feud between my warring sub-personalities I had to rehab my breathing.

Mom, we did our best to love each other, but nonetheless we repeatedly hurt each other. I wrote this letter to extinguish that hurt. Each conscious breath I take now helps me release my hurts, shame, and poverty mentality. Wow, just now, I just took a long exhale. More proof that I am healing myself one breath at a time.

Love,
Natazha

Exhaling My Whole Truth   October 2016

A PBS special commemorating the 100th Anniversary of the Irish Easter Uprising inspired me to write this letter. After watching fewer than five minutes of this PBS special, I felt spooked to my core and suffered intense diarrhea. Bob needed to hug and soothe me for the rest of the evening. The program talked about the role the Black and Tans played during the Irish War for Independence. The very next day I looked up Black and Tans on Wikipedia and found articles about them terrorizing the small village Kilkishen, the hometown of my Mom's mother, Nanny, and her brother, Uncle Mickey. Black and Tans were temporary constables hired to assist the Royal Irish Constabulary during the Irish War of Independence. They were infamous for their attacks on Irish civilians and their property. Imagine the Ku Klux Klan put in charge of policing Blacks in America's South during the 1950s and 1960s.

My mom told us Uncle Mickey and Nanny suffered incredible atrocities. They were pathologically enmeshed with each other, a very common response to trauma. Uncle Mickey never married. For his entire life he lived with Nanny and my Mom while she was growing up. During high school, I was haunted by horrible visions of Nanny, Uncle Mickey and other Kilkishen villagers being raped and beaten. I most often daydreamed about these attacks during Mr. Brown's honors English class. Daniel Siegel and many others discuss how humans use stories to heal from their traumas and tragedies. Stories help us interpret our suffering through a lens of inspirational meaning and hope.

I feel discussing novels in Mr. Brown's class granted me permission to examine the insane relationship between my Uncle Mickey and Nanny. Treating them as literary characters granted me a safe distance from the consequences of what happened to them in Kilkishen. And how those atrocities affected my Mom, my family, and myself. Back in high school I was still blocking out Uncle Mickey's brutal attack on me. Decades later, I now regard Mr. Brown's English class as a step toward healing from Uncle Mickey sexually assaulting me and my Mom, and tearing us apart.

Dear Mom,

I just finished meditating. I often see things differently after giving myself the luxury of breathing at my own pace without any agenda or electronic device interfering with my innate breathing style. Meditating helped me fully acknowledge and accept what compelled me to send you my infamous Declaration of Independence audiotape where I screamed at you for not defending us from pedophiles. My meditation practice helped me grow tremendously. Just now I took some long slow exhales as I prepared myself to discuss the real demon behind my personality split.

I wrote this letter to Uncle Mickey yesterday. It explains the most tragic part of our relationship. The Uncle Mickey incident damaged me far more than your institutionalization. I needed 50 years to process this incident. I'm so sorry I blamed you instead of Uncle Mickey for my DID, all this time. I'm sorry we never talked about it. May this letter help us reconcile on a deeper level.

Letter to My Uncle Mickey

Dear Mickey,

Fuck you Uncle Mickey. You killed the relationship between my Mommy and me the day you shoved a crucifix up my vagina with one hand. And silenced me with your other hand. You held me down, and nearly suffocated me as you ripped off my panties. I was only 4 years old. It takes a sick bastard to shove a crucifix up a little girl's crotch in broad day light on a dining room table. You didn't even seem to care if anyone caught you.

My Mom knew what you did. I passed out, and she found me. She didn't know what to do when I told her "Uncle Mickey hurt my wee-wee." That's why I hated her so much from that day on. You bastard, Mickey! You also molested my Mom as a child in her own home. It's no wonder she didn't defend me. No one defended her against your sexual assaults.

I needed her to console me. I needed her to help me get rid of that horrible burning between my legs. My Mom froze. She looked lost in another world. Then she got angry when I told her what happened. She told me to stop saying bad things about you. Then I froze. I realized no one was going to punish you for hurting me. No one was going to protect me. You might do it again. Terror took up residence in my gut. I learned never to ask for help or dare speak my truth. I began believing everyone else, including perverts like you, were more important than me. I stopped trusting my Mommy and myself.

Now I get it. My Mom was already on the verge of a nervous breakdown. When she found me passed out on the table with my legs apart. Seeing my torn panties broke her heart. It served as one more reminder that she couldn't mother so many kids. You took advantage of an exhausted mother with eight kids under the age of ten. You created one more traumatic event that pushed my Mom over the edge. You asshole, you invested heavily in her psychotic breakdown. Seeing her baby girl sexually abused left my Mom feeling helpless and guilty for not taking better care of me. It gave her one more reason to retreat into her deep, dark despair.

Fuck you Mickey. My hands write with rage, but my heart mourns for you. I can't imagine just how fucked up you were after the Black and Tans terrorized you and your family. They raped the women. They destroyed and burned whatever they could. I can't imagine what it felt like living in a country oppressed for over 700 years. The savage treatment of the Irish was condoned for centuries.

Where does the brutality stop? It stops with me. One breath, one almighty exhale at a time. It's time I forgave you and my Mom. I vow to put an end to the legacy of the oppression and its aftermath that continues to haunt Irish descendants. I vow to get back in present time. I'm determined to stop having 40% of my energy held hostage in the past when you attacked me. I forgive you. I never expected to write that, but I do forgive you, Mickey. And I forgive myself for being an innocent, little child who couldn't protect herself from you.

Yes, the day you molested me changed the trajectory of my life. Terror became my constant companion. Over the years that terror took on many forms: the rat phobia, parking meter phobia, fear of intimacy, and fear of enclosed parking lots. I always expected someone was going to attack me. I panicked when I traveled alone. Chronic diarrhea. Yes, your evil energy poisoned my sensitive gut. My stomach has carried the emotional scars of your attack for 50 years. Just recently I learned that it's not normal to have low-grade chronic diarrhea. Today I took another step in releasing the evil tradition of incest that passes shame down from one generation to the next. I'm finally taking herbs to kill the parasites that began residing in my gut after your attack. And I'm releasing your energy from my system.

I now better understand your motives. I believe you were so wounded you couldn't speak or write about your childhood traumas. You, with your crazed-eye stare, raped my Mom and me because it was the only way you knew how to express your pain. It was your perverse attempt to make us understand your incredible suffering. You wanted us to experience what it felt like to live in Ireland over a hundred years ago. When the Black and Tans roamed the back roads of Ireland beating innocent Irish citizens. I even suspect someone raped you with a crucifix. You did actually succeed in making me feel your pain. I never met any of the Black and Tans, and yet I'm truly terrified of them. At times, I'm plagued with horrific visions of the Black and Tans attacking you and your family.

Uncle Mickey, I'm sorry for all the atrocities you and all my other Irish ancestors endured. I vow to never act out your suffering by either molesting innocent kids or protecting pedophiles. One exhale at a time, I commit to living in the present moment. I promise to leave the past in the past. And yet, honor my ancestors, including you, by respecting them for overcoming incredible cruelty and hardship, and thus, paving the way for me to live a privileged life in America.

Love,
Natazha, previously known as Bernadette and Bunny

Mom, I hope that letter to Uncle Mickey didn't disturb you too much. Please know, the longer you're dead, the more I miss you. I keep realizing just how much we truly loved each other, despite all our misunderstandings. I still regret our Cold War and the bitter silence between us from 1987 to 1993. I paid dearly for it. I'm so sorry for all the chances we missed to express our love to each other in person: family weddings, baby showers, baptismal ceremonies, and countless loving mother-daughter experiences. To console myself, sometimes I pretend you're still alive and imagine us: watching gentle waves hit the shore at

Bayport beach at sunset; smelling flowers at the Bayport Flower House; and enjoying afternoon tea parties at the Bayard Cutting Arboretum.

Oh God! You loved me so much more than I ever imagined. Your death changed everything. I finally felt safe enough to feel and trust your love. Your death granted me permission to feel and express my love for you, too. We ended on good terms, even though we never discussed the Uncle Mickey incident that truly separated us.

Now I better understand all of it. This summer I was devastated when John, Ray-Ray, and Noreen (my siblings) told me that Mom said, "I accused her of molesting me on my Declaration of Independence audiotape." I don't remember accusing you for what Uncle Mickey did to me on that audiotape. I sent that audiotape the year after I quit smoking in July 1988. I had smoked to stuff my childhood traumas into the dark recesses of my psyche. When I quit smoking, I became flooded with memories of childhood neglect and abuse.

I recorded that audiotape in a fit of rage and don't remember exactly what I said. But I do remember ranting and raving about all the ways that I felt neglected and abused by you and Daddy Ray, especially you. I screamed it's horribly wrong for parents not to defend their kids against pedophiles. No one held Sister "You-know-who" accountable. You, Daddy Ray, and the Catholic Church never punished her for molesting my sibling and at least three other kids.

In 1988 when I made that audiotape, I still was in the throes of intensive therapy for Dissociative Identity Disorder (DID). I was still experiencing blackouts. I'm so sorry that I never told you all about my DID. I never kept a copy of that audiotape, so I'm not totally sure what I said. I do remember screaming about no one defending me when someone shoved a crucifix up my vagina. I thought I never named my attacker. I don't remember accusing you. Mom, until this summer I never knew you thought I falsely accused you of molesting me. Oh my God! I'm beyond horrified. I still can't imagine what super-hero spiritual strength you mustered to forgive me. I cringe imagining the incredible amount of love it took to forgive my false accusation.

If I said you molested me, I'm sorry. With all my heart and soul, I wish right now I could look you in the eyes and hold your hands. And, say to you, "I'm so sorry if I falsely accused you. I'm so sorry for any unnecessary suffering I caused you. I love you." How the hell did you forgive me? How did you end our Cold War when you believed that I accused you of molesting me?

You and I both know the real truth. Uncle Mickey was mentally ill. In 1965, he was emotionally wounded beyond repair. He not only molested me, but you, too, as a little girl. Now at 54 years old, I can handle the full truth. I'm big enough to house all my love, hatred, fear, hurt, admiration, and appreciation for you, and most of all, my own guilt for all the pain I caused you. I never meant to falsely accuse you. I never believed you molested me. Back in the late 1980s, I really didn't know who tortured me. Decades later, after you went back to therapy and I had more time to heal, I finally pieced it all together.

After years of soul searching and healing, I finally understand that Uncle Mickey molested both of us. When I first started to unearth memories, I could only see his torturous hands. I sensed I knew and loved the person attacking me in my own home. One hand covered my mouth, almost smothering me. The other hand ripped off my panties and shoved a crucifix up my vagina. All of this happened on the wooden, oval, dining-room table that you got rid of decades ago.

Uncle Mickey left me on the dining room table. Looking back at this incident now as an adult, I wonder why he didn't seem to care if he was caught. He acted as if he knew no one would punish him. I learned during our Cold War, a year after I sent my Declaration of Independence, that you went back to therapy to heal from your own sexual abuse. I specifically asked Dad if Uncle Mickey molested you. He answered, "Yes." He also implied that no one came to your defense. Years later, I learned that a priest also sexually assaulted you.

I now get it. Uncle Mickey wasn't punished when he did it to you. That's why you didn't know how to defend me. No one defended you. How horrible for you! Your mother's brother, a pedophile, lived in your house. You found me on the dining room table. I told you, "Uncle Mickey hurt my wee-wee." I desperately needed your comfort. I wanted a hug. You froze at first. Seemed aloof, and then got very angry. Oh, Mommy! I needed more than a hug. Comfort. Reassurance. I needed to be told in no uncertain terms that I didn't deserve to be attacked. I felt crushed when you didn't hug me. I thought you were mad at me, blamed me and felt I deserved to be mistreated. You abruptly got me off the table and told me to change my clothes. You didn't even go upstairs to help me change my clothes.

Oh, Mom! That event changed everything between us. I stopped trusting you and learned never to go to you for help. I interpreted your anger and lack of comfort as proof you didn't love me. I lost my sense of innocence. I thought it was my fault, that I was an evil defective child. For years, I felt horrible whenever the other kids like Ray-Ray said, "No matter what, I always knew Mommy and Daddy loved me." Those statements triggered horrible shame. I believed something must be terribly wrong with me because Mommy and Daddy didn't love me. My Mommy didn't protect me against Uncle Mickey.

I carried an insane amount of shame. Mom, I always loved you. Why did we never talk candidly about this incident while you were alive? I don't regret expressing my rage and hurt on my Declaration of Independence audio. But I deeply regret feeling so unsafe to fully express my love, admiration, and appreciation while you were alive. I'm in awe that you understood underneath all my hurt and rage that I loved you deeply. You expressed your love for me every time you picked up the phone when I called. I so miss our phone calls. No one ever picks up the phone these days. I miss our breath-based phone calls.

I wish we could talk on the phone, and ask how this Uncle Mickey incident affected you. Did it trigger your memories of being molested by him? Did you feel tremendous pain and sorrow when you found your baby girl damaged by the same man who attacked you? I can only imagine how incredibly helpless and guilty you must have felt.

I spent years in therapy learning that I didn't cause your breakdown. But I still wonder if this incident was just one more event that sent you over the edge. Was it one more nail in the coffin that caused your breakdown? I've always felt responsible for your breakdown. This incident now seems like something that hurt you. It could have overwhelmed you with even more guilt. I feel it could have propelled you toward that psychotic breakdown.

I now believe the Uncle Mickey incident was when I began to split into Bunny and Bernadette. That day changed me forever. I still have a hard time believing it happened. But I've always felt the terror of that sexual assault in my gut. I am finally releasing that terror. I also feel so much sorrow over that incident separating us. I felt you didn't protect me and misinterpreted your anger and guilt as blaming me. And I believed you were mad at me. Now looking back at this incident as a grown woman, I interpret it so differently. Uncle Mickey emotionally paralyzed you when he molested you. That's why you didn't defend me.

Although we never helped each other heal the shame of Uncle Mickey's sexual abuse when you were alive, I feel absolutely blessed with your loving support now. I feel your mystic magic healing me now as I write this book. Writing is helping me heal this deep wound. I'm going to sit and meditate in your honor. Let our spirits conspire to celebrate our victory of releasing this ancient emotional crud.

Love,
Natazha

Held by Their Breath   August 2016

Thank you Mrs. Espizito for making it possible for me to see the New York City Ballet's Swan Lake performance 50 years ago. The event made an indelible impression on me. I don't know what was more special to me, alone time with my Mom or the spectacular performance. As a footnote to my readers, should you ever have a chance to provide a child in need with tickets to a live performance, please, please give them the tickets.

Dear Mom,

When I was six years old, seeing the New York City Ballet's performance of Swan Lake with you changed my life. The dark stage, strange lighting, and whimsical costumes and stage sets made me think we landed in an enchanted storyland. I wondered if the spellbinding ballerinas were fairies. You laughed when I asked, "Are they human?" You never answered my question, so I grew up believing ballerinas were supernatural creatures. And, I dreamed of one day becoming a ballerina.

Many years later, I learned the truth about ballerinas when I taught Pilates to the San Francisco cast of Phantom of the Opera. My students included both the dance chorus and opera singers. You can imagine how disappointed I felt when I learned ballerinas are indeed very human. Those ballerinas hardly acted like the goddesses I imagined them to be. Most lived on cigarette fumes, caffeine, and competition. In comparison to the opera singers they were incredibly stingy with their breath. The dancers tended to hold their breath and struggled to fully engage their diaphragms and other respiratory muscles.

Opera singers are professional breathers. They defy what medical doctors say humans can do with their diaphragms. These chanteuses raced up and down the uneven steps of the Curran Theater wearing thirty-pound costumes without showing any strain on their faces or in their sublime singing voices. It takes incredible strength to look soft and vulnerable on the outside while singing arias imbued with deep emotion under strenuous conditions. These singers worked incredibly hard on the inside so they could look disarmed and in love on the outside. Their impeccable breathing skills fueled their physical and emotional prowess. They harmonized their bodies and souls by breathing from the inside out.

The drastic breath-based difference between the singers and dancers inspired me to stop holding my breath and start holding myself together with deep, core breathing: I wanted to emulate the singers who held themselves together with their breathing instead of the ballerinas who held their breath.

Love,
Very glad I didn't become a ballerina Natazha

The Pay Off for Holding your Breath   January 2016

Olympic synchronized swimmers are water ballerinas. Performing a split is a crucial skill for them. While training the Walnut Creek Aquanuts synchronized swim team, I devised 23 different ways to perform a split on various Pilates equipment. I loved both teaching how to do splits and doing them myself. The split became a symbol of my integration. Reaching my legs in opposite directions became my ritual for showing I was now big enough to house all my conflicting feelings, my hate and love for my Mom. One leg represented Bunny and the other leg represented Bernadette. While performing splits I also felt my legs were just like a little kid stretching out its arms as much as possible to say, "I love you this much."

Dear Mom:

It makes total sense that I taught Pilates and yoga to Olympic synchronized swimmers. These athletes excel at holding their breath under water. I, too, was a professional breath holder. Teaching them to fully exhale on land was exactly what I needed to learn myself. These swimmers were exceptionally bright and asked great questions. I'll never forget Gina asking, "If holding our breath is so bad for us, then why do so many of us do it?"

I answered, "It dulls our pain. Breath holding is a potent respiratory anesthesia that has profound effects. It takes us out of our bodies so that we can escape intense, uncomfortable sensations. It dissociates us from painful emotions and spaces us out to avoid troublesome thoughts. It also allows us to ignore scary scenarios running around in our unconscious." That's all I said to Gina because I needed to keep teaching Pilates, but I wanted to say so much more.

Although it's a free, potent anesthesia, breath holding comes at a dear price. Unless there's a traumatic event, pain is usually a warning sign that we need to make a change. Pain is an important messenger, not a problem. Breath holding offers temporary pain relief, but at some point we need to embrace our pain and decode its message. Breathe into our discomfort instead of run away from it.

I understand that pain can necessitate a doctor's visit, but more often than not it necessitates a breath-based conversation with yourself. Pain is one way your heart, soul, mind, and body can express their unmet needs. How can you have a breath-based conversation with yourself? Sit still in meditation: Calm down and settle into your own innate breathing pattern. Meditation allows your heart, mind, soul, and body to openly say what they want instead of using pain to grab your attention.

Here's an example of breathing through discomfort. In 2013 I felt absolutely terrified when I founded my private, unconventional, lifestyle-medicine physical therapy practice. Each morning I woke up feeling utterly overwhelmed. So I began setting my alarm clock an hour earlier so I could practice meditation in two ways. The first method was breathing while Bob hugged me from behind. Having Bob's warm body against my back was incredibly soothing. Literally and figuratively, Bob had my back. Many neurobiologists including Daniel Siegel report conspiring and hugging works wonders for soothing the nervous system. Hugging and breathing together is a wonder drug for bonding and healing emotional wounds. It helped me heal my shame and fear of success that made it difficult for me to step out into the professional world.

After our hug fest, I meditated on our living room couch. I sat and minded my breath for about 20-30 minutes. Quite often I saw in my mind's eye a nighttime scene of a very rough turbulent sea. I slowed my breathing and imagined myself diving to reach the calmer water deep beneath the turbulent surface. This visualization consoled me; it grounded me in my purpose of teaching people breath-based lifestyle medicine. It helped me come from my calm center. I felt less anxious about my unconventional private physical therapy practice.

In my mind's eye, the turbulent sea scene transforms into a sunny day at a serene, crystal clear lake. It's so still that it can reflect my thoughts, emotions, and perceptions. I then ask, *What's the next simple step I need to take for my business?* And then, an action step is reflected on the lake. This meditation routine enabled me to practice physical therapy in a manner that suits me. Instead of running away from my painful terror I embraced it in order to learn from it.

Mom, I'm so grateful you modeled the habit of daily prayer and contemplation. You inspired my daily meditation practices that helped me establish my physical therapy practice.

Love,
Natazha

Access your Endogenous Opioids   December 2016

I'm proud to be a physical therapist and graduate of the University of California at San Francisco and San Francisco State University Physical Therapy Doctoral Program. Dr. Linda Wanek of SFSU demanded her students master the skills of clinical reasoning and patient education. She said, "Any monkey can learn the latest hi-tech treatments, but only astute humans can learn when and why to use those treatments." She challenged us to reason our way through what truly was the crux of a patient's problem, and explain it so well that our patient was inspired to fully participate in their own healing and course of treatment.

I'm upset there's an opiate addiction crisis in this country, when there's a plethora of research on how meditation, mindfulness, and an assortment of breathing techniques are excellent tools for pain management. I'm disheartened most health-care professionals don't get enough time with patients to educate them on the ultimate causes of pain and ways to treat pain without drugs. I wrote this book in part to educate the general public that pain and discomfort are not optional. Research on aging shows "superagers" age exceedingly well by embracing the discomfort that arises when they challenge themselves. To live to the max requires embracing all of yourself, including your aches and pains. In the past, humans fortified themselves with intentional breathing, not prescription drugs, to manage pain and hardships.

I'm horrified our medical system trains patients to expect some pill, surgery, or electronic gadget to fix them. Many patients don't understand they need to take care of their health. Catch-up medicine is unsustainable. No country can support a medical system where patients adopt unhealthy lifestyles and then expect doctors or medical technology to fix them. I love promoting and teaching "lifestyle medicine." I train patients to change their daily habits to improve their health with a focus on breathing and moving well. Both good breathing practices and exercise are well documented to keep us healthy, happy, and wise.

Dear Mom:

We numb out to avoid feeling overwhelmed or too stimulated by holding our breath or over indulging in our vices. We don't hear subtle messages, such as, "It's time to get some rest." When we ignore those subtle messages, our bodies and psyches often resort to pain to grab our attention. After earning my doctorate in physical therapy (PT) and working as a PT, I'm convinced more than ever we need to breathe through our stress and pain instead of holding our breath or taking pain pills.

PTs are on the front lines of America's tragic prescription drug abuse epidemic. I understand opioids are needed post-surgery and severe injury. But Americans are only 5% of the world's population, and yet consume 80% of the world's opioids. What's worse is a group of PTs practicing at Colorado in Motion report 25% of patients given a prescription for opioids go on to chronic drug abuse (https://www.youtube.com/watch?v=heG84JZfuYU &t=13s)

Our health-care system needs to offer more breath-based pain relief options. There's ample evidence that breath-based techniques including meditation, mindfulness, biofeedback, relaxation, and moderate exercise can alleviate chronic pain. Better yet, these interventions don't have the side effects of narcotics and can help you decipher the underlying message behind your pain. Meditation can reveal insights about your pain, especially when it's emotional pain being converted into physical pain, otherwise known as somatic pain.

Besides my professional experience, I have firsthand experience accessing my own innate or endogenous opioids through my breath instead of using exogenous prescription opioids to heal back pain. I suffered with chronic back pain from 1986 to 1993. I felt so bad at times that friends needed to dress and drive me to the chiropractor's office. After several years of receiving chiropractic adjustments, I realized I needed to change how I moved and breathed. That's when I began practicing yoga and Pilates religiously. I minded my breath more consistently. And I learned to exhale fully and inhale into my tight, neglected body parts that were carrying my unexpressed emotions. My position affected how gravity played out on my body and breath. For example, yoga's child pose helped me breathe into my low back to release emotional tension housed there. Breathing more slowly changed my blood chemistry, and thus granted me better access to my inner pharmacy of endogenous opioids.

I easily somatize pain. Most of my back pain was emotional pain being expressed as physical pain. I release my emotions while meditating and practicing yoga. Last year as I grieved your death, I cried during all my yin yoga and meditation sessions. Given that my back pain was trauma being expressed as physical pain, I didn't need prescription drugs. Taking drugs may have actually made it harder to access my feelings. I needed psychotherapy, yoga, Pilates, exercise, meditation, method acting classes, and just plain tuning into my breath to feel, process, and express my feelings.

Here's something else to think about. More and more chronic pain research shows that pain is more about how our brains interpret our lives, rather than indicative of local tissue damage. Quite often, a patient in intense pain shows no damage on an MRI. This finding suggests that pain is a relationship between incoming data from our lives and how our brain interprets that data. This finding also suggests that pain is more than a physical experience. It can in fact be intensified by how our brain interprets our physical experience. No pill, surgery, or electronic device can change the brain's interpretation, but our breathing can change the brain's interpretation.

Back in early 1992 I was correct. I needed to move differently. At the time I thought I just needed to move physically differently. I never realized breathing differently would release tense muscles that would also change how I moved mentally, emotionally, and spiritually.

Mom, I know I'm on my soapbox, but here's one more thing. Opioids have caused such a problem that drug companies are now being rewarded with a new drug market. On top of selling opioids, drug companies sell more drugs to treat the side effects of opioids, namely opioid-induced constipation. Even worse, if someone has chronic constipation I'll bet they also have digestion and other problems that can be "solved" with more drugs. Taking more pills for the side effects of pills is a terrible idea and a classic example of catch-up medicine.

Love,
Natazha

The Spiritual Internet   August 2016

My life experience challenged me to manage group dynamics. I'm number five of a family with eleven children and was always negotiating with a group. That helped me learn how to manage group dynamics. I also possess every characteristic of a highly sensitive person, and that makes me incredibly sensitive to group dynamics, what I call the Spiritual Internet, aka the Collective Unconscious. My meditation and breathing practices enable me to successfully participate on the Spiritual Internet instead of being overwhelmed by it.

Dear Mom:

Breathing is the ultimate act of giving and receiving. There's no finer example of give and take than exhaling and inhaling. Our first cry at birth announces more than we're breathing on our own; it proclaims we now share with mankind by blowing air in and out of our lungs. That sacred act allows us to simultaneously individuate from and participate in humanity. We inhale air into our individual lungs and exhale air into the collective lungs of humanity, what I call the Spiritual Internet. Carl Jung called it the Collective Unconscious. He regarded it as the part of the unconscious mind that's derived from ancestral memory and experience and is common to all humankind. And yet, it's distinct from the individual's unconscious mind.

I began thinking about the Spiritual Internet after learning in a physics class the same atoms have circulated in the atmosphere since the beginning of time. Moreover, breathing allows us to exchange atoms with the entire universe. We inhale the same, exact molecules as our ancestors, Jesus, and all other forms of life across time. Breathing enables us to interact and connect with all living creatures. And, the breathing of all life forms constantly influences the collective unconscious and atmosphere.

That knowledge about atoms led me to re-interpret the atmosphere as our Spiritual Internet. With our breath, we can transmit anything over the Spiritual Internet including intentions, emotions, thoughts, prejudices, or whatever else is in our hearts, minds, and psyches. How we participate on the Spiritual Internet can either reinforce or destroy the invisible forces behind all relationships: love, hate, fear, despair, compassion, community, fellowship, team spirit, connection, and all the other forces that foster or kill relationships.

Mom, you're a mystic. And you probably already know all about the Spiritual Internet. For the less spiritually inclined, I have to justify it with an explanation of how we communicate through the breath and vibes. You may not consciously register the microscopic exchange of respiratory gases, but that doesn't mean you're unaffected by them. A vibe boils down to changes in the air. You can't quite put your finger on it, but instinctively know something's up. That something was unconsciously communicated via your breath. And the more you connect with your breath, the more you tune into the Spiritual Internet.

I also explain that respiration is the quintessential form of communication and self-expression. Long before language, we communicated with changes in our respiration: laughed, cried, gasped, sighed, and so on. Now we exhale to speak, and modulate our voices and emotions by changing our breathing.

I sometimes add that intentions affect your respiration. Casting a wicked spell versus a blessing changes the configuration of carbon dioxide and oxygen in your out-breath. A curse emits quite a different vibe than a blessing, and registers quite differently on the Spiritual Internet. Also, breathing with loving self-awareness versus hatred changes the atoms you exhale into the universe. And over time that's how we change the world, by changing the breath-based vibes circulating all over the globe.

Here's one more super important point about the Spiritual Internet. All this divine, respiratory interaction gets badly disrupted when we habitually hold our breath to suppress feelings, pain, or discomfort. That insidious respiratory anesthesia also disconnects us from the Spiritual Internet. Mom, I can only imagine how hard it was for you when your COPD took your breath away and disconnected you from the Spiritual Internet. I sometimes wonder if your spirit feels better now that it's no longer held back by COPD.

Love,
Natazha

Let Your Food Breathe   January 2017

I enjoyed growing organic vegetables in the 1990s and still miss gardening. Several years ago Bob and I began planning an intentional community with a big old farmhouse that could serve as the community center. We want to grow organic fruits and vegetables not poisoned by pesticides or suffocated in any way.

Dear Mom,

Today I freaked when I walked up to the produce department in our local grocery store. Seeing all the fruits and vegetables wrapped in plastic, I screamed on the inside, "Oh my God, let them breathe. I don't want produce that's suffocating."

Did you know that eggs don't need refrigeration if they aren't washed or sanitized? Thanks to one of Bob's co-workers, Michelle, we now eat truly organic eggs from her backyard chickens and ducks. The outside shells of her eggs are filthy dirty and covered in bacteria. However, each time I crack open one of her eggs, I'm rewarded with an incredibly bright orange yolk bursting with vitality and flavor. Her eggs look and taste so much more organic than produce sold as "organic." Michelle's eggs make me wonder if "organic" produce retains its nutrition after a plastic wrapper suffocates the aerobic bacteria on its skin and in its flesh. Just like you and me, aerobic bacteria need to breathe.

Mom, I know people are trying to eat better when they buy pre-cut and peeled carrots instead of cookies and candy. They probably don't realize the skin often contains the best nutrients plus bacteria, and they use a chlorinated solution to keep that processed produce looking so good. Not only has that produce lost the bacteria and nutrients on the outside skin, they're also ingesting chemicals, and eating food that stopped breathing in the plastic wrapper.

This incident reminded me that everything goes back to the breath, not just you and me breathing, but also letting our food breathe. More precisely, letting the bacteria in our food breathe. Why is it super important to let your food breathe? Because scientists now are discovering the bacteria in your gut affects your health and weight. Your diet influences the bacteria in your gut, especially bacteria-rich foods like sauerkraut. Alanna Collen wrote a great book, *10% Human: How Your Body's Microbes Hold The Key To Health And Happiness*. She discusses in detail how diet affects the bacteria in your gut. Her book got me thinking how our ancestors ate produce without sealing it in plastic. On top of suffocating the bacteria, research shows that plastic can emit BPA, bisphenol A. It has been linked to all sorts of health problems, including hormonal imbalances that can lead to obesity.

Collen's book affected me so much that I stopped buying the sanitized sealed bags of salad greens. Those sealed veggies last longer than bunches of kale or salad greens, but lack the bacteria of unpackaged veggies. From firsthand experience, I know the sterilized, suffocated produce in the store today is very different from freshly picked produce. When I grew my own fruit and veggies, I ate scrumptious tomatoes right off the vine, and mouthwatering apples and pomegranates right off the tree. All those fruits and vegetables were loaded with flavor and bacteria, and I felt great eating food that breathed freely.

Love,
Natazha

Dramatize Your Respiration to Make it Real   October 2016

I used to wonder why I was so much harder on my Mom than my Dad. I worried about being sexist until I found a thank-you note I wrote to my Dad when I was 17 years old. I thanked him for apologizing to me in my senior year of high school. One day after school he drove me to the Patchogue Library, about 25 minutes from our home. After he parked the car, my Dad looked at me with terribly sad eyes and a guilty look on his face. I got scared he was going to reveal some bad news when he finally said, "I'm so sorry, so sorry. As a little girl you were incredibly happy. You sang and danced with the flowers like Shirley Temple. I'm sorry we burdened you so much. Put too much pressure on you. I hate to see you smoke. You never smile or laugh anymore. Promise me one day you'll quit smoking. Perhaps the world doesn't need another Shirley Temple, but you need to quit smoking." I remained silent for several moments, but eventually said, "Dad, I promise to quit smoking someday. I know you love me."

Long before he died in 2012, I had "forgiven" my Dad. I never actually needed to forgive him. I totally accepted his heart-felt acknowledgement that my childhood was traumatic. We never fought and pretty much always respected and loved each other. Whatever father issues I had, I worked them out with several boyfriends who were 15-20 years older than I. Along with his apology, I want to thank my Dad for sharing his love of the sea and swimming. It's one of the best gifts I've ever received.

I now know my Mom loved me, too. But my Dad always had much less shame than my Mom, and that made all the difference in the world. He could apologize for his mistakes without feeling like he was a mistake. My Mom's shame crippled her. Any attempt to apologize left her feeling like she herself was the mistake. My Mom and I made amazing progress before she died. But my brother John's funeral speech shed the light on her shame that enabled me to better understand her motives and fully forgive her.

Dear Mom,

I joined the Dolphin Swimming and Rowing Club in 2003 to use their sauna after swimming in the Aquatic Park cove. That was two years after your visit to San Francisco. Otherwise, I'd have given you and Dad a tour of the Dolphin Club. You'd have loved their historic rowboats, swimming trophies, and photos dating back to the 1870s. I'd have gladly rowed you around Alcatraz and tried to get both of you to swim or at the very least soak your feet in the bay.

I'm grateful Daddy Ray shared his love for swimming and the sea with me. Swimming in the frigid San Francisco Bay is my favorite form of active meditation. It dramatizes my respiration and makes my breath more real. When asked, "Isn't it painful to swim in 50° water without a wetsuit?" I respond, "It's perversely pleasurable, absurdly sensual. It revives my breath: I can't hold my breath or take half-assed exhales swimming in the bay."

Before I swim, I stand at the edge of the Dolphin Club shoreline. I set an intention for my swim, such as, "I'll swim a mile in honor of my Mom and finishing our book, *Rescued by My Breath.*" I then walk up to my waistline in the water. And, let my feet, legs, and belly register we're back to our First Mother, the water. It's not as warm as the womb, but it still feels good to be back in water. With my head and neck out of the water, I skim across the surface of the bay. The instant the cold water hits the back of my neck, my skin screams as it senses this high sensation. That's when I mother myself with several long exhales. As my friend Kevin Whalen puts it, "We induce a panic attack by jumping into the bay, and then we rescue ourselves with our breathing." After a couple of doggy paddle strokes, I turn on my back to warm up with a bout of backstroke. I connect to my breath more easily with my face out of the water, and love rotating my upper back with each stroke as I lie in a gentle backbend. I express my power through my long purposeful exhales that engage my core muscles.

It's a privilege to enjoy such easy access to raw Nature in a big city that's just a fifteen-minute bike ride from our home. Seeing the sun change its role at sunrise and sunset with Marin and the Golden Gate Bridge in the background fills me with awe and delight. Kiki (my sister) told me Daddy Ray also loved the magic moment of gloaming, the sun's last orgasmic gasp of light that showcases the sky with an iridescent blue just before it turns completely black. I love seeing San Francisco's landmarks illuminated just before the Ghirardelli Square lights sparkle full tilt against the black sky. And on special occasions I swim in moonlit water.

Those glorious sights inspire me to stop taking my life and breath for granted. I instinctively breathe in and out more fully. Bay swimming makes my exhale come alive. I see proof of this invisible life force with bubbles in the water. My breathing sounds so much richer and vibrant underwater. The taste and smell of saltwater spices up my respiration. This winter's heavy rains watered down the salinity of the bay. It tastes and smells downright sweet. So much so I find myself opening my mouth wider to taste and smell the water. My sense of touch verifies if I'm fine and dandy with my ribs, diaphragm, and abdominal muscles widening and contracting with each breath cycle.

I've been hypothermic several times. Just recently I restored my confidence and got back to swimming a mile. Swimming in the San Francisco Bay is like scuba diving with a faulty timer on your oxygen tank. You have a vague idea of how long you can stay in the water based on recent swimming experience. But you always need to stay aware of your core temperature and verify when you might need to get out of the water. You may routinely stay in the water for 30 minutes, but on any given day conditions in the bay or yourself may warrant a shorter swim. For example, the water temperature may have suddenly dropped one to two degrees or you're unknowingly fighting off a virus or slept poorly the night before. Bay swimming keeps my mind from wandering off into the past or the future. I must constantly evaluate my energy level and the forces of nature at hand and stay present with my respiration and five senses.

My respiration provides the necessary feedback to avoid life-threatening hypothermia. I continually monitor my respiratory rate to avoid wearing myself out. I take long, powerful exhales to get more air out so more oxygenated air can rush into my lungs. I regularly sense my body temperature, especially in my belly. It's okay if my feet and hands are freezing, but it's absolutely essential that I keep my core warm. The sound of my breathing reveals the quality of my respiration. Whenever I wheeze, it's time for me to leave the water.

One glorious winter morning about five years ago I suddenly felt terrified for no apparent reason. My psyche screamed, *I don't care if this sunrise is amazing; get the hell out of the water. Right now.* I begrudgingly swam to shore. Later in the sauna I found out a seal had bitten two people, pretty much in the same spot where I was swimming. One of them went to the emergency room and needed a heavy dose of antibiotics. That incident taught me the value of connecting to myself physically, mentally, emotionally, and psychologically by dramatizing my breath. Each aspect of myself provides vital information that my gut instinct compiles on an unconscious level. I may not consciously understand why my gut's yelling to get the hell out of the water, but I need to follow my gut instincts.

Mom, I love minding my breath as I swim. It's become my favorite way to pray. I enjoy worshipping this way because it honors both you and Dad. You taught me to pray and he taught me to love the sea. Before you died, I often dedicated my swims in your honor. And I still blow bubbles in the bay to send you my love.

Love,
Natazha

Breathing With You, Not For You   January 2017

Last Christmas, I gave myself the gift of better boundaries. My loved ones noticed a dramatic difference in me even though they had no idea I had changed my subtle, invisible boundaries. In their book, *Boundaries: When To Say Yes, When To Say No To Take Control Of Your Life*, Dr. Cloud and Dr. Townsend write "Boundaries help us keep the good in and the bad out. They guard our treasures so that people will not steal them." My joy and love skyrocketed as I held in the positive and kept out the negative. I also learned several valuable lessons. When I choose to donate my time and energy I always feel great about helping others. However, I feel resentful when people "steal" my time and energy. And the truth is no one actually ever steals my time and energy. But it's there for the taking if I don't set boundaries that protect me from other people taking advantage of me. More importantly, breath-sponsored mindfulness makes me aware of when my boundaries have been violated.

Dear Mom:

I know you loved Pema Chodron. You admired her journey from being a divorcee and mom in New York who became a Tibetan Buddhist nun, teacher, and author. You read her books and visited her Tibetan Buddhist monastery in Nova Scotia. I'm a huge fan of both Pema and Brené Brown, a TEDx Talk celebrity, storyteller, and Houston University professor who researches shame. I've read most of Brené's books and took four of her online courses. Anyway, my Monday night meditation group is discussing Pema's book *Uncomfortable with Uncertainty* and Brené's teachings often come up. They both teach empathy requires courage to feel or imagine another's pain. It requires putting yourself in someone else's shoes, even when imagining their predicament causes you intense pain.

Brené depicts empathy in a cartoon video that can be seen at www.youtube.com/watch v=1Evwgu369Jw. In the video, a fox falls into a deep, dark hole. A bear climbs down, sits beside the fox, and empathizes with the fox by feeling its pain. There's also a deer that both figuratively and literally looks down on the fox. Never sits and feels with the fox. Instead the deer minimizes the fox's situation, what Brené terms *"silver lines"* it. Brené reinforces the cartoon with these research findings:

- Empathy fuels connection whereas sympathy fuels disconnection.
- We connect by feeling with people.
- Rarely does a response make things better. Connection or authentic empathy is what makes things better for someone in suffering. And connection is emotional and spiritual rocket fuel that provides immunity to burnout.

Connection or authentic empathy is what makes things better for someone suffering. It requires:

1. Perspective taking, or the ability to take the perspective of another person or recognize their perspective as their truth
2. Staying out of judgment; it's implied not judging the other person
3. Recognize emotion in other people
4. Communicate about the other person's emotion

What Brené says about empathy parallels the Buddhist concept of Tonglen, a compassion practice Pema discusses in *Uncomfortable with Uncertainty*. Years ago, I learned Tonglen as the practice of giving and receiving. With compassion, you take on all the various mental and physical sufferings of all beings: their fear, frustration, pain, anger, guilt, bitterness, doubt, and rage. I saw that aspect of Tonglen as acting like a human vacuum cleaner for all the suffering in the world. With Tonglen, you also lovingly give all your happiness, well-being, serenity, healing, and fulfillment to those suffering. In many ways, Tonglen sounded like Jesus Christ taking on the sins of the world by dying on the cross and spreading the Word of God and His love.

For years, Tonglen and initially Brené's definition of empathy totally pissed me off. I regarded them as recipes for co-dependence, martyrdom, and burnout. Ironically, I now regard them as cures for co-dependence, self-inflicted martyrdom, and burnout, and regularly use these practices to rejuvenate and energize myself. What changed my mind? Setting healthy boundaries. I stopped skipping the step of self-empathy. Just as you need to love yourself first in order to truly love others, I needed self-compassion before I could empathize with others.

As Brené puts it, compassion without boundaries is a recipe for resentment and burnout. I now read Brené's work through a lens of healthy boundaries, breathing, and self-compassion:

- Empathy fuels connection *with myself and others* whereas sympathy fuels disconnection *with myself and others. I disconnect from my and other people's feelings by divorcing myself from my breathing, in particular holding my breath.*
- We connect by feeling with people *including myself. I connect with my own and other people's feelings by connecting to my breath. I maintain my boundaries and avoid burnout by breathing and feeling with people instead of breathing and feeling for them. Conspiring, breathing with each other is*

one way to connect with people. Holding my breath disconnects me from my feelings and sets me up for codependence and burnout.

- Rarely does a response make things better. Connection or authentic empathy is what makes things better for someone in suffering. *And connection is emotional and spiritual rocket fuel that provides immunity to burnout*

Empathy requires:

1. Perspective taking, or the ability to take the perspective of another person *and myself* or recognize their perspective as their truth *and my perspective as my truth. Honor my own truth as well as the other person's truth.*
2. Staying out of judgment; it's implied don't judge the other person *or myself. And stay out of judging my own feelings or reactions to the situation.*
3. Recognize emotion in other people *as well as my own feelings.*
4. Communicate about the other person's emotion *as well as my own feelings.*

You know what Mom, I never had a problem with compassion, but I did have a HUGE problem setting boundaries. I'm living proof of Brené's comment, "Compassion without boundaries causes resentment and hatred." To avoid my own repressed pain and traumas, I left my body by incessantly holding my breath. That bad habit disconnected me from my own feelings so I more easily took on other people's feelings. I felt and breathed for them instead of for myself, and then deeply resented them for it. I stopped suffocating myself by learning to exhale: talk out my feelings, sing, cry, and laugh, get regular aerobic exercise, and so on. That's when I began breathing *with* people instead of *for* them and enjoying my relationships again. That breathing style helps me set boundaries and notice when my boundaries get violated. I'm a much more compassionate person now that I've established better boundaries.

Love,
Natazha

Solving the Homeless Problem   July 2016

This letter was inspired by a talk on shame. A female student at the lecture discussed a Twilight Zone episode where a man from a small town stole something. His punishment was being ignored for a year. Before the year was up, he went insane and died. She compared San Francisco's homeless population to that man and asked, "Do the homeless become mentally ill from being completely ignored or are they mentally ill in the first place?" I cringed as I acknowledged I shun the homeless. Fearing for my safety, I regard them as wildlife on my morning runs, as if I were avoiding bears around garbage cans in Lake Tahoe or snakes on sunny paths in the high dessert. I always choose a path devoid of open garbage cans where the homeless hunt for food.

A week later, I attended a meditation talk where a young man said, "As individuals we can't do anything about the homeless problem. We can only solve that problem at the group level of society." I disagreed with him. Once again, I see what others classify as a political problem as a breathing problem. We need to find a way to breathe together, and motivate ourselves to take care of each other instead of eschew or fight with each other. We at the very least can always breathe with anyone. Whether I'm afraid for my safety or disagree with your politics, I can always respect and acknowledge you by breathing with you. Exhale to bless you and inhale to receive your presence.

Dear Mom,

I loved your deep commitment to social justice. I'm scared just walking by homeless people whereas at 83 years old with only 30% lung capacity you provided them food and shelter. Homelessness is a huge problem in San Francisco, and it's getting worse all the time. Folks camped on the sidewalks is only the tip of the iceberg. Too many people live outside their bodies, leaving their spirits homeless.

To me, vagrant spirits haunting our communities is an even bigger issue. Drugs, alcohol, trauma, shame, and stress evict our souls from our bodies. It's the ultimate cause of tremendous pain and suffering in our society. I know all about being a lost soul. When I was younger, I was tortured by poor boundaries and mental illness. My soul wandered everywhere except inside my body. To get back into my body, I quit smoking and drinking and joined the Berkeley Psychic Institute's clairvoyant program. I also engaged in many other activities: psychotherapy, meditation, aerobic exercise, yoga, Pilates, Rosen bodywork, method acting classes, journaling, and visualizations. Intentional breathing is the common thread running through all those modalities.

Conscious breathing seduced my spirit back into my body. Connecting to my breath helped me expel emotional toxins and landmines and transform my body into a safe haven for my spirit. Over time, my breath-based habits slowly reset my physiology. Fully exhaling altered my autonomic nervous system that governs my ability to heal from trauma. It granted me some freedom from my painful past. It calmed me down to where the mere thought of a past trauma no longer immediately overwhelmed me. Innocuous things no longer automatically triggered past traumas. For example, in my twenties visiting the suburbs cued my childhood, whereas in my thirties I lived in the suburbs.

Here's a better example: Bill's (my college sweetheart) paranoid schizophrenia. Initially his illness reignited my guilt and terror around your psychotic breakdown. I just shut down and left my body when Bill got ill. Thank God, I was already in therapy with systems in place to process my paralyzing feelings. I meditated and swam, which taught me to breathe fully and feel and express my feelings instead of smoking and holding my breath.

My therapists talked me through how your institutionalization paralleled Bill's illness. I had no control over Bill's schizophrenia; however, I could control what I thought and imagined about it. Humans don't distinguish between what's real versus imagined. Humans feel what they imagine just as profoundly as any actual events taking place.

After knowing Bill for seven years, out of the blue he became a paranoid schizophrenic. Once again, I felt helpless about a loved one's illness. I blamed myself for his illness to delude myself that I controlled his illness. It was the only way I knew how to combat my helplessness and anguish. If I only changed my "bad" behavior, I could prevent loved ones from getting sick. My therapists helped me breathe through my terror and guilt as I accepted that loving someone comes at the price of being vulnerable. We can't control what happens to them, whether it's our Mom or boyfriend. Bad things can happen to our loved ones for no apparent reason.

I eventually reinterpreted Bill's illness as an act of Nature instead of something I did wrong. And, accepted what I learned from my Grinnell College professors: imbalanced neurotransmitters, not girlfriends, cause schizophrenia. Realizing I didn't cause his illness made me also realize I didn't cause your illness. Nor could I fix you or Bill by being perfect.

Living in San Francisco afforded me easy access to many breath-based tools to heal from the tragedy of Bill's illness and my other traumas. My psychiatrist used breath-based hypnosis and meditation techniques. Instead of prescribing drugs she advised, "Sober, it will be hard enough for you to figure out who you are. It will be nearly impossible on alcohol or drugs."

Back in the late 1980s, when drug companies began popularizing mood-altering drugs to manage anxiety and depression, she advised meditation instead of medication. She painstakingly talked me through many traumas, and took my weekend phone calls. She coached me to neutralize traumatic memories with intentional breathing and soaking in hot Epsom salts baths. Trained me to focus on my breathing to stay within my body and the present moment while experiencing intense, excruciating feelings.

I'm so grateful she recommended meditation, not medication. My friend, Dr. Igor Mitrovic who teaches physiology to the UCSF medical, pharmacy, and physical therapy students, recently explained why her advice works so well. The problem with drugs is they're not specific. Drugs affect our entire system. They can't be directed toward a specific, haunting memory or issue. A pill can't specifically target my feelings about your institutionalization or Bill's illness. By affecting us on the global level, pills interfere with feelings that shouldn't be modified.

Osteoporosis runs in our family so I'll use it as an analogy. Drugs for osteoporosis increase bone density in **ALL** bones, not just your osteoporotic bones. What normally increases bone density is weight bearing and other mechanical stresses applied to our bones. Pushups increase your wrist bone density and walking increases leg and spine bone density. The problem with most osteoporosis drugs is they increase bone density in all bones including the jaw. Since the jaw has no room to grow, these medications can lead to many dental problems.

Mom, I can't emphasize strongly enough how learning to breathe through my pain enabled me to get back into my body. When I breathed life into my body and soul, I stopped living up to my teenage moniker, "Bernadette's a space cadet." Unlike pills, breathing can address specific painful traumas. I repeatedly breathed through my anguish over Bill's illness instead of holding my breath to numb my feelings and float outside my body. Breathing and expressing my feelings about his illness changed my experience of his illness. I accepted what happened and learned to stop leaving my spirit homeless.

Conscious breathing affected me positively in other ways. Hours of meditation, paying attention to my breath changed my mindset. One heartfelt breath at a time, I learned that my feelings only reveal how I'm interpreting what's happening in my life, such as Bill's mental illness. My feelings weren't the problem, but rather a messenger. Killing the messenger doesn't solve my problems. Honoring my feelings helps me heal and ease my woes.

I'm still so proud of myself for staying off cigarettes. Back then I sobbed every day for almost two years as I processed Bill's and your mental illness, and many other suppressed memories. What specifically helped the most was emphasizing my exhalation by singing or whistling. I also often discreetly sighed and exhaled longer than I inhaled. Exhalation helps us stay in our bodies. At the Berkeley Psychic Institute, we called that being grounded. Exhaling is linked to the parasympathetic side of the autonomic nervous system that soothes and heals us. That's why focusing on breathing out is so healing and comforting.

Going back to the homeless, I do want to make eye contact with them. But I don't feel safe doing so. I feel guilty looking the other way, ignoring and ostracizing them. On really bad days, my first instinct is to hold my breath, which disconnects me from my feelings and psyche. And thus, I too become a homeless spirit.

Once again, the almighty exhale rescues me. I bless homeless people and return to my own body by breathing out fully. As I exhale, I imagine blowing out exactly what they may need to meet their needs so they can live with grace and dignity. That breathing practice also reconnects me with you. I feel like I'm following in your footsteps by taking a small step toward social justice. I got the idea to bless the homeless with my exhales from reading John O'Donohue's book, *Blessing the Space Between Us* out loud to you on your deathbed.

Love,
Natazha

Secondhand Trauma   July 2016

Dr. Elaine Aron, author of *The Highly Sensitive Person,* has shown that 15-20% of the population is highly sensitive. They possess an innate, biological trait reflecting a certain type of survival strategy of being observant before acting. Highly sensitive people (HSP) are more aware of subtleties than the rest of the population. I'm a classic HSP. I cry easily, feel my emotions very intensely, experience hypersensitivity to external stimuli, have high emotional reactivity, and engage in deep cognitive processing. Like other HSPs, I'm more inclined to sense subtle energy shifts in my environment and experience secondhand trauma. HSPs are more easily overwhelmed as they notice everything, so they are more over-stimulated when things become too intense, complex, or chaotic. I instinctively managed my HSP sensitivity through meditation and breathing techniques. In May 2015 I attended a lecture by Dr. Aron at the Palace of Fine Arts. I learned she highly recommends meditation for all HSPs.

Dear Mom:

When bad things happened to the other kids, it also traumatized me. When someone else was the victim, my tricks for spacing out didn't work. Leaving my body only made it worse. When my spirit left my body and floated onto the ceiling, it got an even better view of the crisis. While I easily repressed my own traumas, I couldn't erase the incident of one sibling throwing two other siblings down the stairs. The second sibling got thrown down for helping the first sibling. I left my body, closed my eyes, and plugged my ears with my fingers. But I still heard all the screaming and shouting, and sensed the violence and hatred in the air. I imagined a dead sibling with her head cracked wide open at the base of the staircase. I ran out of the house terrified I'd also be killed.

Therapists treated me for survivor's guilt, but I'm not talking about feeling guilty for being spared getting thrown down the stairs. I'm talking about vicarious or secondhand trauma. Just like secondhand cigarette smoke pollutes a non-smoker's lungs, bystanders experience trauma when someone else gets victimized. Whether you witness an incident live or only hear about it, it impacts you. Humans are connected through our collective lungs, and the air we exchange gets polluted when anyone gets persecuted. I'm super sensitive and it doesn't have to be "real" people. I even feel traumatized when I watch a character in a scary movie or cartoon being tortured.

Secondhand trauma is on my mind because I had lunch with Cara (my niece) today. We talked about a blog I wrote on Title IX, a law that protects college coeds from sexual assault. The stats on sexual violence on college campuses are terrifying. One in five female college students and 6% of male college students are sexually assaulted during college. 11.5 million women and 8.7 million men attended American colleges in 2015. That means 2.2 million female and 530,000 male college students will be sexually assaulted over the next four years. Experts believe those numbers actually underestimate the crisis. It also ignores the secondhand trauma experienced by friends and loved ones of these sexual assault victims.

Knowing Cara is a recent college grad, I gingerly asked if she'd had been sexually assaulted on campus. She said, "No, but a friend of mine was. And she never received justice." I could tell by her tone of voice and facial expression that Cara was experiencing trauma. And she didn't want to talk about it.

I relied on my breathing to heal the third-hand trauma I was experiencing. Breathed deep into my belly to soothe myself as I witnessed Cara's pain and sensed her friend's injustice. Then, silently exhaled love and compassion to Cara, one small step toward clearing the air of poisonous second-hand and third-hand trauma smoke.

Love,
Natazha

Holding Resentments by Holding Our Breath   April 2016

My breathing indicates whether my silence is truly golden or I'm actually holding resentments.

Dear Mom:

When you were on your deathbed, I was shocked when you asked, "What made you so interested in breathing?" I quickly blurted out, "Mom, you don't know why? Isn't it obvious?" I sensed immediately I had hurt your feelings. I didn't want to start a fight, but was terribly hurt you didn't understand how terrified I felt watching your asthma attacks. Mom, I was traumatized each and every time you had a violent asthma attack. I'm still haunted by visions of you sitting at the edge of your bed, slouched over, shaking violently, and wheezing uncontrollably. You clutched your bed sheets and hung on for dear life. You were attempting to speak, but none of us could understand what you were saying. I just knew to run for the tiny, light-blue pills and make you hot tea with milk and sugar. Every time I ran to the kitchen, I feared you'd be dead when I got back. I couldn't understand why you smoked when you had such horrible asthma. I still resent your doctors who got you hooked on cigarettes.

I distinctly remember last January closing my eyes to catch my breath. Exhaled. Inhaled until I felt connected to Source instead of my hurt and building rage. I prayed to Source, "Please help me not explode on her." Still feeling shocked and hurt, I resisted the overwhelming urge to hold my breath and lose myself in the story of my wicked mother. I refused to allow my heart and spirit to escape to another dimension, leaving my mind and body to fend for themselves.

The awareness of those urges gave me just enough space to choose another course of well-rehearsed action. I slipped into my comforting meditation habit, closed my eyes again and took about eight slow cycles of breathing in and out. I then sensed you knew I was praying with my breath. I opened my eyes. Your apologetic eyes, defenseless posture, and shallow breathing expressed your bewilderment and remorse. Seeing your fragile, vulnerable body automatically softened my emotions. Instead of holding my breath, I breathed deeply to get even more grounded and express my feelings with both compassion and honesty.

Once again, we had injured each other's feelings, and we knew it. Our long, complicated history of deeply wounding each other circulated through the air in the room, attempting to pollute the space between us. But, seeing you as a fragile, painfully thin, dying woman in front of me broke open my heart. In the past, I expressed my hurt by holding my breath and ostracizing you. Ironically, this time I chose silence to express my love and appreciation for you. No more fighting. I exhaled an "I love you despite it all. I know you did your very best." Your face softened with relief as we breathed together and acknowledged our need to drop the subject. We chose to stay in the present, blissful moment of reconciliation by inhaling and exhaling in unison instead of holding our breath.

Love,
Natazha

Section Four

Breathing Life
Into Your Life

Bonded by Shame and Smoking   September 2016

Caroline Myss is a five-time New York Times bestselling author in the fields of human consciousness, spirituality and mysticism. She writes about how we often bond over our wounds. I clearly bonded over shame and smoking with my Mom. I'm eternally grateful to everyone who taught me to bond through love, especially my husband, Bob.

Dear Mom:

"Let her breathe. God damn it, Shame, let her catch her breath." How often I dream of going back in time, screaming at the top of my lungs, "You evil bastard, Shame, let her breathe." I felt so helpless watching you be tortured by your asthma. Mom, as a little girl, I felt you were fighting an evil spirit whenever you fought to breathe. Today I label that evil spirit Shame. I swear your lungs were poisoned by the ancestral pollution of shame and wracked by the grief and unworthiness shared by generations of Irish. Somewhere, somehow, your genes transmuted the shame of the Irish into your very being.

As a Berkeley Psychic Institute student, I looked at your heroic soul and realized you willingly signed up to transform Irish shame, alcoholism, sorrow, and trauma into self-love. I saw your soul's mission so clearly because I have the same mission. Never had my own kids. But I fight fiercely, one breath at a time, to clear ancestral shame so future generations can more easily love and mother themselves with their breath.

Asthma has an emotional component. At first, your asthma was a manifestation of you wrestling with shame. You were challenging the voice in your soul: "You Irish piece of shit. Your kind isn't even worthy of breathing." Smoking changed all that. Shame stole your breath only during your asthma attacks. Smoking stole your breath, period. It left you permanently decimated with lung cancer and emphysema. You no longer felt you made mistakes, but smoked as if you were a mistake. I still can't fucking believe they taught to you to smoke at Central Islip. How could they recommend smoking in 1967 after the Surgeon General's warning? You needed contemplation, not cigarettes, during your dark night of the soul.

What compelled me to start smoking at age 11? My unconscious desire to be closer to you, and share a bond that none of the other girls shared with you, smoking. I also wanted to help you conquer your shame. I also wanted the obvious flaw of smoking so that the other kids would criticize me for smoking instead of attacking me personally. I distinctly remember standing in front of the mirror adjacent to the window in the bedroom where we five oldest girls slept. I looked into my eyes with shame and disgust. I thought, "Now you can put me down for smoking," as I inhaled my first drag and blew out a death wish. I felt perversely pleased sharing your shame-based death sentence. And I quickly became a professional smoker as I learned to smoke an entire cigarette with never flicking the ash. I acted as if my entire-size-of-the-cigarette ash was a trophy. Very quickly I graduated to smoking 2 to 3 packs a day.

It's hard to say which was more addictive, nicotine or the shame of deliberately hurting myself. Instead of razor blades I cut into my being with poisonous inhales. Shame fueled my intense self-hatred that made quitting impossible. Ultimately, self-love is how I won my battle against nicotine and shame.

During my fourteen-year smoking career, I quit hundreds of times and tried many techniques: hypnosis, visualizations, expressive art therapy, various smoking cessation reward systems, and all types of aerobic exercise: swimming, running, dancing, hiking, martial arts, yoga, and biking. I tried nicotine gum, but it made me sick. I also tried aromatherapy, meditation, sucking on various candies, and chewing on cinnamon sticks and gum. The American Lung Association's smoking cessation program offered group support, but still lacked the one ingredient that mattered most: examining why I wanted to smoke. What was my payoff for smoking? It seemed counterintuitive at the time, but I successfully quit once I understood why I smoked cigarettes. Smoking allowed me to act out my shame and self-hatred.

Embracing my shame and self-hatred made all the difference in the world. On Monday, June 29, 1987 at 3:21 p.m. I officially quit smoking. That's when I threw my cigarette off the Larkspur Ferry into the San Francisco Bay. That moment marked my commitment to loving myself through many breathing practices instead of hating myself through smoking. I transformed my shame-based smoking into self-love through these breathing habits: meditation, exercise, expressing my feelings.

My favorite self-love breathing technique was imagining I was pregnant. I'd breathe deep into my belly and pretend I housed fraternal twins who looked like Raphael's angels. One twin was a wild, red-haired, high-spirited boy I called Francis who loved dangerous adventures. The other was a girl twin with curly black hair, bright blue eyes, and a contagious laugh. I named her Regina. While I struggled setting boundaries for myself, I had no problem setting them to protect Francis and Regina. It was okay to harm myself with cigarette smoke, but my maternal instincts forbade me from even imagining exposing them to cigarette smoke. I would lullaby them with deep, loving breaths. Sometimes I wondered when I did get pregnant, hopefully with twins, would my babies love or hate it when I swam. Would swimming make them fuss and kick in the womb or mellow out?

I'd pretend for hours these loving spirits lived inside me, and whenever I experienced a shame-induced nicotine craving, I'd express my love for these twins and myself with deep, heart-felt breaths into my belly instead of lighting a cigarette. I taught myself to mother myself with my breath by imagining I was a mom.

The folks at the Berkeley Psychic Institute called Francis and Regina baby beings, spirits without a body looking for a mother. In 2004, when Bob and I learned we couldn't have kids, I stopped conspiring with baby beings. That breathing practice caused sorrow instead of joy. I also took down all my images of Raphael's angels in our condo.

I can now appreciate my imaginary pregnancy breath practice as one of my many steps toward learning how to love myself through my breath. Loving myself helped me reconcile with you. Those imaginary pregnancies taught me to bless the distance between us instead of polluting it with cigarette smoke.

Love,
Natazha

Mining Your Resistance for Gold   August 2016

I routinely explore the payoff for my "bad" behaviors. What part of me is fed by my "bad" behavior? For example, I have an inner rebel. When I find myself speeding and breaking other driving laws, I know it's time to go skinny-dipping. That's a fun way to rebel without putting anyone's life in danger or paying for expensive traffic tickets.

Dear Mom,

A big part of me wanted to smoke. The issue was not why I wanted to quit smoking. The real issue was why I didn't want to quit. By honestly examining my motivations, I discovered the misdirected, shame-based part of myself that felt compelled to smoke. It appeared to me as an internal cartoon character I called Smokey.

Smokey suddenly popped up in my awareness on my walk to work one day, way back in 1987. I had just stamped out a cigarette, and hated myself for smoking first thing in the morning. That's when I saw Smokey in my mind's eye. I intuited that my psyche created Smokey in response to my self-loathing. He looked like a chimney sweeper living in my lungs, and symbolized parts of me addicted to smoking that kept sabotaging my efforts to quit. No wonder I couldn't quit; I had disowned my shame-based motivations for smoking. I disregarded them as evil desires that didn't belong to me.

That morning I received a big insight: to quit smoking I needed to embrace and compassionately communicate with Smokey. He needed coaching, not criticizing. In the ensuing months, I used writing, visualizations, and deep breathing to love and coach Smokey. I felt a little crazy, but I did it anyway. I stopped writing my reasons to quit and began writing my reasons NOT to quit. I deliberately connected with Smokey and even wrote the following story to honor him.

Smokey, Help me

Smokey was a classic fallen Angel. He fell from the heavens and crashed headfirst, smack in the middle of an ashtray. Besides a whopping headache, his body was crushed down to half its original size. His angel costume was tattered beyond recognition. No one got close to him because he smelled like a half-used cigarette begging to be put out of its misery.

The crash changed more than Smokey's appearance. His whole outlook changed as he forgot his guardian angel heritage and became a chimney sweeper. He used his broken, completely torn-off wing to sweep ashes. And he scraped tough tar stains with his broken halo. He was quite lopsided, with only his left wing attached to his body. That strained his back and caused him constant pain. He escaped his pain by distracting himself, sweeping cigarette ashes nonstop. His life purpose changed from being a guardian angel to seducing smokers into smoking more cigarettes and leaving more ashes for him to sweep away. Not once did he flashback to his angel days of helping people quit smoking or never smoke in the first place.

Success made Smokey feel miserable and lonely. The more he seduced smokers to inhale cigarette smoke, the sooner they died, leaving him in the depressing spot of needing to find a new victim. Deep down, Smokey felt guilty about luring smokers to their suicide. He wanted to quit his chimney sweeper job, but couldn't think of anything else he could do. Living inside smoker's filthy lungs is a lonely place. He had no friends to help him envision a new purpose, and felt hopeless, destined to chimney sweep forever more. So he decided his only choice was to charge full speed ahead with this chimney-sweeping career. He started sending subliminal messages to his smokers to ease his loneliness and guarantee they never got the stupid idea of quitting. The mere idea of smokers quitting gave him an instant anxiety attack, as he feared losing his job security.

Smokey never realized his subliminal messages were a throwback to his days as an angel, when he whispered sweet words of inspiration into peoples' ears. Now his sinister words sounded like a never-ending, incoherent, old-fashioned TV cigarette commercial. "You've come a long way, baby. Have another cigarette. I'd rather switch than fight. Be a Marlboro man." He first spoke in a heavenly whisper, but over time he started screaming his messages. On this particular day,

Smokey was extremely loud. His current smoker, Grace, was a twenty-four-year-old co-ed who after 13 years of sucking down cigarette smoke was determined to quit. Smokey used every trick in the book on Grace, and he feared somebody would die before this will of wars was over. Smoky became terrified watching Grace slowly wean off cigarettes. He panicked and got stuck on the phrase, "Be a Marlboro man." He shouted it over and over again so Grace couldn't ignore it.

Grace couldn't ignore Smokey's screaming as she engaged in the breath-based technique of self-hypnosis. She was connecting to disowned parts of herself and just couldn't block out Smokey's ranting and raving. Spiritually inclined, all along she suspected some kind of demon possessed her to smoke. As she breathed more deeply and went deeper within herself, she encountered Smokey head-on. There was no denying it. Right there, smack in the middle of her lungs, was a lopsided chimney sweeper screaming, "Be a Marlboro man." She instantly sensed Smokey was the demon thwarting her attempts to stop smoking. Her first impulse was to kill him. But curiosity inspired her to take a closer look, and find out more about this tiny, filthy, crooked creature. He looked so helpless with his tattered clothes and broken wing that Grace felt obligated to help Smokey, not punish him.

With a clear, loving tone, she whispered, "Hello, I'm Grace. Who are you?" Smokey almost died. He had no idea what to say. Was she really talking to him? He froze in fear. His need to connect with her got the best of him. He growled, "You talking to me? Are you talking to me? Who am I? I'm Smokey, the chimney sweep who lives in your lungs, Missy. And don't you forget it."

Shocked and delighted by Smokey's spunk, Grace replied, "I'm pleased to meet you, Smokey." Smokey was stunned by her kindness. She talked directly to him. He started sobbing. No one had talked to him since the crash. Grace visualized a tissue for him to wipe his tears, an act of compassion that took him back to his angel days.

Grace visualized hugging Smokey, cleaning his clothes, and healing his broken wing. Her love transformed Smokey. He called it "mystic magic" when her sweet intentions transformed his clothes back into his pearly white angel costume.

"Oh my God, you're an angel, not a chimney sweep. Can you please help me quit smoking? Would you be my guardian angel? Smokey, help me. Please help me."

Smokey felt honored by her request, and loved having a chance to connect to her. He couldn't resist helping Grace. Her confidence in him renewed his guardian-angel skills. Grace helped him to return to a state of Grace.

Smokey thrived helping Grace quit smoking. He loved having a human being speak directly to him. First thing in the morning when Grace got plagued by urges to smoke with her morning cup of coffee, she called out "Smokey, help me. Smokey, help me."

Smokey felt wonderful singing "You can do it, Grace. Breathe deep. Love yourself with your breath."

At lunch, all her coworkers would go outside to smoke. Grace felt lonely and wanted to smoke with them. But instead she whispered, "Smokey, help me. Smokey, help me."

Smokey answered, "I'm here for you. Remember, exhale to soothe yourself." Those words of encouragement helped Grace resist smoking at lunch. Over time, her lunchtime ritual evolved into conversing with Smokey. They spoke all about what she wanted in life, rather than letting her dreams go up in smoke.

With Smokey's help, Grace did stop smoking. Long after she quit, she continued saying, "Smokey, help me. Smokey, help me." Smokey always answered her and became Grace's official guardian. And they lived happily ever after.

I originally saw myself as Grace, but eventually identified more with Smokey when I realized that I, too, was off course being at war with you, Mom. And I needed to change my life by forgiving you. After quitting nicotine, I stopped squelching my feelings and began expressing them more freely. That shift inspired me to revise Smokey's story. As my lungs got cleaner, I made Smokey an artistic guardian angel with a new job as an artist. Just like the first version, at first Smokey was terrified to stop chimney sweeping. I breathed deeply to console and persuade him that painting on my clean lung walls could be much more rewarding than cleaning them. As I stayed away from cigarettes, my lungs healed and I expressed my own creativity and feelings more freely. Smokey started feeling safer to express his creativity. He evolved into an artist of many media: painting, drawing, dance, creative writing, poetry, singing, and playing musical instruments. He actually loved producing art so much more than sweeping chimneys.

I stayed off cigarettes permanently by relating to Smokey and myself differently. I also learned how smoking met many of my needs. Staying thin appealed to my vanity. Providing a circle of smoking buddies appealed to my social self. Staying awake to study long past my bedtime appealed to my intellect. Smoking justified taking desperately needed breaks. That appealed to my reflective self.

Learning new ways to satisfy those needs enriched my life and Smokey worked even harder on helping me stay off cigarettes. I swam to stay thin, and made new friends who didn't smoke at the local YMCA and 12-Step meetings. I learned breathing exercises to help me concentrate and focus. That allowed my reflective self to integrate the events of my hectic workdays. Moreover, I learned I felt guilty taking breaks in my twenties. I had used smoking to cue myself to take breaks. Eventually I realized I absolutely need breaks to stop and smell the roses and move my body. At first glance, breaks appear to be unproductive but they actually help me organize my thoughts and renew my energy.

In stark contrast to my smoking days, I now have no trouble taking breaks. I routinely stop to breathe; practice meditation and yoga. I conspire with all the characters running around inside my psyche, including Smokey. One breath at a time I'm staying connected to all of me. It's great now to have Smokey work for me, not against me.

Mom, I wonder if I got the idea to embrace Smokey from growing up with a mystic like you. It turns out my practice of loving and breathing life into my demons rather than suffocating them mirrors a Tibetan Buddhist mystical practice called Chöd.

A Buddhist monk, Tsusltrim Allione wrote *Feeding Your Demons: Ancient Wisdom for Resolving Inner Conflicts* in which she explains when we fight our demons (addictions) they only grow stronger. But if we feed and nurture them, we can free ourselves from the battle. Her description of Chöd parallels my practice to quit smoking. Just like Chöd, I breathed deeply to connect with my inner demons, such as Smokey. And like Chöd I imagined my demons in vivid detail, and asked them about their motives and needs. Similar to the Tibetan practice I, too, found creative ways to meet their needs. I sometimes repeat this process as I change over time.

I feel sad realizing we rarely shared our favorite ways to express our souls' desires and explore our creativity and spirituality. I never shared my *Smokey, Help Me* story or many of my other spiritual adventures with you. You never told me about your spiritual pilgrimages. Anyway, I hope you enjoyed this story. Journal writing and creative writing really helped me start loving myself more. It helped me release so much shame and grief.

You know what, these days, I don't say, "Smokey, help me." I say, "Mommy, please help me." Book writing is even harder than quitting smoking. I'm healing my shame and fear of success on a much deeper level. I'm more than giving up an awful habit. I'm saying I'm worthy of being published. That goes right up against my sense of unworthiness. Thanks for being a healing presence by my side reminding me to "Breathe Write (right) now."

Love,
Natazha

Breathe Write (Right) Now   March 2017

I'm a world-class breather who has no problems breathing as I run marathons, row over 100 miles from San Francisco to Sacramento, bike the hills of San Francisco, and swim without a wetsuit in the frigid San Francisco Bay. However, as I write I often hold my breath, even though I'm trying to pour my heart and soul out on paper. Writing is an emotional act that requires me to emote through my breath. Breathing with my Mom's spirit while writing this book taught me to breathe as I write.

Dear Natazha,

Be kind to yourself. Breathe write now. Of course you're struggling with your book writing. It puts you smack up against your shame. You feel unworthy of being published. I watch you procrastinate to avoid your fear of success. I know that anxiety all too well because I passed it on to you. Please know you're absolutely worthy of being published. You were always a talented writer. We loved the heartfelt and incredibly insightful letters you wrote us as a kid. You've always confided in a journal. And wrote great papers. That's why Grinnell College and San Francisco State University honored you with awards for your scholarship and creativity.

I'm so glad you trust me now. You now understand I was never jealous of you. I absolutely wanted you to succeed.

I'm here for you, and will help you publish your book on breathing that's been brewing inside you for a lifetime. You have so much wisdom to share about your graduation from smoking to healthy breathing habits: meditation, exercise, and expressing your feelings. I love watching you mother and love yourself with your breath.

Natazha, you've always had all the compassion, brilliance, and talent to teach, lecture, and write about breathing. You courageously grow from your mistakes by minding your breath. I'm so proud of you for sticking with your book even when your inner critic and perfectionist kept screaming lies at you, "You're not good enough to publish. Don't embarrass yourself by publishing your awful book." I love watching you tame those demons by breathing through your fear, not running away from it.

Please believe me. You're worthy of all the love and success you've ever dreamed about. You've done the really hard work of staying present as you transform your shame to self-love, one breath at a time. Please share your wisdom about mothering yourself with your breath with the world. Stay with it. Please keep writing your book. I share your vision and will continue to bless your efforts from afar.

Love,
Mom

Dear Mom,

You wise wicked woman, you used your mystic magic on me again. You seamlessly seduced me into writing my book even when I felt overwhelmed by self-doubt, shame, and my inner critic and perfectionist. Those two shame thugs terrorized me with their lies that I wasn't good enough to publish a book. I got waylaid by their harsh criticisms, and almost gave up. But I felt obligated to honor my vow to you that this time I'd publish my book.

Thanks for helping me when I needed it most. Starting last June, whenever I sat down to write, I'd quickly get distracted, and felt compelled to water plants, wash dishes, make a cup of tea, text friends or clients, go for a row or swim or bike ride or run or hike or dancing – anything but write. Then I felt more and more scared and discouraged, which only made it even easier for my inner critic and perfectionist to pick on me. I felt guilty about procrastinating and easily fell prey to their ridicule.

In my hour of need, you urged me to keep writing despite my terror and shame. I flashed back to memories of you conquering fear: leaving the Central Islip insane asylum, swimming for the first time at 60 years old, battling the IRS three times, receiving chemo for breast cancer, undergoing surgery for lung cancer, and many other memories.

You inspired me to write by showing me examples of you feeling the fear and doing it anyway.

Those visions got me writing again. I missed you more than ever, but couldn't call you on the phone, so I started writing you letters. I let my right-hand channel encouraging letters from you to me. At first, I wrote about regretting and not sharing more of my life with you. Eventually I wrote what I wanted to say in my book about breathing. Writing letters from my heart and soul released me from the tyranny of my inner critic and perfectionist. Best of all, it got me back to writing consistently.

All summer and fall, I felt safe writing letters I thought would never get published. I felt that I was still failing at my book writing until Tom Bird assigned our writing group to hand in our first 10 pages. My first 10 pages were all letters so that's what I submitted. I was quite surprised when my fellow writers loved the letter format. They felt it was a nice way of communicating about breathing in a personal, heartfelt matter. I now see some of my writing about breathing could have been dreadfully dry if it was written in a traditional book format.

Then, the time came to edit those letters. That's when my shame returned with a vengeance. I suffered even worse bouts of anxiety and self-doubt. I saw visions of people attacking me: "You have no right to say 'mother yourself' with your breath. You're not a mother. You treated your own mother like shit. You should be ashamed of yourself."

That's when I began in earnest to BREATHE WRITE NOW. As I wrote I devised ways to mother myself with my breath. That's how I broke my habit of holding my breath to avoid feeling my shame or frustration when I struggled to find the right words to express myself. Unlike writing, I don't attack myself or hold my breath when I exercise. It demands sound breathing to meet my increased demands for oxygen. Otherwise I'll conk out. Movement automatically cues me to connect to my breath, a key ingredient for processing all feelings, especially self-love.

Writing entails no strenuous physical activity to cue my breath. Even worse, revising requires visiting the same neighborhoods in my brain where my inner critic and perfectionist live. Those shame punks don't bother me when I'm writing a shitty first draft (SFD). I don't analyze that writing: I write so fast there's no chance for them to attack me. It's straight from my gut and heart.

Revising is totally different. I'm taking the raw SFDs that only make sense to me because I wrote them in my own peculiar vernacular, just for my consumption. I'm adding or deleting details so others without my unique background can understand. I don't want to lose the heart and soul of my SFDs with word crafting; I need the loving version of my inner critic and perfectionist, their skills minus the shame. I need to BREATHE WRITE NOW while revising. And I realized the Tibetan Buddhist breathing technique of "Feeding your Demon" that transformed Smokey from a chimney sweeper to my artistic guardian angel could help me BREATHE WRITE NOW.

I used breathing to tame my inner critic and perfectionist. Both of them were transformed after I stopped suffocating them and instead exhaled love and compassion to them. I set new boundaries with my inner critic. I taught him to critique only my work, and not ridicule me. I taught my inner perfectionist that I wanted to strive to do my best, not be perfect. And told her, "Done is better than perfect." I explained to her that I have hundreds of perfect versions of my book inside of me. There isn't just one perfect version of my book; it's more important I actually write, publish, and share my book with others. I also gave her some special projects where she could practice some perfectionism, my book cover and table of contents. Those specific features need to be "perfect" to attract readers.

I placed BREATHE WRITE NOW signs throughout our condo to cue me to breathe and process my shame-based feelings as I wrote. Instead of running off to water plants or wash dishes or exercise, I simply sat at my writing desk, and took long slow breaths to conspire with your spirit as well as my own. Prayed through my breath. And most times, after a few breaths, I was ready to keep writing.

For the first time in my life, I truly listened to the lyrics of the Beatles song, "Let It Be." I interpreted that song as a prayer to you when I realized you're my Mother Mary who in times of trouble comforts me. I began singing "Let It Be To You" when I felt paralyzed by my shame. Singing cues extra-long exhales known for reducing anxiety and increasing confidence. That song in particular soothed and energized me; I began enjoying book writing. I also pulled out my aromatherapy oils: Joy, Forgiveness, Believe, and Orange. Those delicious scents enticed me to inhale slowly through my nose to smell compassionate scents. I also exhaled fully to call on the help of all our ancestors, Grandma Winnie, Grandpa Joe, Nanny, plus mothers from all ages.

The BREATHE WRITE NOW signs reminded me of your courage: breathe through your fears and do it anyway. It also reminded me of Tom Bird's advice. He often said, "Consistency is more important than production. Consistent writing is the most important thing." His advice echoed Elizabeth Gilbert's advice in her book *Big Magic*. "Writers write. You need to write consistently." I added, "Writers write while loving themselves through their breathing." And, I told myself I only needed to write daily; no one said only book writing counts. That gave me permission to keep writing letters to you while I renegotiated my relationship with my shame through my breathing.

You're right; I've always loved keeping a journal and writing letters. I never felt unworthy writing those things. Now, I see that a book is a longer version of those things. And I do deserve to be published. Thanks for mothering me from afar and inspiring me to write you all those letters when I was too afraid to "write my book."

Love,
Natazha

There's No Best Way to Breathe   September 2016

Bob's sister Anne Marie is tougher than all five of her brothers combined. She's one of many moms who inspired this letter. Besides touring Bhutan with me, we've traveled down the road of reconciling with our Moms. She's the first person in my life to openly and honestly acknowledge having a "different" mom than her siblings did. I received an incredible healing watching her and Bob laugh about how their Mom treated the girls so differently from the boys. I always believed I was innately defective because my relationship with my mom was so different from my siblings. My mom acted much more lovey-dovey with my younger sisters Noreen and Gabrielle, but I never took into account that my role was to kick my Mom in her spiritual ass. Demand she look at her own sexual abuse and learn how to defend herself and kids against pedophiles and bullies. Annie's honesty fostered an insight: I did nothing wrong; I just had a different relationship with my Mom.

Annie's also one of the best moms I know. She doesn't blindly follow the same recipe raising her kids. Like Annie, my niece Sasha is fierce. If Sasha puts her hat in the ring, she'll die before she quits. Without Annie's mothering skills, Sasha could easily have become a bully. I love watching Annie add some femininity and compassion to Sasha's style. On the other hand, Annie uses totally different tactics with her son Quinn. He's super intelligent, laid back, and excels at many things including sleeping. At times she lights a firecracker under his butt. Lastly, all my sisters are great moms too, but I lost the privilege of watching their kids grow up on a routine basis. That's been one of the most painful consequences of using 3,000 miles to set a boundary with my family.

Dear Mom:

So many people ask me, "What's the best way to breathe?" You even asked me that question several times. I hate that question. It suggests breathing is a problem to be solved. And, implies once you solve the problem with a "best way to breathe" technique, you never again need to mind your breathing.

Instead of being a problem, breathing's a process, just like mothering. You loved us all, but mothered us differently. We wore you and Dad out; you changed your parenting style over the years. You definitely were the strictest with the first five kids, including me. You relaxed your standards with the next five kids. You were most relaxed with Gabrielle and Luke, the caboose kids. By the time they rolled out, you and Dad were like Velveteen Rabbits, so real and worn out from loving us kids that you looked more like their grandparents than parents. I remember Luke complaining that his teenage friends asked if you were his grandmother.

I was jealous of how lax you were with them, and thought you knew all about their shenanigans and drinking. Later I learned that you had no idea. Do you remember what happened the night before Gabrielle left for Belmont Abbey College? Her crazy-ass boyfriend got wildly drunk and climbed up onto the porch roof. He threw pebbles at Gabrielle's bedroom window, yelling over and over again at the top of his lungs, "Gabrielle, I love you. Please don't leave me. Please don't go."

Gabrielle finally woke up. She opened her window, and was trying her best to talk him down off the roof when he suddenly fell off. He hurt himself pretty badly, broke several bones. He screamed in agony on the ground while she called for an ambulance.

Another neighbor called the cops. In no time flat, a large crowd of neighbors, cops, and EMTs surrounded him just below your bedroom window. Gabrielle told you the next morning pretty much the entire neighborhood woke up that night, except you and Daddy.

You were totally different when I was a teenager; you barely slept. You stayed up all hours of the day and night raising kids, attending church, typing papers for Dad during his doctoral program, and sewing clothes. I loved the light-blue cotton dress you made for my sophomore high school prom.

Back then I resented you changing your parenting style. I thought parents were supposed to be rigidly consistent. Now I see good parenting entails responding to the unique and fluctuating needs of each kid, and it's a testament to your mothering skills that you had a different relationship with each child.

Breathing well resembles good mothering. A mother constantly monitors her baby, and doesn't use the same old approach to meet her child's ever-changing needs. We also need to frequently check our breathing. And modulate it to respond effectively to whatever life throws at us. Breathing is how we monitor our control buttons. And, guess what, monitoring our control buttons never ends.

Finding the best way to breathe is not the real issue. Mindfulness is the hard part. Stress, overstimulation, and electronic devices divorce us from our respiration. Mindfulness allows us to stay married to our breath and breathe in our own best interest. Mom, your COPD and shortness of breath forced you to constantly check your breathing. Most people need training to stay aware of their breathing. Humans innately know how to breathe well, and breathe better the moment they tend to their breath.

Mindfulness works wonders. It helps us to stop holding our breath and to quit other harmful breathing habits.

Breathing is like background music. And, there's no such thing as the best background music. A slow, intimate dance with your honey requires completely different music than a raucous teenager's birthday party. Just as different activities require different music, different tasks require different breathing patterns. Writing at your desk requires much less oxygen than running a marathon, so you breathe differently.

Here's the bottom line: just as a mother is devoted to her children, we need to stay connected to our breath during good times and bad times. Constantly check in with our respiration. That check-in automatically cues us to breathe in a manner that suits our needs at any given moment. And our needs change all the time. That's why we need a wide variety of breathing styles instead of one best way to breathe.

In many ways, your asthma and COPD forced you to practice devotional breathing. I often saw you place a hand on your heart to take a brief moment to assess your breathing. I'm so grateful you modeled devotional breathing: one of the most important tools in my healing process.

Love,
Natazha

Findhorn Angel Cards   September 2016

Founded in 1962, the Findhorn Spiritual community in Scotland feels like a modern-day monastery for spiritual growth and learning. I briefly visited this amazing community right after I passed my physical therapy boards, and was truly inspired by what they've done through the art of setting intentions.

Dear Mom:

A better question than "What's the best way to breathe?" is "How do you stay in touch with your breath? Be mindful about it?" Answer: Set an intention first thing in the morning and throughout the day to mind your breath. I know you loved your retreat in Findhorn, Scotland. So you may enjoy my breath-intention ritual with Findhorn angel cards. Do you remember when I gave you a deck of Findhorn angel cards? They were tiny cards, about the size of a return address seal. Each deck has 72 divine qualities, such as love, joy, humor, synthesis, and transformation.

For my breath-intention ritual, I decorated a recycled wooden box with spiritual symbols, and filled it with three decks of angel cards. This box rests on a shelf above my toilet. Each morning when I go to the bathroom, I close my eyes and choose three angel cards: an angel quality for inhalation, exhalation, and a card for breathing well with others.

Some days, I pick the same quality three times in a row. I selected transformation three times one Easter. Felt that was an incredible coincidence. I mean what are the odds of picking 1 out of 72 cards three times in a row? And, on top of that a quality that beautifully speaks to the Resurrection of Christ. Today I chose: to inhale grace, to exhale humor, and to conspire honesty. I loved that I chose humor for my exhalation. In the late afternoon, I expressed my humor through my exhalation. After sharing a truly silly joke about sheep I exhaled long and hard with a raucous belly laugh.

Mom, thinking about Findhorn saddens me. For years, I dreamed of going on a Findhorn retreat with you. I can't go with you now, but still hope someone else from the family joins me. Perhaps Cara or Julia (my nieces) will go with me.

I need to take a breather to process what feels like a bottomless pit of grief. I'll go for a walking meditation. And pretend we're on a retreat in Findhorn, walking together in one of their many splendid gardens.

Love,
Natazha

The Beauty of Informal Meditation   January 2017

I'm always on the lookout for spontaneous, creative ways to meditate. I'm grateful to my parents, nephew Mac, and the Italians for showcasing informal meditation.

Dear Mom,

Today we had brunch with Bob's nephew, Mac. He's a great guy, married to a great gal, Jaime. They have absolutely adorable one-year old identical twins, Audrey and Evelyn. I can't get enough of those high-spirited cutie pies. It's always a special treat when they visit us in San Francisco.

Bob's family knows I'm big on breathing and meditation. Unfortunately, sometimes that makes them feel guilty about not meditating. And sure enough during brunch, Mac said to me, "I just can't sit down and meditate."

I responded, "But you sing and play your guitar to Jaime and the twins. I love your videos of Audrey and Evelyn shaking their booties. You play the guitar really well."

Mac responded, "But singing is not meditation."

I answered, "Oh, yes it is. Think about it. All religions, yogis, and Buddhists sing or chant as a form of worship and meditation. In fact, followers of the Nichiren Buddhist tradition chant instead of meditate in silence. Singing and chanting connects you to your breath."

Mac looked at me with some skepticism. "But, it's not formal meditation."

I said, "Informal meditation like singing is even better than formal meditation. You can do it anywhere, anytime. Besides, Mac, you found one fun activity to meet many of your needs. Singing connects you to your whole family. It allows you to meditate together, and teaches the twins to enjoy music. They sing, express themselves, and connect to their breathing. It's a form of meditation."

Mac smiles back at me. "Thanks, I didn't think about it that way."

I add, "Mac, you're mega busy as a Dad with two little baby girls, a wife, dog, house, and full-time job. I'm impressed you take the time to sing and play the guitar. Don't worry; the day will come when you'll sit down to meditate. In the meantime, just keep singing."

Mom, I'm grateful you and Daddy also modeled informal meditation to me. Dad sang all the time: in the shower, making coffee, driving to Bayport Beach, and anytime the situation got too tense. His singing taught me to use song to tune into my breathing. For instance, I sing, "This little light of mine, I'm gonna let it shine" as I brave the streets of San Francisco by bike. Singing makes me mindful instead of fretful navigating crazy traffic.

Both you and Daddy practiced what I call "Italian-style Meditation." It's one of my favorite ways to meditate informally. You know the saying, "When in Rome, do as the Romans." When we visited Rome that's exactly what we did. We copied the Romans, and sat on the park benches along the Tiber River appreciating the beauty all around us. Simply sat still. Breathed. And, enjoyed the scenery: the river flowing before us, people strolling the sidewalks, birds flying overhead, and an occasional gentle breeze blowing between us.

My favorite souvenir from Rome was rediscovering my habit of sitting still and appreciating beauty. That practice quickly boosts my gratitude and mindfulness. I love that I can do it pretty much anytime and anywhere. Some of my fondest childhood memories include Italian-style meditation. Daddy Ray would drive us to Bayport Beach. I sat in the shotgun seat and the other kids in the back seat. Daddy parked the car and we enjoyed one of those very rare, silent moments. We quietly conspired and appreciated the waves gently slapping the shoreline. We watched swimmers make their way across the enclosed area, and people stroll along the shoreline. Once, you drove me to the Ursuline convent in Blue Point for 5:00 Mass. Again, you parked the car with me sitting beside you. We, too, sat in silence for about a minute or two as we appreciated our surroundings: the long line of fir trees lining the pavement, the birds flying between the trees, and the serenity of the grounds. Your Italian-style meditation inspired my present-day meditation practices.

Mom, there was another way you taught me to informally meditate. Right before leaving the house or having heart-to-heart conversations, I often saw you check your breath by placing a hand over your heart. I'll never know if that was the mystic in you connecting to the Divine or the asthmatic in you checking if you needed more medication. Either way, I find myself copying you. I bow my head, take heart-felt breaths, and place my hand on my heart to set an intention before embarking on activities, such as teaching a class or swimming in the San Francisco bay.

Informal meditation is an incredibly important, life-affirming act. One reason I'm writing a book on breathing is to remind people to stop wandering through life without minding their breath. I want to seduce people to practice informal meditation: sing, practice Italian-style meditation, or simply check their breath every time they check for their cell phones or keys on the way out the door.

Love,
Natazha

Mother Teresa's Creating Miracles Recipe   September 2016

I adore Mother Teresa. I love that she never had any kids, and yet everyone called her Mother Teresa. She acted as a mother to the world by providing maternal spiritual wisdom. She inspired me to express my maternal instincts as a "Breathing Mama," a woman who shares wisdom about how to mother yourself with your breathing.

Dear Mom,

I know you were a huge fan of Mother Teresa. Did you know that when asked, "How do you create a miracle?" she responded, "You perform the smallest acts with the greatest love and attention." Not surprisingly, I believe intentional breathing is a great ingredient to use in Mother Teresa's recipe for creating a miracle. Breathing done with great love and attention creates miracles.

Unlike you, most of us take our breath for granted. Breathing done with great care and devotion can sponsor miracles in our lives. You'd be hard-pressed to find an ailment that meditation doesn't alleviate. Scientists keep proving meditation, also known as paying attention to your breath, cures almost anything that ails you, and enhances everything that makes life worth living. It eases chronic pain, alleviates depression, ameliorates anxiety, improves memory and cognition, slows down the aging process, facilitates weight loss, enhances self-esteem and self-love, reduces reactivity, helps ease addictions, and increases optimism and relaxation.

Breathing with great love and devotion miraculously transforms relationships. Invisible forces play out over time in our daily habits and relationships. Those forces can't be fixed with any pill, surgery, or electronic gadget. No one ever saves a marriage with divorce-prevention pills. However, respiration governs the forces required for a happy marriage: self-awareness, compassion, love, patience, empathy and willingness. You mend the relationship with yourself and others when you attend to your breathing. That's how you save a marriage.

Bob and I are living proof of the research on mindfulness; meditation decreases reactivity that damages relationships. It helps you make wiser choices about how you behave. Bob and I received excellent marriage therapy after learning that we could not have kids tore us apart. I believe my meditation practice played an even bigger role in saving our marriage than therapy. Our therapist pointed out that I needed to stop verbally attacking Bob, but I already knew that long before attending therapy. Knowledge wasn't enough. My daily morning habit of minding my breath while sitting in the lotus pose on our sofa helped me behave differently, and stop accusing Bob of not caring. My meditation practice blessed me with the awareness that stopped me dead in my tracks whenever I was just about to verbally attack Bob. Instead of just knowing what I needed to change, that awareness actually enabled me to change my behavior. And thus restore our marriage.

Mom, my breathing also connects me to you. I confide in you by conspiring with your spirit. Since your death, I feel we created a miracle by blessing the distance between us.

Love,
Natazha

Honor Your Respiratory Signature   December 2016

I believe humans have a respiratory signature, a unique breathing style that's only detectable on a super, subtle level. We just need better technology to measure it. That's why I was thrilled to learn scientists recently figured out ways to use our breath to detect diabetes, cancer, and bacterial overgrowth. To me, it's just a matter of time before they'll devise a reliable way to identify us by our breath, just like fingerprints. My own respiratory signature got wildly off kilter due to trauma. I feel that's why I choose breath-based addictions: smoking and promiscuous sex. It's obvious why smoking is a breath-based vice. Here's why I classify sex addiction as a breath-based vice. A sexual orgasm causes a glorious shift in our breathing. As an incest survivor, I got the message that I was a sexual object. And I used sex in an unconscious attempt to interrupt and thus restore my injured breathing style through orgasmic breathing.

Dear Mom,

We have unique fingerprints and voices. I believe we also have unique respiratory signatures. We each emit a unique volume and set of gases and odors at any given time. Medical technology is now so sophisticated that we can measure never-before-detectable differences in the gases we exhale to determine diseases, like diabetes. You could think of this technology as a camera taking a photo of your breath. And one day it will depict the uniqueness of your breathing, just like a photograph captures your distinctive face.

A camera can also capture how our appearance changes over time. And so I believe medical technology could capture how our respiratory signature or breathing changes over time. I wish I had documented the dramatic improvement in my breathing since I stopped smoking and upgraded to self-love habits: inhaling aromatherapy oils and cool San Francisco breezes instead of cigarette smoke; exercising regularly; meditating; and taking frequent, mindful pauses to exhale fully and honestly express my feelings.

It'd be wonderful if one day we could more effectively track our breathing. Breathing governs all biochemical life processes as well as our psyches. That's why all Eastern health systems use the breath as the basis of health: acupuncture, Ayurvedic medicine, yoga, tai chi, martial arts and so on. It makes total sense to track breathing to get an accurate picture of your health, just like a blood test.

Your respiratory signature fluctuates, just like your voice and breathing. It's affected by many things: lung size, blood chemistry, diseases, diet, stress, sleep, and basically everything else that affects your respiration, including your preferred breathing style. That's your innate breathing pattern that allows you to settle into your bones. Gets your body, heart, mind, and spirit aligned and harmonized. It's the paradoxical unconscious yet conscious breathing style that satisfies every cell in your body and soul. Makes you vibrate with bliss.

Why am I going on about this? I struggled a lot learning how to maintain my own, blissful breathing pattern. It's my gift and curse. All my metaphysical teachers tell me I'm superb at matching other people's energy. That makes me very persuasive and great at selling ideas as a teacher. Here's the downside: we match energy through our breathing. Think about it. Breathing causes our bodies to vibrate and we match each other's vibration or energy through our respiration. And I used to easily lose my space and get off-center conspiring with others. I often stopped honoring my own breathing rhythm as I followed someone else's breath pattern.

As a middle child in our large family, I became damn good at matching others' energy. From day one, I matched the vibrations of a tribe of breathers. I even match the energy of animals and electronic gadgets through my respiration. Visiting Apple computer stores traumatized me until I started grounding and meditating before and during my store visits. Now I stay tuned to my own breathing, so I don't automatically match the high-pitched energy of the fast-paced electronic gadgets and young whippersnappers dealing with stressed customers.

Here's another distinct example. My breathing drastically changed when I moved in with Bob after living with my ex-boyfriend Jim, the 7th degree black belt who I met at the Berkeley Psychic Institute. Jim had excellent breathing habits after decades of karate and meditation. Over five years, he taught me volumes about breathing. I soaked up his good habits by matching his breath that rubbed off on me even while I slept. When I first moved in with Bob, he was a notorious snorer. I, too, began snoring. Inhaled through my mouth and woke up with a dry mouth that causes gum and tooth decay. Bob thought I was "different" when I began taping my mouth shut with bright green tape before going to sleep to stop snoring. That worked sometimes, but I often pulled the tape off my mouth during my sleep. Ultimately meditating before going to sleep at night was the solution. It helped me maintain my own innate breathing pattern as I slept, instead of matching Bob's snoring.

Meditation returns me to my innate breathing rhythm, the way I breathe when I'm centered and at peace. Takes me out of my head, beyond thoughts or words. Back to my raw, divine essence. That calm place where my mind, body, heart and soul harmonize. No part, especially my mind, dominates the others. I become whole again, at one with Nature and Source, my name for God.

Over time, my meditation practice helped me appreciate my gift for matching other's energy as I could more quickly restore my respiratory signature and innate breathing pattern. Individuating my breath through meditation enabled me to conspire better with others. I can now sing in my own octave in the never-ending respiratory chorus of all living things. Appreciate other choir members breathing in a different key from me without being thrown off-key by them.

My meditation practice is almost more important than what I eat. I can skip breakfast, but not my formal morning meditation. My day goes much better when I meditate at dawn. And even better if I take breathing pauses all day long to tune into my breath or spirit. Once again, I'm seeing how much I take after you. My meditation habits parallel your prayer life. You formally worshipped at Mass everyday on top of praying throughout the day.

Love,
Natazha

PS – By the way, changing to a Paleo diet cured Bob's snoring.

Sedentary is the New Smoking   October 2016

I'm heartbroken that so many Americans are motion starved. Like food, we have an innate need to move and we're clearly not meeting our daily requirement for motion.

Dear Mom,

I'll never forget a Little League baseball coach saying, "What's killing kids today is organized sports. Kids used to play spontaneous games of tag, dodge ball, baseball, and basketball all the time. Nowadays, only the minority of kids, selected for organized teams, play sports. The other kids are sent the message that they're not qualified to play sports. And they don't. They sit around playing video games or watching TV. You rarely see kids playing in the streets or parks anymore. Physical inactivity is causing childhood obesity."

Today's reality is such a stark contrast to life on Hampton Street during my childhood. Growing up, over 100 kids played all hours of the day and night on our dead-end street. As a kid I never considered myself athletic, but even I played tag or Ringolevio most days.

Adults are in the same boat. The conveniences of modern life have stripped away movement woven into our daily activities, or what I call informal exercise. The Internet lets us to make deposits without walking to the bank and buy clothes without running to a store. We ride elevators in modern office buildings instead of taking stairs. Adults exercise at organized events: a gym, yoga studio, organized teams, charity-sponsored endurance events like running a marathon to raise funds for Team in Training. And guess what, it's not enough physical activity. Adults are also more obese and sedentary than ever.Even if you exercise for 90 minutes each morning, but then sit for the rest of your day, you're still sedentary most of the day.

Health-care practitioners now claim, "Sedentary is the new smoking." More and more research shows humans are designed to move all day long. Chronic diseases, heart disease, and even some types of cancer are linked to a sedentary lifestyle. Moving throughout the day keeps our bones, connective tissues, and organs strong and healthy.

Here's an example of how movement throughout your day improves your health. Only the blood has a pump called the heart. All our other bodily fluids don't have a pump. That means our lymphatic, synovial, digestive, and other fluids need us to move and breathe deeply to help them circulate throughout the day. Exercise helps pump our bodily fluids. Consider twisting your torso as you reach for something overhead. That rotational motion contracts and relaxes the core muscles surrounding your digestive organs. And thus, it helps to pump your digestive fluids. A twist is like wringing out your digestive organs. Rigorous exercise forces us to breathe faster and harder, which also contracts and relaxes our core muscles and helps pump our digestive fluids.

Weaving movement into our lifestyle guarantees we move throughout the day. For example, climbing stairs at your workplace forces you to move at least three times: morning, noon, and night. You use the stairs coming to work, going to lunch and back, and returning home. Meeting people in person instead of communicating via the Internet also guarantees we move more often. Informal exercise has another hidden benefit. Movement is magic because we breathe better. Aerobic exercise forces us to breathe harder and faster. We must breathe more efficiently. On the other hand, sitting cues our worst breathing habits: shallow breathing and breath holding. Better breathing translates to better health.

Mom, I still regret not helping you weave more movement into your daily routines. There's no cure for COPD. You can't fix damaged lungs. However, exercise can strengthen all the other systems in your body, which is a healthy way to compensate for COPD.

Love,
Natazha

Sensationalize Your Breath   July 2016

I hope this letter inspires you to engage your senses in order to seduce yourself to mind your breath throughout your day.

Dear Mom:

I heavily promote meditation to my students, but many report it's too boring or difficult. They just can't get the hang of it. So I tell them to meditate by sensationalizing their breath. I ask them to use their five senses: sight, smell, hearing, touch, and taste, to enlighten their respiration and meditate.

I use biking to work to teach them how to sensationalize their breath. When I drive, I sit behind my steering wheel sealed off from both the traffic and my vitality. My car engine runs well, but I run on automatic pilot. I space out and hold my breath whereas biking demands I tune into my breath and body, which is also how we meditate.

My bike commute runs along the Embarcadero. You stayed at the Harbor Court Hotel on the Embarcadero when you visited us for our wedding. It's the wide, four-mile waterfront sidewalk that winds around the Giants' baseball stadium, past the Ferry Building, Barbary Coast, and ends at Fisherman's Wharf. With the lawlessness that embodies the Spirit of the Wild West, every day thousands of people and assorted beasts transverse the Embarcadero in every way possible. They come at each other from competing directions on foot, bikes, cycle rickshaws, roller blades, golf carts, strollers, skateboards, a crazy assortment of very-old-to-very-modern scooters, and sadly, every once in a while, an out-of-bounds car. Runners and off-leash dogs zigzag around this unpredictable commotion, adding more spice to all this chaos.

I've been knocked off my bike twice by other cyclists. I often feel like I'm running the gauntlet whether I'm biking on the sidewalk or in the bike lane that's often littered with broken car glass, absent-minded sightseers, and Uber drivers dropping off passengers. I'm hyper vigilant circumventing all this chaos. To combat my anxiety, I transform biking into an active form of meditation by minding my breath. With great awareness, I breathe in and out. I use my sense of touch to feel my diaphragm narrow and widen during each breath cycle, and my handlebar grip. My eyes and ears take in the erratic sights and so I can navigate through the crazy traffic safely. The salt-water scented fog intoxicates my sense of touch and smell. It cools my cheeks and seduces me to inhale fully so I'll better smell that familiar, soothing scent, and free aromatherapy. I check my taste buds to see if my mouth feels dry or has what I call the "panic taste."

When I feel really overwhelmed, I sing out loud "This little light of mine." In the Wild West atmosphere, no one ever notices my singing. I feel totally free to soothe myself with song. My voice reveals my stress level. Off-key singing indicates I'm tensing my neck or shoulder muscles, or I'm sticking my chin out too far. Being a physical therapist I know biking is correlated with neck pain. Singing soothes my nerves and helps me avoid neck pain by aligning my head and shoulders.

I also sensationalize my breath through yin yoga; I began practicing it at Giggling Lotus Yoga Studio in the Dog Patch area of San Francisco. Back in 2001, we briefly visited the Dog Patch neighborhood because Daddy wanted to see where a million soldiers were outfitted and shipped to the Pacific Front during World War II. Our tour abruptly ended when a well-intentioned cop warned us Dog Patch was now home to vagrants and other assorted criminals. He told me to get you back in my car and tour another neighborhood. Today, Dog Patch is an exclusive neighborhood since UCSF's upscale Mission Bay Campus moved in next door along with the Golden State Warrior basketball team, which is building its sports arena four blocks from Giggling Lotus Yoga Studio.

I fell in love with yin yoga when it seduced my senses and put me into an altered state of deep relaxation. The gentle yoga music and soothing voice of Mimi, the yoga studio owner, charmed my ears. The soft lighting, high ceiling, and classic brick walls enchanted my sense of sight. Before class I dabbed one of my favorite essential oils beneath my nose to delight my sense of smell. My sense of touch was in absolute heaven, holding various yoga poses for more than three minutes to induce high sensation, much like bay swimming does. All throughout class, I'd rescue my tight, neglected body parts by mothering them with my breath. Lavished attention on them by exhaling their discomfort, pain, and tension and sending them exactly what they needed by inhaling into them. Sometimes, I even asked these body parts, "What's your favorite color?" I listened for an answer and imagined inhaling air in that favorite color to reinforce healing and loving myself through my respiration. This sensationalized breathing always left me feeling completely relaxed and energized, just the way I usually feel after meditating.

Coming and going to my yoga classes often reminds me of our brief tour of the Dog Patch neighborhood. That was such a great visit. I smile on the inside and outside whenever I remind myself of what Gabrielle told me: "Mom said, 'She felt like she was in heaven when she visited you in San Francisco.'" And, now I sense you really are in heaven.

Love,
Natazha

Good Breathing Begets Good Posture   November 2016

We stand at our tallest when we are in good posture. When I left Long Island at age 21, my height measured 5'2". At age 54 at my last doctor's appointment, my height measured at 5'4". We use the same exact muscles for both breathing and posture. That's why I believe my taller stature is proof of my improved breathing habits.

Dear Mom:

You probably don't know you use the same exact core muscles for breathing, balance, and posture. Breathing directly affects posture and balance. That's why I teach a class called the Better Breathing, Balance, and Posture Class (BBBP Class). I wanted you to take my class, or something like it on Long Island. I hated to see your posture deteriorate as your Chronic Obstructive Pulmonary Disease (COPD) got worse. I felt awful knowing you had so little lung capacity, and your poor posture made matters even worse. I used to fantasize about taking a sabbatical to provide you pulmonary rehabilitation. I never acted on that fantasy fearing that I'd miss Bob and my life in San Francisco too much. Now I regret not doing that. I teach classes in your honor and still fantasize about teaching you basic pulmonary concepts and exercises.

Do you remember doing a posture-breath experiment with me right after Dad's death? You sat on the edge of your bed. First, you slouched and took several breaths. I asked, "How easy it is to breathe as you slouched?" Then you sat up tall and took several breaths, and I asked, "How easy is it to breathe when you sit erect? Was there a difference between slouching and sitting up tall?" You answered, "Yes. There was a big difference. I breathed more easily sitting up straight." I explained, "That's because bad posture begets bad breathing and good breathing begets good posture. You can't separate those two functions because posture directly affects the diaphragm as well as all the other respiratory muscles."

Breathing and posture are married in another profound way. Your breath-based posture speaks volumes about how you feel about yourself, the story you tell about yourself to yourself. That's why criminals pick victims based on posture. It tells them if you'll put up a fight.

Speaking of criminals, I worried about you serving ex-convicts, mentally ill patients, and the homeless. I worried with your compromised posture that they'd consider you easy prey. Many times, I assuage my anxiety by reminding myself of your amazing courage and victories. You won so many battles against incredible odds. You came back from insanity, beat both lung and breast cancer, and you raised 11 kids on a teacher's salary. Winning your battle against the IRS amazed me the most. It still pisses me off that the IRS didn't have anything better to do than harass you and audit you three times. They just couldn't believe you fed and educated all of us on so little money. That's enough for now. I'll say more about the BBBP class tomorrow.

Love,
Natazha

The Diaphragm is a Super Hero   September 2016

Graduate school was grueling. I went from teaching and practicing yoga and Pilates to sitting full time in class. Dr. Kim Topp lived up to her surname and demanded the very best from her students. Her anatomy course lived up to its reputation for being notoriously hard. Her final exam posed one bonus question for an easy five points, "What's your favorite muscle and why?" I had some difficulty choosing between my favorite respiratory muscles: transverse abdominus and the diaphragm. I cherish transverse abdominus that I nicknamed the "I love you muscle." This muscle wraps around your low back like someone giving you a hug from behind. On my final exam I chose the diaphragm. This letter expands upon what I wrote on my exam. Lastly, Dr. Topp had an insane teaching and administrative workload; nonetheless she found time to praise my assignments for being exceptionally well written. Her positive feedback reminded me my ultimate goal was to write a book on breathing.

Dear Mom,

In my last letter I explained that we use the same group of muscles for breathing, posture, and balance. Our breathing directly affects our posture. With your COPD you couldn't get air out of your lungs, which caused your lungs to become overinflated with stale, deoxygenated air. Ironically, not getting enough oxygen compels people with COPD to take even more ineffective, shallow breaths. This breathing pattern seriously compromises posture.

Breathing affects your ability to move. Diaphragmatic breathing distributes the workload more evenly, so no body part over or under works as you move. Breathing with your diaphragm is like dropping a pebble in the middle of the pond that causes ripples to move evenly from the center outward. If you drop that pebble off to one side, the ripples become dominant on one side of the pond. Your breathing ripples more evenly throughout your body with diaphragmatic breathing; it engages more muscles and reduces the chance of overworking any one particular muscle. That more equitable distribution of the workload creates cohesive teamwork that improves your balance and movement. Shallow breathing and holding your breath, on the other hand, set you up for poor balance, wearing out body parts, inefficient movement, and injuries.

Let me use the movie *"Gladiator"* to better explain those breathing concepts. Daddy was a huge fan of this classic movie. Russell Crowe earned an Oscar for portraying Maximus. The movie depicts a dramatic reenactment of the Battle of Carthage. Because the Romans won, they loved to re-enact this battle in the Roman Coliseum. Maximus and other slaves were cast as the Carthaginians and slated for massacre. But before the staged battle begins, Maximus advises the other slaves, "Whatever comes out of these gates, we have a better chance of survival if we work together. You understand? If we stay together, we survive."

Maximus successfully inspires the slaves to "stay together." They beat the Roman Gladiators. That astonishes the Romans, especially the Roman Emperor. The Roman Gladiators always won this ceremonial battle because the men portraying the Carthaginians always fought in an "every-man-for-himself" manner. Working as a united team, the slaves overpowered the better equipped and more numerous Roman Gladiators.

Diaphragmatic breathing creates a powerful synergy in the body. When your diaphragm spearheads respiration, your muscles work together rather than against each other. The diaphragm reminds me of

Maximus: unique, incredibly powerful, and multi-talented. Like Maximus, the diaphragm has no partner or opposing muscle. It is a floating floor at the bottom of your rib cage that separates your heart and lungs from the digestive organs.

The diaphragm is the only muscle that is both a primary muscle for inhalation and exhalation. That allows the diaphragm to exert extraordinary leadership over your body. Your diaphragm commands your muscles to "Stay together! Work together!" when you move and breathe. By participating on both sides of breathing, the diaphragm sets the stage for cooperation instead of competition between your inspiratory and expiratory muscles. Ideally your inhalation and exhalation are in balance. One side of respiration doesn't dominate the other.

Mom, unfortunately your COPD made your inhale dominant. Your inhale team over-powered your exhale team. You inhaled much more easily than you exhaled. Given that your lungs were permanently damaged by emphysema and lung cancer, you couldn't improve your lung capacity. However, you could improve how you used your respiratory muscles, including the diaphragm. You could also improve your cardiovascular fitness through exercise. That's how pulmonary rehabilitation works.

As you learn to tolerate more vigorous exercise in pulmonary rehabilitation you strengthen the super hero diaphragm. It returns to center stage in your breathing performance. You stop over-inflating your lungs. You stop breathing shallowly and overusing the inhale performers in your neck, shoulder, upper back, and chest muscles. You stop excluding or minimizing your exhale performers, namely your abdominal muscles and diaphragm. And guess what, as more muscles participate, you distribute the workload for breathing more equitably. So no muscle gets over or under worked.

Just one last thing about Maximus's adage to "Stay together. Work together." Stress often tears us apart. It affects how well your mind, body, heart and spirit move together. How well they synergize. When we get stressed, our minds race ahead of our bodies and feelings. Minds can move lightning quick, but our bodies and feelings can't move that fast. It takes longer to fully process feelings and physically move. It's as if stress triggers your mind to adopt an "each-man-for-himself" attitude and races ahead of your heart and body.

That's when you need to rescue yourself with your breath. Allow your diaphragm to act like Maximus. Shout out: "Stay together. Work together." It's well documented that conscious, slow, steady, diaphragmatic breathing unites or yokes your mind, body, feelings and spirit. That's what yogis have done for centuries.

During my last visit, it was painful to watch you breathe. You no longer could breathe diaphragmatically. You reminded me once again to be grateful that I breathe with such ease.

Love,
Natazha

Quit Smoking: Change Your
Breathing To Change Habits   February 2017

I'm supremely grateful to the mystical force that helped me quit smoking. I still consider it a miracle I stopped without any nicotine gum or patches. I truly believe my Grandma Winnie's spirit guided me through my tortuous withdrawal from cigarette smoking. I feel blessed whenever I have an opportunity to help someone else quit.

Dear Mom,

Today I felt exhilarated after sharing tips on quitting smoking with Kerry at the Dolphin Club. Just like me, she began smoking at age 11. It's tough for her to stop smoking after 30 years. We commiserated about how awful it feels on all levels: physically, emotionally, mentally, and spiritually. Smoking is a breathing habit, and since breathing affects everything, quitting affects all aspects of you. Physically, you're tired and weak. Emotionally, you're anxious, grouchy, and just out of sorts. Mentally, you're foggy, forgetful, and just not on top of your game. Spiritually, you don't feel like yourself. It's disorienting and gut wrenching to break up any friendship of 30 years, especially one with cigarettes.

I told her I cried almost every day for two years when I quit. And I stopped having cigarette dreams after five years. She confided that the first week she dreamt she went to buy cigarettes but stopped herself. But last night she dreamt that she did buy them and it scared her. She also worries about gaining weight. I explained, "The odds are in your favor. When I quit, the American Lung Association told me most ex-smokers don't gain weight. One third lose weight; one third weigh the same, and only one third gain weight. I was thin before I quit, and stayed thin. You won't gain weight if you exercise. That's the best thing to stay off cigarettes, especially open-water swimming that forces you to breathe well."

That got us on the topic of oral gratification. Smoking is not about oral gratification. In my experience chewing gum, sucking lollipops, and chewing on cinnamon sticks or carrots was useless. Smoking is first and foremost a breathing habit, not an oral gratification vice. You need to change your breathing patterns to successfully quit. When I quit, no one discussed how smoking changes your breathing. I didn't lick my cigarettes like a lollipop or chew them like gum. I emphasized my inhaling to get more nicotine. I sucked smoke through the filter and held my breath to allow more nicotine into my system. Smoking systematically trains you to breathe poorly and disobey the tenets of healthy breathing.

1. It's ideal to breathe air as clean as possible. Smoking infuses your lungs with poisonous toxins. It's the number one cause of preventable deaths and disease in America.
2. Western medicine teaches you to inhale through your nose not your mouth. Smokers inhale through their mouth to suck in toxic smoke.
3. Ideally you don't want to hold your breath, but smokers hold their breath to infuse more nicotine into their lungs.
4. Smoking cues longer inhales than exhales. Biofeedback research shows exhaling longer than you inhale helps us relax and combat stress.

I then shared with Kerry how I used aromatherapy to retrain my breathing habits. My girlfriend, Eunice, taught me to inhale uplifting essential oils instead of smoking cigarettes. Aromatherapy retrained me to inhale through my nose instead of my mouth. I also replaced my cigarette break with an aromatherapy ritual. Instead of smoking, I went somewhere nice and put several drops of basil essential oil on my handkerchief. I brought the handkerchief to my nose to smell the basil oil. Eunice recommended basil to quit smoking. Through experimentation I found orange is also very uplifting. I still use soothing scents each morning to seduce myself to breathe deeply and meditate.

Kerry and I also chatted about breath holding. Smoking caused me to emphasize my inhalation and then hold my breath and short shrift my exhaling. When I quit smoking, I worked hard to break my inhale-dominant breathing pattern.

I told Kerry I used cigarettes to repress childhood traumas. When I quit, boatloads of repressed grief, terror, shame, and despair boiled up to the surface of my psyche. I felt emotionally ambushed because smoking had been my tool to dissociate from my feelings. And now I was drowning in intense feelings. I was feeling all the grief and terror that I had suppressed by smoking. Exercise and slow, steady exhaling helped me process those intense feelings.

We both smiled when I said, "That's when I began to exercise. Bay swimming is great." Cold water demands you exhale forcefully to keep yourself warm and fuel yourself with more oxygen to meet the extra demand for oxygen. I boosted my yoga practice, and began Pilates, running, hiking, biking, and dancing. I moved whenever possible, and changed from a desk job to teaching Pilates, yoga, and fitness classes for a living.

We also emote and express our feelings through exhaling. Singing, talking out our feelings, laughing, sobbing, and sighing are just some of the ways we express ourselves through exhaling. I could have talked for hours about changing breathing habits to successfully quit smoking. I truly believe to change any poor habit, such as drinking, procrastinating, and self-sabotaging, you need to address your breathing. But Kerry had to leave so we ended our chat.

To end on a high note, I looked Kerry in the eyes and said, "I treasure the moment I threw my last cigarette into the San Francisco Bay. I changed my life forever by trading the worst breathing habit for the life-affirming habit of devotional breathing. I now tend to my breath as if it were my beloved. To the core of my being, I know I'm happily married for 16 years, have the aerobic capacity of a male college student, and truly love myself because I quit smoking."

As we hugged goodbye, I gave her my business card as I said, "I can't emphasize how tough it is to quit smoking. Please, please call me anytime if you feel like smoking or just need to talk." I repeated, "Everything starts with the breath. You're changing every single aspect of yourself by dropping this breath-based vice. You're dealing with mental, physical, emotional, and spiritual side effects. That's a lot coming at you all at once. Be kind to yourself."

Mom, as she walked away, I realized I never shared my secrets for quitting smoking. I felt sad and ashamed that I thought you were jealous of me when I quit smoking. It was the beginning of our five-year feud. I so wish we had helped each other through the agony of giving up cigarettes. I know you were hospitalized for your COPD during the first week you quit smoking. You couldn't smoke in the hospital, but cigarette cravings go on for years. How did you manage your cravings after your hospitalization?

I'm sorry we weren't there for each other. But I do feel we can be here for each other now. And that's been incredibly healing. Writing a book brought out my shame demons in full force. It's one thing to quit something harmful, but writing and publishing a book requires much more worthiness. I'm not just settling for releasing a harmful behavior; I'm claiming that I'm worthy of being heard and have something valuable. That's a huge freaking step for me.

Mom, I've been feeling your presence every step along the way. Just today I told (my sister) TC, "I'm sad mom had to die for me to finally feel safe to receive her love. Yes, she was mentally ill, but out of love for us she did an amazing job of healing herself. I really, really feel her love for me now. Just wish I could have felt that when she was alive."

TC responded, "It's great you've grown. And, now you can receive it. Better late than never." After I hung up, I realized your love also lives on through my relationships with my siblings. Thanks for giving me so many brothers and sisters. Each one carries a special part of you.

Love,
Natazha

Naked Lady Wisdom   April 2016

I love the wit and wisdom the other naked ladies share with me sitting in the Dolphin Club sauna. It's icing on the cake after a glorious swim in the cold San Francisco Bay. And, I know why being naked makes us speak with more insight. Being naked enables us to breathe more freely. Tight outfits and belts restrain our breathing. Clothing inhibits our respiration by sealing off our skin; that's considered the "third lung" in traditional Chinese medicine.

Dear Mom,

I'm still helping my friend Kerry at the Dolphin Club quit smoking. I gave her a Valentine's gift of basil essential oil to sniff instead of smoking. Today in the women's sauna, we talked about her payoff for smoking. What does she miss about smoking?

She's so honest that she said, "I miss being a rebel. I loved saying fuck you to the world by smoking. Now I need something bad to replace it with." Then she looked down at the floor, and said, "Today I stole a pack of gum."

I said, "Did you do it accidentally?

She looked at me sheepishly. "No, I stole it deliberately."

I continued to make excuses for her, and said, "Are you sure the gum didn't accidentally fall into your purse?"

Kerry responded, "No, I definitely stole it on purpose. I need to find something for my inner rebel to do now that I'm not smoking."

I smiled at her and said, "There's always skinny dipping. You know it's now illegal to run around naked in San Francisco. Technically, you're breaking the law when you swim naked in the bay. That's my favorite way to be naughty."

She smiled and said, "I already skinny dip. I need something else."

That's when some of the other women in the sauna joined our conversation. I was surprised how many of them had also stolen gum. Oddly enough, I felt like a delinquent for being the only one who hadn't stolen gum. We also discussed ways to rebel. Some of them suggested having sex with strange men. Eventually, Kerry in all her wisdom said, "I really think rebelling is about being seen. It's a way of standing out." She went on to say, "I think creating art satisfies both the need to be seen and rebel. I guess I need to find a creative outlet."

"Wow, Kerry, that's an awesome insight." I said. Then I shared how I began journal writing when I quit smoking. I expressed my feelings and point of view first to my journal and eventually ventured out to sharing them with other human beings. My writing practice evolved into writing a book, *Rescued By My Breath.*

We then stopped talking and communed through our breath. The sauna's heat seduced me to close my eyes and breathe more slowly. Both Kerry's sage comment and my deliberate breathing raised my consciousness. As the pores in my skin opened up, I inhaled and exhaled with my third lung, my skin. And I digested my conversation with Kerry on a deeper level.

Kerry's insight stirred up my fears. Being seen still scares me. I expect to be attacked when I promote myself. After all these years, I still expect a jealous sibling to call me names or hit me if I outshine them. Even though it's painful and scary, I'm slowly but surely releasing those traumas by consoling my frightened inner children with heartfelt exhales. I also exhale pleas for your support. And I inhale your comfort and support.

My breathing practices are definitely helping. But, to be completely honest, I'm still scared to publish *Rescued by My Breath*. Mom, you did an amazing job helping me write this book. Now, I need your help to promote this book.

Love,
Natazha

PS–After chatting with Kerry, I drove to a dinner party. While driving I realized both artistic expression and being naughty feed my soul. At the dinner party, I asked the other couples how they rebel or earn naughty points. They mentioned playing practical jokes. I beamed and giggled as I planned some silly pranks to play on Bob.

Oral Culture is A Respiratory Morse Code   October 2016

During my last visit to my Mom on her deathbed, I found myself singing, "Tura lura lural, Tura lura lie, Tura lura lural, that's an Irish Lullaby," over and over again. I hadn't heard or sang that song in decades. My voice instinctively switched back and forth from my present day fairly bland California accent to my childhood Long Island accent to my ancestors' Irish brogue. Somehow my singing helped me stay in the present moment while I time-traveled through all those different phases of my development.

A similar experience happened to me when I visited New Orleans in October 2016. During that trip, the air was charged with the acrimonious presidential election and the ongoing schism between cops and people of color. On that trip I also learned a family friend had committed suicide by jumping off the Golden Gate Bridge. She left behind a husband, twelve-year old son, E-Roy and ten-year old daughter, Lulu. I had cut Lulu's umbilical cord at her birth and felt somewhat suicidal myself as I processed the painful consequences of her mom's suicide.

My spirit was scattered far and wide while visiting New Orleans. I felt spacey and tired, even though I kept tuning into my breath. No wonder my spirit felt so split. All last Fall I felt compelled to take sides on the presidential election, the police controversy, and now my friend's suicide. Raised in an emotionally enmeshed family, my psyche perceived all those issues as good causes to slice my consciousness into tiny pieces and divvy myself out. I gave one piece to my girlfriend who must have felt incredible pain to kill herself. Lulu received another slice of me. She'd live without a mom for the rest of her life and be burdened by the shame of her mom's suicide. I came to New Orleans with a slice of my soul committed to Hillary Clinton, and planned on voting for her. Another slice was being served to Trump supporters because I totally understood why they wanted a nontraditional politician. I also felt torn apart by the cop versus minorities issue. Many of my relatives were and are in law enforcement. My Uncle Phil and Mom's Dad were cops, and many of Bob's relatives are cops. All along I've felt guilty about the American "justice" system that ironically doesn't serve justice in many cases. Racial tension haunted my spirit as I roamed the streets of New Orleans with its history of Irish immigrants coming to escape the Potato Famine and slavery. I felt suffocated not only by the hot humid air, but my compulsion to divide my breath among all those warring factions.

On Sunday, October 16, when I heard the soul-piercing music of two superb violinists, Wael and Anna, I finally found my breath again. These talented Pied Pipers inspired me to abruptly leave our tour group and track them down to listen to their music. They blended Celtic, African, French, you-name-it, into a harmonious, divine sound that reverberated throughout every cell of my body, but most of all freed my soul from the shackles of divisiveness. Their music seamlessly honored and represented all creatures in the universe. And I began breathing on such an authentic, heartfelt level that I simultaneously breathed for my dead girlfriend, Lulu, my Irish cop relatives, all minorities who are mistreated by our justice system, Trump supporters, Hillary supporters, black slaves, Irish immigrants, antebellum slave owners, and everyone else on the planet. Wael's and Anna's sensual music led me back down to my pelvic floor, the all-important basement dance floor of breathing. Their music seduced me to breathe with my entire body, all my senses, and my vagina, that's center stage of the pelvic floor. I enjoyed a spiritual orgasm right there on the corner of Bourbon Street that shattered all the divisional lines carving up my psyche. Their music redeemed me. Restored me to a whole human being breathing with everyone in the universe.

Dear Mom:

You would love being in New Orleans to celebrate Doc Ray's 60th birthday. TC (my sister married to Doc Ray) rented a mansion for twenty five of us: me, Bob, Gabrielle, Luke, Jackie, Zoltan, Teddy, and Doc Ray's sisters, their families and his cousins from Louisiana. Today, we started with a tour of the French quarter. We ate beignets at the famous Café du Monde, and walked along the Mississippi river. Then we prayed inside St. Louis Cathedral before visiting art galleries and enjoying amazing street musicians and singers. In the late afternoon we saw City Park with its stately botanical gardens. Yesterday, we toured the Garden District with its beautiful homes and gardens and learned about all the famous authors who lived there or nearby: Anne Rice, Ernest Hemingway, John Kennedy Toole, Tennessee Williams, and Walt Whitman, plus Dad's favorite, William Faulkner. Last night we celebrated Doc Ray's birthday at the mansion.

Two days ago, we visited the Oak Valley plantation. Back in the1980s, I fell in love with Oak Valley after seeing it in so many movies and TV commercials. I even tore a picture of it out of a magazine and taped it to the back of my journal. Thirty years ago, I began dreaming about visiting Oak Valley with its quarter-mile avenue of 28 giant live oaks leading up to the splendid Greek Revival style mansion that sits on 25 acres. That's why I was so excited when our friend, Allison, drove Bob, me, and the rest of the gang to this plantation for a tour. When I stepped out of Allison's car, I felt like I had landed on the movie set of *Gone With The Wind.* I loved that movie as a kid and dreamed of growing up to be just like Scarlett O'Hara.

The mansion and grounds were stunning; however, the tour guide's talk bothered me. That's when I began feeling tired and out of sorts. And, I still haven't shaken off the haunting grief and shame I experienced walking through the black slaves' pathetically small "cabins." Just now I'm finally sorting out what spooked me on that tour. The juxtaposition of the plantation owner's wealth and the slaves' abject poverty and suffering disturbed me. I'm also ashamed I showed up at Oak Valley wanting to emulate Scarlett O'Hara, a selfish, spoiled brat who disregarded the suffering of others.

Bob and I visited Auschwitz two years ago. We prepared beforehand to honor the Jews and Poles who suffered in the Holocaust. We acknowledged we'd be visiting grounds where humans were tortured and persecuted; I prayed for their souls. I'm embarrassed I arrived at Oak Valley ready to celebrate the old South's Golden Age, without any respect for the slaves who experienced that place as a concentration camp. I never prayed for their souls before or afterwards.

No wonder I left Oak Valley all discombobulated. I wanted to see that place for decades and it turned out to be haunted by unspoken shame and pain. Auschwitz is a memorial to the human spirit. Poles and Jews remind us to never allow atrocities like the Holocaust to happen again. I feel guilty that I took so long to notice Oak Valley has no reminders to make sure slavery never happens again. Brené Brown teaches shame festers when it's unacknowledged or unheard. At Oak Valley, the slaves were regarded as merely low-paid workers, not slaves. No one openly talked about the white elephant in the room, slave abuse, and the need to ensure it never happens again. You can understand why this situation bothered me so much. You're my Mom and know I need to clear the air by talking about white elephants. I go bonkers when no one's addressing the emotional shit beneath the surface.

Mom, New Orleans triggers pain for another reason. Our tour guide, Libby, gave us a great Garden District tour. She briefly mentioned the Irish Channel and explained the Irish were considered lower on the totem pole than the slaves. They came over in boatloads in the1850s to flee the Irish Potato Famine, and did all the dangerous jobs like building canals, as they were considered expendable. You paid good money to replace slaves, but you Micks were free. This chapter of Irish history left me feeling ashamed. Our kind was regarded as "worthless lowlifes" that cost nothing.

After the tour, I couldn't enjoy Doc Ray's celebration. I felt pulled out to sea by an undercurrent of shame as I realized our Irish ancestors were treated as slaves in their own country. This trip caused me to reflect on my trip to Ireland when I met your cousin, John Madden in Kilkishen, Ireland. When I visited him, I didn't understand why he complained about Americans visiting the Irish castles. He said, "Those castles aren't Irish castles; that's where my ancestors were treated as slaves." Now I understand what he was saying. The British used enslaved Irishman to staff those castles. Just like Oak Valley plantation, there are no signs about trying to prevent seven centuries of oppression. Now I see why John Madden was so upset when visitors weren't told his, and our, ancestors were treated as slaves. Moreover, the Irish were regarded as unfit to run their own land for centuries. That's a profound statement of unworthiness and shame.

Mom, although I felt an incredible undertow of shame here in New Orleans, this morning two street musicians revived me. I felt sick to my stomach after drinking coffee and eating sugar-loaded beignets. As we walked down very humid, hot streets, I heard off in the distance some sublime violin music serenading my soul. I quickly excused myself from our tour and hunted down Anna and her husband, Wael with their baby girl Mia strapped to his back. Their eclectic mix of Cajun, classical, Celtic and African music vibrated through my bones and uplifted my heart and soul, and instantly rejuvenated me. I immediately bought their CD and checked out their website on my cellphone www.waelanaviolin.com.

Hearing jazz on the streets of New Orleans showed me how the Irish and slaves endured such harsh lives. They poured their grief, shame, and trauma into their music and singing, and eventually developed jazz, an exquisite example of oral culture. They beautifully blended Celtic, African, and French music, and thus created a common oral culture to communicate with each other. I believe jazz music and singing enabled them to rescue themselves with their breath. Mom, please hear me out as I explain how jazz helped save them from hardship. Jazz singers and musicians produced a unique sound that reverberated through their bones and souls; it soothed their bodies and psyches. They couldn't help but think and feel differently after playing their wind instruments and singing the blues. It also made them move and breathe differently. Jazz is famous for its soul piercing signature singing and wind instruments, including saxophones, clarinets, trombones, trumpets, and tubas. Both singing and playing wind instruments are forms of breathing. They used their breath to express themselves through jazz that uplifted their spirits and inspired them to think, feel, and move differently. Their breath-based music became their way to release their sorrows and woes. That's how they rescued themselves with their breathing.

The oral culture of New Orleans includes much more than jazz. Language, speaking, and dialects are also part of any oral culture. Culture is the collective spirit of any group and spirit responds to both sound and breathing. To me, oral culture is a respiratory Morse code orchestrated by our breathing. To understand how oral culture is a Morse code I first need to explain how the Morse code works. It's a universal language used primarily by the military. It's based on two basic sounds, *dah* and *dit.* Those sounds are used to create an alphabet of letters. Proper spacing is essential in the Morse code. You need uniform spaces of silence between the characters to create words. And longer uniform spaces between the words. And even longer spaces between phrases and sentences. The spacing needs to be exactly right. Just as in music the rhythm needs to be exactly right.

Similar to Morse code, spacing between our breaths is the basis of oral cultures. Look at it this way. All cultures are based on the breath-operated spoken language. And, how we modulate our breath affects our speaking voice and regional dialects that are based on the spacing between our words and phrases. Culture also revolves around singing, playing wind instruments, theatrical plays that are oral forms of art, chanting and other oral versions of worship, and other forms of breath-based self-expression and creativity. How a society breathes together forms their culture; culture affects how a society breathes.

Let's take the example of New Yorkers versus folks from New Orleans. New Yorkers talk very differently from folks from the South. New Yorkers tend to be in a hurry and leave less space between their words. And their quicker speaking rate affects the sound of their voices. Their fast-paced respiration gives rise to an entirely different accent than a Southern drawl. In New Orleans as my breath pushes against the barrier of hot humid air, I'm forced to speak more slowly, and change the rate, sound, and quality of my speech. I begin to approximate a Southern drawl, and believe over time my speech would change if I lived in New Orleans for a long enough period of time.

Did you know when I arrived at Grinnell College after 18 years of living on Long Island both my American and international classmates thought I was speaking a foreign language? They could barely understand me. I had adopted a super-fast-paced speech to compete for airtime in our home, and eliminated as much space as possible between my words. I can now see this was another way I avoided breathing in and out fully.

On top of promoting meditation and second-hand smoke laws, San Franciscans also taught me to breathe well by their slower speaking style. I dropped my New York accent after living in San Francisco for decades by learning to breathe like a Californian instead of a New Yorker. Listening to their more mild-mannered speech slowly over time trained me to breathe more serenely when I talked. I blessed my speech with space between my words. This change in my breathing healed my spirit that's so sensitive to breath and sound.

Love,
Natazha Raine O'Connor
Proud to be a dual citizen of Ireland

Section Five

You Must Be Present To Win

Repossessing My Sexuality   May 2017

I'm amazed no one ever asks me about sex and breathing. How we breathe absolutely affects our sexuality. We make a sublime shift in our breathing and being when we connect through sex. A full-blown sexual orgasm is a glorious, explosive exhale on both the inside and outside. We engage the same exact muscles in our pelvic "dance" floor to breathe deeply and make love. I allowed the Church, shame, Uncle Mickey, my ancestors, cultural taboos, ex-boyfriends, and family to possess my sexuality. In December 2016, after decades of conscious breathing and finally setting boundaries, I revolutionized my life. I finally felt secure enough to repossess my sexuality. And own it anywhere on the planet, not only at home with my husband.

As a young woman, my Dissociative Identity Disorder (DID) wreaked havoc on my life, especially my sex life. I finally hit bottom and sought professional help in 1989. When I was about six months sober from drinking I received three disturbing phone calls. Three different men claimed we had sex and wanted to arrange more rendezvous. I had no recollection of any of these sexual encounters. I blew off the first caller as a wrong number. The second phone message made me very nervous, but I ignored it. I screamed at the third caller to leave me alone as I slammed down the phone. This experience occurred during the height of the AIDS and herpes epidemic in San Francisco. I realized my life was in serious jeopardy. Despite feeling very ashamed, I finally acknowledged my blackouts were more than just a drinking problem. My sexual behavior was also a cause. That's when I sought professional help to resolve my Bernadette and Bunny sub-personality split caused in part by sexual traumas.

Writing this book made me see my tremendous progress with my sexual sobriety. However, I also realized I still had much more healing ahead of me. After writing the series of letters below about my deep desire for "3rd Road" relationships, I became terrified that I'd be misunderstood by anyone who read these letters. I define "3rd Road" relationships as interactions with men who are sexually attracted to me and I'm sexually attracted to them. And yet, we consciously choose to neither deny nor act out our sexual desires. I became scared people would misinterpret "3rd Road" relationships as cheating on my husband and thinly disguised affairs.

To ease my fears, I meditated, prayed, and of course wrote to my Mom seeking her guidance. My Mom's spirit insisted I include these letters because my sexuality defined the very fault line that ran through my fragmented psyche and bad breathing habits. I felt so overwhelmed with conflicting emotions about including these letters in this book that I returned to couples therapy to discuss "3rd Road" relationships. I also tuned into my breath via hiking, rowing, swimming in the San Francisco Bay, running, journaling, meditating, and talking out my feelings. And I read and listened to some of my favorite spiritual teachers, including Oprah and Deepak Chopra.

I'm a huge fan of Oprah and Deepak's Twenty-One Day Meditation Series. During this time, I listened to their Hope in Uncertain Times series. This meditation series, especially the messages on Day 6 and 9 about trusting yourself, made me realize my desire for "3rd Road" relationships was actually a testament to my growth. I didn't need to feel ashamed of my need to have "3rd Road" relationships. I realized my DID had destroyed my trust in myself. I needed "3rd Road" relationships to rebuild my self-confidence and prove to myself I was more than sexually sober. I now was an integrated, trustworthy, conscious human being who made sound choices about her sexuality instead of sexually shutting down in Bernadette mode or blindly running on her animal instincts, unable to turn down sex, in Bunny mode. I wanted to confirm I could feel and express my sensuality and sexuality appropriately. My desire for

"3rd Road" relationships was my way to verify I had in fact fully integrated Bernadette and Bunny.

Dear Mom,

Long ago, journals became my most trusted confidante, a place to express my darkest fears, most cherished dreams and fantasies, and musings I didn't necessarily want to act out. My journals still house what's truly going on in my heart and psyche, but would never dare to say in the "real" world. In many ways my journal acts like a priest hearing my confession.

Uncle Mickey deeply wounded my sexual boundaries. The series of letters I'm about to share with you are fictitious conversations that enabled me to heal those sexual boundaries. I wrote these letters to an imaginary male archetype, Horndog, who haunts my psyche. Horndog is an imaginary guy who represents all the men with whom I failed to set sexual boundaries. I refer to him as Horndog because it was a nickname an old boyfriend gave me. I also wrote to my "Bunny" and "Bernadette" parts as they, too, needed to learn about "3rd Road Relationships." I loved writing these letters. They enabled me to imagine myself saying and receiving exactly what I wanted and needed from men. Writing them transformed my perception of men and cleared crap that's been festering inside my psyche for decades including my own part in my victimization.

LETTER # 1 TO MALE ARCHETYPE HAUNTING MY PSYCHE

Dear Horndog,

The often-used phrase, "The road less traveled by," comes from Robert Frost's famous poem *The Road Not Taken*. Please bear with me, Horndog. Read the poem below to better understand the points I'm about to make later on in this letter.

The Road Not Taken - By Robert Frost

Two roads diverged in a yellow wood,
And sorry I could not travel both
And be one traveler, long I stood
And looked down one as far as I could
To where it bent in the undergrowth;

Then took the other, as just as fair,
And having perhaps the better claim,
Because it was grassy and wanted wear;
Though as for that the passing there
Had worn them really about the same,

And both that morning equally lay
In leaves no step had trodden black.
Oh, I kept the first for another day!
Yet knowing how way leads on to way,
I doubted if I should ever come back.

I shall be telling this with a sigh
Somewhere ages and ages hence:
Two roads diverged in a wood, and I—

I took the one less traveled by,
And that has made all the difference.

Horndog, I began wondering, why had this poem resurfaced in my psyche? Only to realize it's about our relationship that both delights and tortures me. On the surface that poem is about two roads. One road symbolizes honoring my marriage. I shut down sexually and completely ignore my intense attraction to you, and your sexual attraction to me. I've chosen that road in the past and it also shut down my sexuality, period. The other road leads to giving into my carnal desires and ravishing your body. That road leads to shame, self-loathing, and heartache all around.

Being who I am though, I see a third road, the truly less traveled road. So rarely taken, even Robert Frost's traveler didn't see it. It's the "make your own path in the woods" road by accepting the agonizing challenges to grow that our relationship demands of me. I grow large enough to house my sexual longings for you and yet honor my vows of holy matrimony, the truth that my exclusive sex life with Bob means the entire world to me.

I know in this day and age we could so easily cheat. We don't live in some tiny Irish village where everyone knows each other's business. We live in a big cosmopolitan city with easy access to romantic getaways like the Pelican Inn. But my heart and soul know Bob is my Prince Charming who truly loves me.

Without a doubt, he'd forgive me, but I could never forgive myself. I need him. I love him, and cringe whenever I peek ahead and sense I may out-live him.

You've reminded me I'm Irish, a rebel at heart. I don't need to rebel against the British Empire or Bob. I'm rebelling against being an infinite spirit living in a finite human body. Just like the traveler in Robert Frost's poem, I too can only walk down one road. My curious nature wants to wander down the road of having an affair with you, whereas my authentic, heartfelt commitment to Bob and my vows of Holy Matrimony call me to take the shut-down-my-sexuality road.

Thank God my daily practice of tuning into my breath directs me down the third road that meanders between the other two roads. People very rarely see the third road because it's so rarely traveled. There are no footsteps advertising it. There will only be my own footsteps, and I pray yours, too. Will you take a pledge to engage in a 3rd Road relationship that includes the agonizing awareness of our sexual attraction along with a commitment to never act on it nor deny it?

Please accept my invitation to enjoy a heartfelt, sensual but nonetheless nonsexual, 3rd Road relationship. Trust me, a full-blown 3rd Road relationship guarantees we both grow exponentially. We set a boundary that allows both of us to access our heart's true desire.

Let's help each other grow,
Natazha, Your 3rd Road Relationship Buddy

LETTER #2 TO MALE ARCHETYPE HAUNTING MY PSYCHE

Dear Horndog,

During our last conversation, you asked with a very snide attitude, "What's the difference between a 3rd Road Relationship and an affair?" You strongly implied 3rd Road Relationships are affairs cleverly wrapped up in rhetoric. I completely shut down. At the time I just couldn't respond. After some reflection and talking things out with Bob during couples' therapy, I can now address your question. Furthermore, I'm even more convinced we both would greatly benefit from a 3rd Road Relationship. It's absolutely not an affair. Spouses like my husband Bob and all other concerned parties know all about 3rd Road Relationships, whereas affairs are conducted in secret.

I'm now willing to reveal my background which will help explain why I need 3rd Road Relationships. Many years ago, I suffered from Dissociative Identity Disorder (DID). Many people call this split-personality disorder. To survive my childhood traumas, I split into my Bunny and Bernadette parts. Each part breathed and carried herself very differently. I worked very hard to heal. Today I call myself Natazha because the name honors my present day, integrated self. Please review the chart below to learn more about my Bunny and Bernadette parts. Let me know if you have any questions.

Bernadette **1st Road** **Relationship** Ignores sexual attraction & sexually shut down	**Bunny** **2nd Road** **Relationship** Acts on all sexual attractions and hyper-sexual	**Natazha** **3rd Road** **Relationship** Acknowledges sexual attraction & makes sound, conscious choices
Named for a saint who saw visions of the Blessed Mother in Lourdes, France	Nickname given to me a kid when I jumped up & down like a bunny	Name I gave myself to signify I had integrated my Bunny & Bernadette parts.
Blindly followed Irish Catholic traditions & sacrificed for the family. No boundaries. Incapable of intimacy	Rebelled against the family. Hated making sacrifice for the family. Can't set boundaries. Incapable of intimacy	Accepts the whole truth about her mentally ill parents who loved her. Sets boundaries. Capable of intimacy
Pathological Breath Holding to avoid feelings and sexual sensations/urges	Pants like a dog in heat. Fast, shallow breathing from her vagina and lower belly	Intentional Breathing: connects to her breath as much possible
Slumped, Mother Teresa posture	Hussy posture: weight on one leg with that hip pushed out to the side	Stands tall. In a relaxed yet upright posture.

When I quit smoking in 1987 an intense civil war ignited between my sub-personalities. I experienced deep conflicts around my sexuality that led to blackouts. Bernadette pursued 1st Road relationships and Bunny pursued 2nd Road relationships. Natazha enjoys a happy healthy marriage to Bob that has ignited another level of growth. Miracle of all miracles, I truly bonded with Bob. I often thought I'd never bond with anyone because I didn't bond with my mentally ill parents. Bonding with Bob has given me the confidence to explore 3rd Road Relationships. I want to prove to myself that I can handle sexual temptation without falling into either Bunny or Bernadette mode, but rather staying integrated in Natazha mode. I recently realized that I freely express my sensuality and sexuality with Bob in the privacy of our home, but suppress it in public because I'm still afraid of men and worry about how I'll manage unwanted sexual passes and flirting. And in the back of my mind, I still worry about splitting again.

I want a 3rd Road Relationship with you to prove I've integrated permanently. I'll never go back to splitting and can freely express my sensuality and sexuality in public. I need to know I can respond to flirting and sexual passes appropriately with my newly acquired boundaries, and can trust myself. I want to be confident that I'll make sound choices about my sex life under any circumstances. I hope you better understand where I'm coming from now.

You may wonder, why I have chosen you? First of all, you're always staring at me and look like you're ready to jump my bones. It's pretty obvious you're attracted to me. Second, I see the way you drool over your nieces and nephews. It's so obvious that you want to settle down and have kids, but you're terrified marriage requires giving up your sexuality. You appear as someone who thinks he will need to stop looking at other women when he gets married. Mastering 3rd Road Relationships is one way to enjoy your sexuality while honoring your marriage. Also, you're a surfer who enjoys high intense sensation, just like me. You love the thrill of communing with Nature in the cold, wild ocean just as I love open water swimming without a wet suit. Acknowledging your sexual attraction without acting on it creates intense sensations and requires living in the limbo of never knowing what may happen next. I sense you can handle the high sensation of a 3rd Road Relationship. I hope you still want to try a 3rd Road Relationship that could greatly benefit both of us.

Let's help each other grow,
Natazha, Your 3rd Road Relationship Buddy

LETTER # 3 TO MALE ARCHETYPE HAUNTING MY PSYCHE

Dear Horndog,

I need to update my offer to you, Horndog. I still want a 3rd Road relationship, but for totally different reasons than I previously stated. After sorting out my feelings, I realized I'm actually not sexually attracted to you. Please hear me out. Let me explain. I'm not trying to hurt you or be difficult or confuse you. You need to understand that I'm an incest survivor who was raised in an emotionally enmeshed family. This means I often pick up other people's feelings and then get overwhelmed when I regard those adopted feelings as my very own. I easily flip-flop between identifying with my own versus other people's feelings. My penchant for swamping feelings is very confusing for me, and I can only imagine how confusing it must be for you.

I'm sorry I got confused and labeled your emotions as my very own emotions. Believe me, I desperately want to stop feeling for other people. I fear that breaking my deeply ingrained habit of emotional enmeshment will take some time and effort. Here's why. I grew up believing my family's survival superseded my own. I must feel with my family's heart and head instead of my own. Now, one breath at a time, I'm reprogramming my being to feel my own unique emotions instead of defaulting to other people's feelings. With great self-love and patience, I'm consciously breathing to sort through my emotions and distinguish my feelings from other people's feelings.

Trust me. Being emotionally enmeshed sucks. It's a wicked handicap. I get confused and can't distinguish my own feelings and desires from my partner's. I flip-flop between my own feelings and my partner's and other characters in my life. It makes all relationships, especially sexual relationships, problematic. One of many reasons why I cherish my marriage is that Bob is the first person who I successfully bonded with, despite my emotional handicap.

Anyway, I'm still convinced a 3rd Road Relationship would greatly benefit both of us, and help us grow beyond our wildest dreams. It could help me clarify my feelings from your feelings. That would be a wonderful first step toward repossessing my sexuality and kicking out everyone else in my sexual space. I'm very embarrassed that my sexual space is such a disaster area.

As I've previously explained, thousands of times I only wanted emotional comfort expressed through cuddling or a hug. Sometimes I clearly stated my needs, but all too often I just caved in and endured unwanted sex, some more traumatic than I care to remember. I want to heal from that trauma, and finally get the non-sexual cuddling that my inner hug monster desperately needs and wants from someone other than Bob. Horndog, you smirked at me, and replied, "If you enjoy such a happy marriage with Bob, then why do you need cuddling outside your marriage?" Then you took an emergency phone call and had to leave. We never finished that discussion.

Here's why I want to cuddle with you. To me, hugs are a non-sexual expression of affection. Even though they can be a prelude to sex, they belong in a 3rd Road Relationship. More importantly, for once in my life, I want a man with a strong sexual attraction to me to put my emotional needs before his sexual needs. For once, I want to experience a guy honoring my request for just a hug without any sex to erase all the times I felt abused by men. I want to be self-assertive. I stay with my own feelings and the guy takes care of his feelings.

For many reasons, Bob can't do this for me. For starters, our fulfilling sexual relationship never has been the problem. It's been part of the solution. And, Bob already does give me hugs, and only a hug, whenever I ask for one. I don't think it's fair to ask him to give up sex with me given that we're married and exclusive sexual partners. And, quite frankly I don't want to give up sex with him. I love having sex with him. Lastly, Bob's faithfulness, openness, and honesty has greatly healed me and helped me get this far. I just want to get more healing.

And here's one more thing. Unlike other boyfriends, Bob never doubted my fidelity, whereas my last boyfriend repeatedly threatened to kill me if I ever cheated on him. And, being a 7th degree black belt he had the skills to carry out his threat. That made me shut down my sexuality, fearing he'd be threatened if any other guy looked at me. Bob's never been jealous. His faith in me makes me loyal to him.

There's another issue, my Grandma Winnie. When I was four, my mom was institutionalized for a year and Grandma Winnie took care of me and my seven siblings. I adored Grandma Winnie, who made me feel safe and secure in a horribly traumatic time. She hugged me all the time. When my Mom returned home, I wanted both my Grandma and Mom to mother me. But my Mom was too threatened by Grandma and asked her to stop living with us. I never wanted my "Grandma" to replace my Mom. I just wanted her hugs. I always felt ashamed of loving my Grandma because it felt as if I was having an affair on my mother. I need a 3rd Road Relationship to heal my Grandma Winnie wound. Bob can't play both the role of my Mom and Grandma Winnie. I need someone other than Bob to play Grandma Winnie hugging me.

Oh God! I feel so vulnerable. I've told you so much about me, and you haven't shared anything about yourself. What I know about you comes only from observing you. I pray you don't abuse my trust. That's enough about my needs. How do you feel about my offer to be friends without any benefits? Do you see how you could grow?

Horndog, your reward for a 3rd Road Relationship is gaining some control over your sexual instincts. You'll still have plenty of your sexual charisma, but will spice it up with some consciousness. You'll finesse it so you don't automatically mow down your dates by pouncing on them sexually, and then get stuck making love to road kill. You'll learn to slow down to enhance your partner's sexual pleasure as well as your own. Temper your love-making to enjoy a more erotic, blissful connection.

Let's help each other grow,
Natazha, Your 3rd Road Relationship Buddy

LETTER #4 TO MALE ARCHETYPE HAUNTING MY PSYCHE

Dear Gentleman previously called Horndog,

Thank you! Thank you! Thank you! Our 3rd Road Relationship helped me grow exponentially. You shocked me by never taking advantage of my vulnerability. I felt outrageously selfish for putting my needs first. That left me in a very foreign and disorienting place. It felt like I was tittering on the brink of internal civil war. My long-entrenched emotionally enmeshed self was at odds with my newly emerging healthy-boundaries self. Any country or person on the brink of civil war is incredibly vulnerable to attack, as they don't have their resources aligned to defend themselves. Thanks for recognizing I was even more vulnerable to swamping feelings and less emotionally grounded. Bob's support plus you nursing me with sexually neutral hugs helped me nurture my newly acquired sexual boundaries. I'll be eternally grateful for your support.

I owe you and men in general an apology. I always assumed the worst of men. Considered them barbaric apes. Why should I bother setting sexual boundaries? Apes can't respect them, anyway. That's why I never before demanded a 3rd Road Relationship. You actually surprised and terrified me by acting so honorably. I can no longer automatically blame you or other guys for my problems with feeling unsafe to express my sexuality. You stood by your word. You had sexual feelings for me, and yet never acted on them. I can't believe how difficult that was for me. I kept anticipating you to go back on your word. I kept expecting for me to somehow, somewhere become your victim. But, you never hurt me. You acted honorably, and never flinched when I tested you by wearing more provocative clothing. You stuck to our 3rd Road Relationship rules.

To tell you the truth it's been downright painful to see my part in my past sexual conflicts and traumas. And take more responsibility for it. I saw why I had such difficulty setting boundaries with men. That's become a rich and powerful area for new growth that I'm exploring with Bob.

Congratulations on your upcoming wedding. Thanks for inviting us to it. You know I'm a terrible matchmaker, but I'm 100% accurate at spotting matches made in heaven like you and your fiancée. You deserve only the very best. May the insights and skills you cultivated in our 3rd Road Relationship bless your marriage. May you enjoy more 3rd Road Relationships that enhance your marriage. I've decided I should stop calling you Horndog. You've graduated to Hot Diggity Dog status. Please stay in touch. Let me know if you ever need my counsel.

Let's help each other grow,
Your 3rd Road Relationship Buddy,
Natazha

Mom, writing those letters provided an amazing healing. I felt transformed by imagining myself getting exactly what I needed. I initially felt terrified to set sexual boundaries. It felt great having Bob and Horndog support me until my boundaries fully grew in and became a permanent fixture in my psyche. I still feel uncomfortable but now I behave according to what I want rather than what guys want. I'm setting better boundaries in my professional life as well.

However, I'm devastated seeing how much I played the victim in the past. I even played the victim with a fictitious guy named Horndog in my journal. In this imaginary scenario, Horndog was behaving himself and that terrified me. I desperately wanted to cave in and have sex with him in order to be in control. If I had sex with Horndog, I determined the outcome of our encounter. The uncertainty of our 3rd Road Relationship drove me crazy. I hated living with our sexual attraction and yet not acting on it. I felt like I was living in limbo rather than setting a sexual boundary. My love for Bob helped me weather that sickening feeling of chaos that I so often felt as a kid. To console myself, I exhaled "I love you" to Bob. That helped me sit still with my perverse anticipation of the worst to come. Staying connected to my breath held me together as my inner voice screamed, "You don't know when Horndog will go back on his word. Don't trust him. Take control. Have sex with him now. Put an end to your misery of waiting for him to fuck up."

My love for Bob shut down that screaming ghost. My love encouraged me breathe into my fears until they slowly but surely vanished when these ghosts realized I was now immune to their spooking. I was no longer easy prey as I spent hours hugging Bob. We often don't talk out our problems. Bob and I just breathe about them. Being held by Bob and breathing together helped me hold myself together as my inner civil war raged inside my tummy. Bob could actually see my insides convulsing as I battled my inner demons. Eventually my newly acquired sexual boundaries won out. Those shame specters stopped spooking me.

After I finally trusted Horndog and myself in a 3rd Road Relationship, I was hit by another emotional tsunami. I ached from head to toe when I realized my inability to set boundaries instigated so much unnecessary self-abuse, mental illness, sexual trauma, agony, missed chances to celebrate life and love, and even played a role in us not having kids. I felt overwhelmed by grief and regret as I processed many different realizations:

- I held my breath as a pathetic replacement for setting boundaries. That made my needs invisible to others and myself.
- I numbed myself with smoking and promiscuous sex to avoid feeling the painful consequences of having poor boundaries.
- My DID was an attempt to escape the self-sacrificing tenets dictated by the Irish Clan mentality. Instead of creating boundaries I sliced my psyche into parts. Bernadette blindly followed the clan mentality. She felt obligated to fulfill the needs of the family. Whenever she felt overwhelmed by the demands of the family, Bernadette could say, "I didn't disobey, Bunny disobeyed."
- My phobias acted as psychological placeholders to revisit traumatic events when I was strong enough to process them. For example, my parking meter phobia served as reminder for me to revisit the incident when I hit my head on a radiator at 4 years old. It happened just before you were institutionalized, and barely coping. Back then, I couldn't stand up for myself and say, "I need medical care and affection to heal this life-threatening head wound." I became phobic of

parking meters because they are round metal objects that vaguely resembled the round surface of the radiators in our home.

- Moving 3,000 miles away from Sayville was the only way I knew how to set a boundary. That's how I said, "No" to putting my own life aside to take care of the endless problems that cropped up in our family. I'm heartbroken that caused me to miss out on watching my nieces and nephews grow up and living near my siblings and you.

This brings me to another point. What helped me work through all this emotional pain was reading *Boundaries: When to Say Yes, How to Say No to Take Control of Your Life* by Dr. Henry Cloud and Dr. John Townsend. They explain in the chapter entitled "How Boundaries Are Developed" that at birth babies are completely dependent on their moms and have no sense of self. Babies believe, "Mommy and me are one and the same." After this bonding phase, a phase called "hatching" or "differentiation" arises. Babies learn "Mommy and me aren't the same." And they assert a need for autonomy.

Dr. Cloud and Dr. Townsend explain that mothers who never fully "hatched" themselves have a very difficult time when their infants "hatch." They resist their baby's need to become more independent and set boundaries. These moms often conceive lots of children. Mom, I sobbed and howled after reading that chapter. I curled up into the fetal position to soothe myself for about an hour. And, consoled myself with healing exhales.

This book explained what I could never understand about you. Your obstetrician, parents, and Catholic Charities advised against you having more kids. So why did you have four more kids after being institutionalized? I felt you rejected me, and set me up for more neglect when you chose to have four more kids. You already struggled to meet our basic needs and yet you signed up for more kids. That guaranteed I'd face even more neglect and abuse.

Growing up, I wracked my brains to figure out your motives. I never felt the Catholic Church was to blame. After reading *Boundaries,* my soul said, "Bingo, Dr. Cloud and Dr. Townsend nailed my Mom's motives and the major cause of my own poor boundaries." I clearly saw what happened to me as a toddler. I sensed you didn't want me to individuate and set boundaries. And, the Irish Clan mentality reinforced this message. The group's survival was more important than my individuation. You struggled when your children hatched and were no longer fully dependent on you. As a toddler I got the message loud and clear: I can choose between my own independence and setting boundaries, or have your love. That's why I never felt worthy of setting boundaries. It meant losing you. I've battled all my life with setting boundaries until I read *Boundaries* last December. Now I feel worthy of setting them.

Mom, I still feel super vulnerable enforcing my boundaries. I'm afraid when I reveal exactly what I want, the other person will use that information against me. When anyone knows what's important to me, they can either honor my needs or deliberately hurt me. I felt hurt as a kid when you couldn't honor my needs. Now I understand you really tried to honor and love me, but not being fully "hatched" yourself got in the way of you expressing your love for me.

I'm supremely grateful you didn't commit suicide like my friend, and worked your butt off to heal yourself. You're now in a very different place and your spirit is much more enlightened. Mom, it's

Mother's Day and I so dearly miss you. Let's take a moment to breathe together to reset our boundaries. I now understand you must have felt miserable being "not hatched" yourself. Let's hatch together. With this exhale, I grant myself full permission to set boundaries, and fully forgive you and myself for not setting healthy boundaries in the past.

I sense your sorrow and regret too. We both suffered and we both grew. You, by far, fostered more growth in me, more than anyone else in my life. Thank you. I love you. I truly love you.

Love,
Natazha

End Your Story On Your Resurrection, Not Your Crucifixion
March 24, 2017

The Irish Rebellion of 1916 is also called the Easter Rising. A PBS Special about this event depicts how Britain poured 20,000 troops into Dublin to quash the poorly armed band of 2,000 Irish rebels during Easter week of 1916. Rebel leader Padraig Pearse felt in many ways the purpose of the Easter Rising was not to win, but to lose. Pearse imagined the rebels' executions would be an even greater rebel weapon. He reasoned, "Yes, they'll kill us, but our fame will live on." And it did. The New York Times devoted 14 days of front-page coverage to the Easter Rising. After six days of fighting the rebels were forced to surrender. But their actions changed the course of Irish history, and Ireland eventually became an independent nation. The Irish proclamation of independence inspired freedom movements all over the world and heralded the end of European colonialism in the 20th century.

I believe it's no mere coincidence the rebels chose Easter to revolt. Both the rebels and Christ knowingly sacrificed themselves and were executed to save their brethren. On the PBS special, Liam Neeson's voiceover states, "As the men and women take on the might of the British Empire they have little hope of success, and yet the time has come, the most momentous week in Ireland's history is about to begin." The statement reminds me of Christ accepting his fate in the Garden of Gethsemane. I feel the Easter Rising rebels' sacrifice wasn't born out of shame or self-hatred. Their sacrifice is actually a sacred example of sacrifice born out of a love that extends out to everyone and everything in the universe.

This all-encompassing love inspired many noble acts. The Irish finally won their independence and paved the way for other colonies to win their political freedom. One rebel leader, Joseph Mary Plunkett, married his sweetheart, Grace Gifford, seven hours before his execution. This love also inspired Pearse to write a poem for his mother the night before his execution. I dedicate this letter to all moms who have lost their sons and daughters to noble causes. May their grief be heard and shared. May their hearts seamlessly release all the sorrows associated with raising sacrificial lambs. That's so eloquently expressed in Pearse's poem, 'The Mother:'

> I do not grudge them: Lord, I do not grudge
> My two strong sons that I have seen go out
> To break their strength and die, they and a few,
> In bloody protest for a glorious thing,
> They shall be spoken of among their people,
> The generations shall remember them,
> And call them blessed;
> But I will speak their names to my own heart
> In the long nights;
> The little names that were familiar once
> Round my dead hearth.
> Lord, thou art hard on mothers:
> We suffer in their coming and their going;
> And tho' I grudge them not, I weary, weary
> Of the long sorrow – And yet I have my joy:
> My sons were faithful, and they fought.

Lastly, the theme of this letter is Easter. About 15 years ago, I got in the habit of celebrating Easter with the Eastern Orthodox churches as well as the Roman Catholic Church. After talking to Rev. David McArthur I actually wrote the letter below to my Mom on Sunday, May 1, 2016, when the Greek Orthodox Church celebrated Easter. In 2016, Roman Catholics celebrated Easter on March 27. These Churches also differ in their interpretation of Christ's crucifixion. Many Eastern Orthodox Churches believe that God himself, not his son, came down to Earth to be crucified. That version of the Easter story is much easier for me to swallow.

Dear Mom,   Letter written on May 1, 2016

Today I rewrote the most important story I'll ever tell: the story I tell about myself to myself. Buried under all my accomplishments, I still felt like a weak, defective girl who left Sayville. I was the only one who couldn't handle the family and split into sub-personalities. Today I healed myself on an even deeper level by truly acknowledging I used strength, courage, and integrity to leave Sayville. I had felt crucified by neglect and abuse as a child, but never acknowledged how Source helped me heal through meditation, breathing through intense feelings, yoga, therapy, and a healthy marriage. More so than ever before, I now appreciate how my breathing practices enabled me to get in present time. They helped me update my story and end it on my resurrection instead of my crucifixion. Source resides in our breath. No wonder I was redeemed through my breathing.

What triggered this growth? A few days ago, I met with Reverend David McArthur from Unity of Walnut Creek to discuss my shame and fear of success. He asked me, "What do you think is causing your overwhelming sense of unworthiness?"

I said, "My mom's institutionalization and what I learned about Christ's crucifixion in the Roman Catholic Church." I then gave him a synopsis of why I split into Bunny and Bernadette. I explained I renamed myself Natazha, which means Resurrection, because I felt that both Bunny and Bernadette had died. I told Rev. David, "It's strange my nickname was Bunny as in the Easter bunny and

I named myself Natazha, which means resurrection, given how much I hate the Roman Catholic version of Easter. To me, that Easter story is a tale of child abuse. If God was so omnipotent, why didn't He get his own sorry ass down to Earth to die on a cross?" I sobbed as I said, "He sent His son to do His dirty work, just like men send their sons to war and Irish Catholic families sacrifice their sons and daughters by looking the other way when nuns and priests molest their kids."

We also discussed the notion that Christ took on the sins of the world, and that concept makes me afraid to act on my deep desire to help mankind. It makes me feel I have to take on the sins of the world and be crucified if I want to help humanity. And it triggers my childhood feelings of being obligated to sacrifice myself for my family or some other worthy cause. I said, "My Bunny part resented making sacrifices for my siblings and society, whereas my Bernadette part felt guilty if she didn't sacrifice herself. I feel like a loser no matter what I did."

Rev. David gave me permission to reinterpret the Easter story. Be a Christ who modeled love and light. He reframed Christ's crucifixion by explaining that Christ chose to be crucified. His Father never forced him. Christ wanted to show the most powerful empire ever to rule over the world at that time, the Roman Empire, that it had the wrong idea about the body. He wanted Romans to understand that humans are much more than just a body. They have a spirit or soul. The Romans tortured and killed His body, but Christ resurrected His dead body and came back stronger than ever. Christianity spread all over the world and His spirit has lived on long after the fall of the Roman Empire.

His interpretation made me see I had been stuck on my crucifixion. He pointed out I was happily married and that's the truly hard part. Anyone can be a famous author, but it takes integrity, love, and being whole to have a healthy marriage. My breathing practices had in fact resurrected me and blessed me with the divine qualities that make a happy marriage possible. After listening to him, I also realized on some level I chose to be crucified and dissociate so I could fully embrace the power of intentional breathing and teach it to others.

I don't want it to sound like all this change just happened suddenly. Many years of intentional breathing, therapy, my healthy marriage, and talking things out with wise people like Rev. David contributed to this shift. Although it feels like a sudden revelation, decades of conversing with my breath slowly but surely sponsored this breakthrough. Now, I'm taking the revolutionary step of fully forgiving myself. I just plain love myself more than ever. Best of all, that makes it easier to love you, too.

Love,
Natazha

I Left My Lungs in San Francisco   August 2016

It pays to follow your gut instinct. In 1984, I just knew I needed to move to San Francisco, a special city truly ahead of the times. I'm eternally grateful to the countless Bay Area residents who inspired me to love and heal myself through my respiration. When I die, I want my epitaph to read, "I left my lungs in San Francisco."

Dear Mom:

Today I stood in the glorious sunshine right in front of the Harbor Court Hotel where you stayed during your visit to San Francisco. As hundreds of people buzzed by me on the waterfront, I flashed back to you standing in the exact same spot in 2001. In utter bewilderment you asked me, "Why are so many people jogging? I never see so many people running on Long Island. Do they get paid to run? Is there a race going on?"

I answered, "No, there's no race. It's normal for this many people to jog here. Our climate and spectacular seaside scenery seduce you to exercise outdoors. San Franciscans love communing with Nature as they run, hike, bike swim, and row. Even I hike and run outdoors."

These days I also swim, row, and bike, on top of my Pilates and yoga practice. Living in San Francisco transformed me and actually saved my life. I converted from chain smoking and a destiny of COPD and lung cancer to becoming an elite athlete with excellent cardiovascular fitness. At 52 years old my VO2 Max tested at 47 ml/kg/min. That is off-the-charts great for my age group and gender. I also ran my first marathon at age 42 in 3 hours and 43 minutes and qualified for the Boston marathon. I now feel invigorated when I row over 100 miles to Sacramento. I credit my transformation to living in a city that sponsors so many breathing practices. For instance, if you stop and think about it, exercise requires us to breathe well. And, San Franciscans taught me to work out rather than wear out my body by minding my breath when I exercised.

During your trip I shared my favorite spots in San Francisco, but I didn't share how it was uniquely qualified to be the most perfect place in the whole wide world to stop smoking and redeem myself. I feel so blessed for all the second chances that coming to San Francisco afforded me. Literally thousands of San Franciscans helped me transform my suicidal breathing habits into life-affirming ones. You know what Long Island culture was like during the Studio 54 era of the eighties. Abusing your body with cigarettes, alcohol, and drugs was considered hip. I chain-smoked and held my breath to look tough and hide my sensitivity. I was like one of those notorious Biblical sinners who habitually cheats, steals, and murders. Until one day, they miraculously change their corrupt ways after they're mysteriously converted into a loving instrument of peace.

My mystical conversion occurred on Monday, June 29, 1987, at 3:21 pm on a ferry from Larkspur to San Francisco. After spending $75 in a hypnotherapist's office, I smoked four cigarettes in less than 45 minutes. Back then, $75 was an awful lot of money to me and I was pissed about wasting it. I impulsively threw my lit cigarette into the San Francisco Bay, not realizing that I had actually quit smoking 2-3 packs a day. I still can't believe I smoked so much. But, back then smoking was permitted almost everywhere: offices, restaurants, airplanes, and libraries, so I had a lit cigarette dangling from my mouth pretty much all day long. All that changed on that glorious day in 1987 with the help of countless San Franciscans who had adopted many breath-based practices and laws long before the rest of the country. They showed me how to love myself by befriending my breath. I can't thank Bay Area residents enough for role modeling and experimenting with unorthodox breathing practices.

San Francisco became my haven for so many splendid reasons. In the early 1980s, UCSF's Stanton Glantz fearlessly fought for second-hand smoking laws. He ignited a movement that blazed a trail from San Francisco all across the world and my personal life. His work inspired my friends and co-workers to pressure me to quit smoking. He's a super hero to me. I felt honored taking statistics from this brilliant character in graduate school.

Mom, please hear me out as I explain how San Franciscans taught me to meditate instead of medicate. It's so ironic you worried about me getting hooked on drugs in San Francisco. As it turned out, I'm the only one who never took prescription drugs for my mental illness, whereas other family members who sought professional help were prescribed drugs including Prozac, Zoloft, and Xanax. Although prescription drugs for depression and anxiety became super popular in the 1990s, my therapists believed in meditation, not medication. They trained me to mind my breath to change my biochemistry and mood. My therapists were influenced by the San Francisco and Palo Alto Veteran's Administration that pioneered the work on Post Traumatic Stress Disorder (PTSD) in the1980s. My mental illness was a form of PTSD.

Since your death, some of the other kids have asked me about healing from trauma.

You were a big fan of Carl Jung who popularized the concept of the collective unconscious. Did you know Dr. Stanislav Grof, a Bay Area resident, further developed Jung's theory of the collective unconscious by linking it to breathing? He is the father of Transpersonal Psychotherapy, a theory that the unconscious, including the collective unconscious and other states of mind, can be accessed through his breathing technique called Holotropic Breathing.

I owe a huge thank you to Tav Sparks, a leader in the Holotropic Breathing Community. After attending his weeklong retreat in Taos, New Mexico, in June 2006, Tav took me aside and said, "I've witnessed thousands of Holotropic Breathing sessions and strongly advise that you get professional help. Only one other time during a Holotropic Breathing session did someone show evidence of a split like you did." He referred me to Mireya Alejo. Mireya's Holotropic breath retreats were a perfect venue to continue healing my traumas and deep ancestral wounds. They allowed me to access wounds in my own unconscious as well as the collective unconscious. I was able to heal those wounds, and thus integrate more fully.

Here's another reason why San Francisco was a perfect refuge for me. Its strong Asian influence primed the Bay Area to embrace Oriental breath-based medicine and other energy-based healing practices. And I definitely needed breath-based medicine to heal my wounds, including the Uncle Mickey incident. Easy access to Oriental medicine is why I was the first one in our family to receive acupuncture. In 1988 Misha Cohen, an acclaimed acupuncturist, began giving me treatments to harmonize my energy channels to help me integrate my sub-personalities. She also stressed the importance of breathing. I feel this Asian influence helped create an audience for energy-based organizations like Berkeley Psychic Institute. It offered psychic readings, energy-based healings, and meditation long before they were mainstream. Folks on Long Island weren't ready for BPI in the 1980s. I fondly remember John (my brother) and some of the other kids teasing me. They called my psychic training, "my psycho training."

This Asian influence primed San Francisco to host many breath-based disciplines such as yoga, Pilates, and martial arts. Those disciplines helped me stop holding my breath. It was easy for me to continue practicing yoga in San Francisco after being introduced to it at Grinnell College. In 1993 I started Pilates at the Embarcadero YMCA a decade before it became popular. I learned in my Pilates teacher certification program the valuable lesson that breathing organizes our movement. Our breathing needs to shift to suit the demands of our activities and that's why each Pilates exercise has a distinct breathing pattern. I studied Aikido, which emphasizes breathing and mindfulness. I know you didn't like my boyfriend Jim, the 7th degree black belt. But he deserves some credit for teaching me many martial-arts breath techniques.

Asian immigrants exported many types of meditation to San Francisco. Meditation trained me to mind my breath instead of focus on my woes. My meditation career began at BPI and the San

Francisco Zen center. I lived across the street from the Zen Center from 1990-1993, and enjoyed easy access to its programs. It opened in 1962 and founded the first Zen monastery outside of Japan in 1967. Governor Jerry Brown practiced mediation at the Zen Center in the 1970s. That earned him the nickname, Governor Moonbeam. His nickname shows just how far ahead of the curve Jerry Brown and San Francisco were.

Mom, please know Buddhism is not a religion but a philosophy that encourages us to relieve our suffering, primarily by minding our breath. I had incredibly mixed feelings about the Roman Catholic Church. Bernadette overdid Catholicism and Bunny rebelled from it. I, too, am a mystic and was always super curious about Spirit, but afraid of organized religion. Buddhism provided a venue to process and integrate my good and bad experiences with the Catholic Church. I never gave up my Catholic heritage.

Besides the Zen Center and BPI, I've joined numerous other meditation programs. My love affair with meditation trained me to engage my breath everywhere I go, especially swimming and rowing on the San Francisco Bay. The bay is my favorite exercise partner. I love how it demands me to be conscious of my breath. I'm blessed to be a member of the Dolphin Club. With the support of this community, I swim in frigid water all year round. Did you know swimming in cold water acts like steroids for the parasympathetic nervous system (PNS)? The PNS is the part of the nervous system that allows us to heal and relax. And research shows swimming in cold water is great for healing trauma. San Francisco is a mecca for open-water swimming races. It hosts the famous Alcatraz and Tiburon One mile swim races.

San Francisco's tradition of tolerating alternative lifestyles granted me some breathing room to heal my mental illness. That tolerance gave me permission to put my energy into healing my dissociative identity disorder instead of following the traditional path of getting married and having kids right after college. During my twenties and thirties, when I visited Long Island, people asked, "When are you going to get married?" On Long Island, I felt pressured to follow the traditional family route. No one in San Francisco even blinked an eye when I followed my own path. They never harassed me about marrying late in life, my parking meter and rat phobias, changing my name to Natazha Raine O'Connor, or being estranged from my family.

Bob and his family living here is the most precious reason why San Francisco is uniquely qualified as my special healing spot. Bob truly is my prince charming. His unconditional love restored me. Bonding with him helped me rebuild my trust in myself and set better boundaries. I just love cuddling and breathing with him each morning. It helps me breathe more easily.

I can't emphasize strongly enough how San Franciscans' enlightened ways of breathing made it the ideal place for me to recover. Here's one last thing. You liked Tony Bennett's song, "I left my heart in San Francisco." If I could write a song to pay tribute to this city by the bay, I'd entitle it, "I left my lungs in San Francisco."

Love,
Natazha

Breathing Mama's Mission   December 2016

I hope to carry out my mission of training people to mother and rescue themselves with their breath. More and more, I feel worthy of receiving the assistance to make this dream come true. It is a dream I suspect many other moms share with me.

Dear Mom,

Do you remember that my first job out of college was in advertising? I followed in Grandpa Frank's footsteps; he loved promoting ideas and selling products. I want to use my advertising skills to promote breathing. No one ever talks about selling breathing. It's so innate to life, just something so basic that we take it for granted. But I believe all the pain and sorrow in the world goes back to us losing touch with our breath, our humanity. I want to teach people to exhale fully before they reach for drugs, sugar, junk foods, alcohol, or pick a fight, or whatever else they do to numb out and cheat themselves out of an authentic life, a life worth living.

Unlike you, I'll never have children this lifetime. Not having kids almost tore Bob and me apart. It took me more than a decade to heal from that heartache. Now I want to express my maternal instincts as a Breathing Mama who teaches people to love and mother themselves via their breath. Moms train their kids how to take care of themselves, love and relate well to themselves and others, and contribute to the world. Connecting to one's breath provides the most easy-to-access, universal path to fulfill our mothers' wishes: love yourself and make the world a better place than you found it. Befriending your breath equips you with the energy and fortitude to manifest your destiny.

You, Clara Barton, Quan Yin, Mary, Mother Teresa, Mary the Mother of God, and mothers across all ages and galaxies inspired my mission. You earned your Master's degree in your late fifties and coordinated the Saint Lawrence Outreach Program for 23 years, until you were 83 years old. By the way, Gabrielle (my sister) told me yesterday, "They renamed the Saint Lawrence Parish Outreach program building in your honor."

Just like me, Clara Barton never had her own kids and lavished her attention on her nieces and nephews. She founded the American Red Cross at 60 years old in 1881. And like you, led it for 23 years, until she was 83 years old. You and Clara make me feel at 54 years old I'm starting my mission early in life. I got my Doctorate in Physical Therapy at the young age of only 49 and will publish my first book as a young 54-year-old whippersnapper.

After I publish and promote *Rescued by My Breath,* I want to establish a non-profit organization to fulfill this mission: 1) Promote breathing skills through Public Service Announcements. Inspire people to exhale before reaching for cigarettes, alcohol, drugs, junk food, or any other vice they use to numb out and cheat themselves out of a life worth living. 2) Motivate and train people to breathe and move well through social media, online courses, live seminars, and lectures all over the world. 3) Collaborate with "Clean Air" non-profits and governmental agencies to protect air quality so the atmosphere is safe for us to breathe.

Going back to my advertising days, I'd produce the following Public Service Announcements designed to inspire people to breathe well.

PSA #1: "HAIL THE EXHALE"

It's a stormy, wet night on a gritty city street, reminiscent of a scene from the movie, The Matrix. A svelte, athletic woman dressed in a slick black-leather outfit dashes off on her motorcycle. The background music suggests she's in grave danger. She looks over her shoulders, then darts to an industrial building without taking off her motorcycle helmet. Uses her thumbprint to unlock the outside door. Avoids taking the elevator. Instead gallops up four flights of stairs like a gazelle. Once again her thumbprint unlocks the door to her massive 4,400-square-foot loft.

The moment she enters her home, all hell breaks loose. About 80 ninjas immediately pounce on her. It becomes clear her leather outfit is bullet proof when bullets bounce off her body. And swords can't cut through it. You just keep hearing her distinct, powerful exhale with each ninja she takes out.

She swiftly kills off all but one ninja. He cowers in the dark behind a floor-to-ceiling water fountain. He's frozen with terror. She takes a moment to recalibrate her breath. You can see her slow deliberate out-breaths fogging up the face of her helmet. When she finally takes off her helmet, you see she's over

65 years old with thick, long gray hair flowing past her shoulders. Think Helen Mirren.

The terrified ninja blurts out, "How did that Old Bag do that?"

With the speed of lightning, she exclaims, "Dimwit, I know how to exhale."

She blows an air kiss across the room that knocks him down dead.

This PSA ends with this tagline: **Exhale - Your life depends on it.**

PSA #2: I'D LIKE TO TEACH THE WORLD TO BREATHE

Do you remember the Coca-Cola TV ad back in the 1970's with a big group of people on a hill singing, *"I'd like to teach the world to sing"*? This PSA is a knockoff of that ad. Instead of "I'd like to Teach the World to Sing" the words are changed to "I'd like to Teach the World to Breathe in Perfect Harmony, etc."

It starts with only the music and provocative pairings of people. Donald Trump (look alike, don't think he'll do this ad) helps a Mexican immigrant family find a place to sit at a soup kitchen for the needy; Ku Klux Klan members serve African Americans food at a barbeque; Muslims in their traditional garb in a mosque greet stereotypical over-weight, white-male Texans with big ol' cowboy hats, blue jeans, and boots. I'm still dreaming through the pairings of people, which will change according to what's going on in the world. The last 10 seconds of the PSA shows all the pairings holding hands on a big hill and singing "I'd like to teach the world to breathe in perfect harmony," just like the 1970's Coca-Cola commercial. This PSA ends with this tagline: **Singing helps you breathe well.**

Mom, I'm still amazed at how much you accomplished in your life. And, you never, ever gave up. Thanks for inspiring me to DREAM BIG. I'm still musing about ideas for other PSAs. In my wildest dreams, I want to air these PSAs as Super Bowl Ads.

How I wish you were still alive. I'd love to know what PSA could have motivated you to quit smoking long before it was too late, before you got irreversible emphysema. Before you got lung cancer that metastasized into lethal bone cancer. Seventeen percent of American adults still smoke. Given all we know about how horrible cigarette smoking is for your health, that's just plain ridiculous! I feel blessed I quit 30 years ago, and destined to help millions of smokers quit cigarettes because I've got the conviction, experience, and talent. Creating a PSA to inspire smokers to quit is definitely on my to-do list. In the meantime, I'll meditate and pray that one day soon I'll help people quit smoking in your honor. Create a PSA that inspires millions of smokers to quit and a Mary Connors Smoking Cessation program.

Still miss you,
Natazha

P.S. We engage in a special form of breathing as we sleep. I'd love to devise a technique so people would dream about my PSA's. I suspect breathing would be the key for reaching people as they dream in their sleep.

Patron Saint of Prostitutes   March 2017

Lewis Botswick, the founder of the Berkeley Psychic Institute (BPI) gave me a psychic reading only one time. At the time, I was confused and somewhat insulted by his remarks about me. Was Lewis suggesting I petition Pope John Paul II to become the Patron Saint of Prostitutes? But, now after processing my Irish shame, I have come to a fuller understanding of his reading. It now makes perfect sense to me.

Dear Mom,

Out of the blue, I began thinking about the psychic reading Lewis Botswick, the founder of BPI, gave me way back in 1993. You'll be happy to know that I worked very hard for social justice in another lifetime, according to Lewis. Let me first tell you what he told me, before I explain why his reading has resurfaced in my awareness.

Lewis excitedly explained in a previous life I owned a sewing factory in London during Victorian times. I despised the hypocrisy of British law in that era. Men hired prostitutes and got off scot-free, whereas the hookers got jailed. I believed these ladies of the night needed help, not prison time. I risked everything, including my livelihood and reputation, to take in as many prostitutes as I possibly could. I was the exact opposite of Jean Valjean, the factory owner in *Les Miserables* who kicked out Fantine. I helped prostitutes by letting them sit and pretend to sew when the London police raided my factory.

In 1993, Pope John Paul II was canonizing saints left and right. I was bewildered by Lewis's reading and with some sarcasm thought, *Maybe I should petition the Pope to become the Patron Saint of Prostitutes.* I forgot all about his reading until recently when I inadvertently insulted another woman in the Dolphin Club sauna. San Francisco is a "blue" city, and most people assume their fellow San Franciscans are against Trump. I'm not a Trump fan, but when this woman started talking about press reports that our First Lady was previously a call girl, I instinctively came to Melania's defense. She deserves her privacy, especially around her past. Who cares if she had worked in the world's oldest profession? She clearly graduated from her past circumstances and is now raising a small boy under very trying circumstances.

And, speaking of First Ladies, I still feel bad for Hilary Clinton. I interpret the Monica Lewinsky sexual Rorschach test very differently than most Americans. I admire Hilary for forgiving Bill. I don't understand why the general public vilifies her for standing by her man. I also identified with Bill Clinton, as I, too, cheated on past boyfriends. My infidelity had nothing to do with my boyfriends, but everything to do with my shame and mental illness. Bill Clinton publicly stated his sexual misconduct had nothing to do with Hillary, but rather he felt pushed to the brink by the Kenneth Starr investigation. Just like Melania, the Clintons deserve a private sex life or at the very least a kinder interpretation of their behavior.

Sorry about that tangent. Getting back to my story about Lewis Botswick's psychic reading. The Dolphin Club sauna wasn't the first nor will it be the last time I defend sex workers. I angered many of my fellow physical therapy school classmates when I strongly advocated that PTs prescribe sex for patients. We were discussing the case of a 23-year-old man who at 13 years old was permanently incapacitated from a stroke. He wanted to visit the infamous Bunny Ranch in Nevada. I argued physical therapists strive to treat the whole person, not just their bones and muscles. We aim to enhance our patients' overall health and wellbeing. Research shows having sex improves your overall health, immune system, cardiovascular fitness, and self-esteem. This young man was already deprived of so many of the pleasures that his peers enjoyed. Why should he be deprived of sex?

There's a link between Lewis' reading and shame around sexuality. Prostitutes have always been doused in shame, and I've often felt ashamed of my sexuality. And sexuality is shamed in our culture. My job allows me to see how shame plays out as an assortment of aches and pains in my patients' bodies. It's one reason I'm such a fan of breathing, which is a neutral, yet incredibly effective tool for healing almost everything that ails someone, including sexual shame manifested as physical pain. Many of my female patients don't realize that pelvic-floor exercises not only improve their core strength but also help them enjoy a sexual orgasm. Our pelvic-floor muscles are used both for breathing and sex. One innocuous exhale at a time, I'm also helping them release emotional scars around sex and other traumas by teaching them pelvic floor exercises. Lastly, as a physical therapist I go beyond the physical, mechanical causes of pain. Several times, I've evaluated low back pain (LBP) patients. I found some physical causes for their LBP, but also found evidence their pain was also related to pent-up sexual energy. Some of them needed to have sex just like the 23-year-old gentleman we discussed in PT school.

Now, I see Lewis was correct. I do have a big soft spot for sex workers. Here's another reason why I'm thinking about that psychic reading. Lewis emphasized over and over again that I created some awesome karma in that lifetime. I sacrificed wisely for others and deposited boatloads of positive karma in my spiritual bank account. That's the link I now see between his psychic reading and my current life. I sacrificed and worked my heart and soul off to write *Rescued by My Breath.* It speaks about Irish shame, and many of the girls I saved back in Victorian London were probably Irish women who were forced to prostitute themselves on the streets of London during and after the Potato Famine. Of course I felt for these women. How could anyone have turned their back on them during their time of need, and worse yet, shamed them? I wrote this book to heal from shame, and help my readers heal from their own shame, including Irish shame. I wonder if the amazing support I've received writing this book is how I'm cashing in on that "awesome" karma per Lewis' reading.

Another reason why I'm thinking about Lewis' reading is I'm struggling with fear of success. I'm excited and terrified *Rescued by My Breath* is turning out so well. Just last night, Bob and I were looking at the San Francisco Bay from our living room. After feeling how much I cherish our marriage, I blurted out, "It's scary to enjoy such a sweet life. I'm afraid something bad is going to happen." The Buddhist in me thought impermanence is just part of life, but I also thought shame is poisoning my joy. I still don't feel I deserve happiness. That's when I told Bob about Lewis' psychic reading and how I'm using it to help convince myself I earned this sweet life in San Francisco, back in Victorian London. For all I know, Lewis may have made up that story about me, but I might as well use it to feel worthy of my happiness and success.

Bob smiled and said, "I get scared our life is too good to be true, and worry it will suddenly be destroyed. I don't believe in all that psychic stuff, but your Lewis Bushwick story does make me feel better. You're definitely rubbing off on me." We both laughed and continued to enjoy our view of the moon rising over the bay.

That's when I realized that experiencing my discomfort associated with success is a wise, loving way to sacrifice for my loved ones. I feel better about succeeding knowing that somewhere, somehow, when I raise my vibration by enjoying the sweetness of life I'm also raising my tribe's and the rest of humanity's vibration. I'm not being selfish but rather of service by shining and enjoying myself. It truly is time to release my shame.

Love,
Natazha

PS–Pope Francis recently announced he's willing to explore priests getting married. That got me thinking, he may be the only Pope willing to hear why we should have a Patron Saint for Prostitutes and people suffering from shame about their sexuality.

PPS–You were an excellent seamstress. And my fondest childhood memories revolve around dresses you made for me. Those dresses became a symbol of your love when I was in the throes of healing childhood traumas. Anyway, I wonder if you're making clothes for me was somehow related to my "Patron Saint of Prostitutes" past life.

You Have To Be Present to Win   February 2017

What sold me on meditation and mindfulness? Because so many times I successfully soothed myself with my breath in times of trouble. Besides navigating stress and pain with greater ease, minding my breath raised my consciousness. It also enabled me to notice very subtle progress and easy-to-miss joys. As I became more present, I more readily received and appreciated invisible blessings, including friendships deepening, feeling more connected to myself and others, greater self-confidence, and the bliss of becoming more whole.

Dear Mom,

People often ask, "How did your life improve with meditation?" I start off by saying, "I'm much more patient and considerate, especially when I'm driving. I no longer assume I'm the only one on the road; I allot extra time for traffic instead of cursing under my breath when I need to slow down for fellow drivers." Trust me. That was a huge shift. When I started dating Bob 20 years ago, he was horrified at how much I cursed at fellow drivers.

Now, I smile on the inside and outside, and tell them, "It makes me more present. I now notice the invisible blessings in my life that are never formally announced by an email or phone call; I need to be aware to appreciate them. It's like the familiar raffle prize disclaimer, "You have to be present to win." Meditation makes me more cognizant so I fully enjoy gifts from the Divine. Most of the best things in life sneak up on you: your marriage ripening into unconditional love, a long-standing emotional wound melting, newly acquired insights, learning more quickly from your mistakes, and forgiving more easily."

Here's a sweet example. One sunny morning about two years ago I was meditating on our living room sofa. I was just luxuriating in my respiration. Breathing at my own pace without any agendas. I was so still I heard my spirit ask, "If you had to pick between being married to Bob or having kids, what would you choose?" I didn't even need to think about it, I immediately chose Bob. That tiny moment changed my life and marriage.

The Irish Catholic message I received was loud and clear: "A woman is supposed to have kids." I felt defective for not having any kids. After a decade of grieving, I assumed I'd never feel good about not having kids. It caused so much pain that we almost got divorced.

Before we married, Bob and I agreed we wanted kids. We handled our grief over infertility quite differently, and that caused severe problems. To me, Bob's "understated" expression of grief proved he only said he wanted kids to trick me into marrying him, after I told him I broke up with my last boyfriend because he didn't want kids. Truth was he just expressed his grief differently than me. Unlike Bob, I expressed my grief frequently and dramatically. I talked out my feelings in therapy, swam endless miles in the San Francisco Bay, wrote and wrote and wrote about it in my journal, and cried my heart out for years. Bob began wondering if my "overstated" grief was proof that having kids was more important than being married to him. It left him feeling I could only enjoy our marriage if we had kids; Bob alone wasn't enough for me.

Answering my soul's question before work that morning helped me finally see Bob's point of view. I realized how I overtly expressed my grief about our infertility, but understated my appreciation for his unconditional love. I needed to start expressing my love for Bob more often and stop taking his love for granted. That insight enabled me to claim our unconditional love for each other. As I recognized our love for each other, I also recognized how fulfilling our life was even without kids. We enjoyed a sweet life even though we had deviated from our Irish Catholic heritage.

I also opened my eyes and saw I did have a brood of kids in my life. I was an aunt to 16 nieces and nephews and a great aunt to five grand nieces and nephews. I needed to fulfill my role as an aunt and act as a "Back-Up Mom." That morning, I became fiercely proud to be a "Back-Up Mom" to my nieces and nephews and grand nieces and nephews. That brood keeps growing. And, I need to stay present and aware so I can step in and help whenever I'm needed.

There's one more special gift meditation bestows upon me. Along with writing letters to you, meditation is how I connect to you. I feel your presence when I settle into my body by tuning into my breath and exhale to call out to your spirit. Meditating lets me hear your spirit's loving response. I feel so blessed to still have you in my life.

Love,
Natazha

Setting Boundaries With My Breathing   March 2017

At the Berkeley Psychic Institute I learned how to handle feedback. Take what rang true for me and leave the rest. Feedback came in the form of psychic readings at BPI. I'd often ask the same question of several psychics and get completely different, contradictory answers. That's why I often disregarded my psychic readings. However, when it came to my rat phobia, I was always told the same exact thing. "You were a young man in a Polish prison during the 1500s. You were thrown in jail for a crime that you didn't commit. You got sick and rats ate you alive." The spooky consistency of that answer convinced me that I needed to find out how this past life was relevant to my current life.

I didn't want to suffer from "past life-itis." I define it as avoiding your current life by fixating on your past lives. I tried, however, to figure out when in my current life did I feel eaten alive by rats? Self-reflection made me realize this past life symbolized feeling eaten alive by my family's conflicting emotional needs. I'm a sweet being who wants everyone to be happy. Enmeshment was the golden rule in my family that trained me to feel all the conflicting emotions of everyone in my family. I tried to simultaneously embrace opposing sides of family fights. And often wound up losing myself in the process. I didn't stand up for myself because I was too busy trying to win the approval of others.

I was eaten alive by another conflict. I was the classic lost child, highly imaginative and creative who often disappeared into the world of fantasy. I spaced out to a happier place where everyone got along with each other. Living in my fantasy world made me invisible. At the same time, I felt compelled to stand out. I wanted to be a family hero and shine brightly to make the family look good. My conflicting family roles chewed away at me. Those insights helped disintegrate my rat phobia. And prompted my journey toward feeling safe to succeed and setting better boundaries.

Dear Mom,

Today was a classic example of what happens when I don't get a chance to meditate first thing in the morning. I was completely ungrounded and couldn't maintain my boundaries until I finally got a chance to catch my breath. Praise still stirs up shame storms in my psyche. Two days ago, Tom Bird gave me positive feedback on our book, *Rescued by My Breath*. He loved my writing and just wanted more of it. He told me to write an introduction to the book and for each letter. His praise triggered intense feelings of unworthiness and shame. My energy's been bouncing off the walls ever since. I've been unmotivated to get centered and keep sabotaging myself.

Last night I procrastinated for hours instead of preparing for this weekend's writing retreat in Sedona. I didn't start packing until after midnight even though I had to wake up by 3:45 a.m. to catch my 6:00 a.m. flight. I went to bed around 2 a.m., and slept through two alarms. Bob woke me up at 4:50 a.m. saying, "Don't you need to get up for your flight?"

I jumped out of bed. Bob volunteered to get my car out of the garage and meet me in the circle driveway out in front of our condo complex. Completely out of it, I ran around our condo like a banshee. Got dressed lickety-split. I skipped all my routine morning rituals of essential oils, angel cards, and meditation. I packed my final incidentals at 5:01 a.m. I then locked our condo door, ran down the corridor and took the elevator down 11 flights to the front lobby. I was almost out the lobby door of our building when I realized I didn't have my cell phone.

So I left my luggage by the security guard's desk and dashed back to the elevator. Rode it back up to the 11th floor, and then ran down our hallway and opened our condo door.

I frantically looked for my cell phone. I ran into our bedroom, our bathroom, and back to the kitchen and living room. Seeing no sign of my phone, I got really scared I was going to miss my flight. After hyperventilating, I exhaled a prayer to you. Asked you for help. Suddenly I was inspired to look under a pillow on the living room couch, and there was my phone. I ran out of our condo. Relocked the front door. Sped down the hallway back onto the elevator. Jumped out of the elevator. Grabbed my luggage and rolled it as fast as I possibly could to my car.

I felt like Bob's accomplice in a bank robbery. He was parked in front of our condo building with the back and front passenger doors wide open. I threw my suitcase into the back seat and jumped into the front seat. We sped out of the driveway in record time, and communicated only through our breathing. Sitting in the car, I started exhaling loud and clear. Bob automatically joined me on countless rounds of the "Almighty Exhale." Our pronounced exhales sounded like we were exercising really hard, when in fact we were only exorcising our fears about me missing my flight. No words. Just exhaled our prayers to the powers to be with our every out breath.

I love we're at a point in our marriage that we instinctively match our respiration to express our feelings. Bob exhaled with all his heart and soul to send me nourishing compassion. I'm humbled by his generosity. He gives me Simon Cowell honesty, always has my back, and has earned my complete trust. He never complains when I do stupid things that spill over into his life. He just goes with the flow. In many ways he reminds me of Daddy Ray. This morning once again I was grateful he was there for me in my hour of need. We were about five minutes from SFO airport when I squeezed his thigh. And said, "I'm self-sabotaging. I have felt awful ever since Tom Bird gave me positive feedback on my writing. I hope I still catch my flight."

SFO airport is always busy. I've taken many 6:00 a.m. flights. And, know the TSA lines are crazy busy even at 5:30 in the morning. I'm convinced I'll miss my flight when we arrive at the American Airlines curbside at 5:27 a.m. Bob told me he left his cell phone at home, but still wants me to call him if I miss my flight. He'll come back to the airport to pick me up. He kissed and hugged me good-bye. Waving good-bye to him, I cried.

I ran into the airport. Looked for the nearest monitor to reconfirm my gate number. Then, I blindly ran toward the nearest TSA counter. A young male custodian with a broom in his hands saw my face and sensed my panic. He instinctively cocked his head and broomstick toward another man with a TSA uniform and said, "Just let her in. Don't worry about it. Just let her through." I'm confused why a custodian is telling a TSA agent what to do, but I'm supremely grateful when the TSA agent looked at my **not** preapproved TSA boarding pass, and let me through anyway. I realized he's done me a huge favor when I saw no one in line and flew through this TSA pre-approved line.

I was in terminal one and needed to walk to terminal two to get to my gate. Along the way I passed the TSA line I should have used. It was about a mile long. It would have taken over 30 minutes to get through that line. That's why the alarm was set for 3:45 a.m. I ran so fast that I almost knocked down a little old lady. I shouted, "I'm sorry" as I picked up my running pace. I got to my gate just as they announced they were boarding groups 5 and 6. I was group 6. Eight minutes later I sat down in my plane seat, and took a huge breath of relief. It was 5:57 a.m. when I texted Bob, "Thx, I made the flight. Luv u." He was already home and texted back, "Great. Luv u. Call me tonight."

I took my airplane seat and retrieved the manuscript copy of my book from my backpack. I looked at the cover of my manuscript, when tears began streaming down my face. Just then a guy took the aisle seat. I quickly turned away to hide my tears. When I finally looked at him, he introduced himself as Rick. I told him "I'm Natazha." He saw the cover of our book, *Rescued By My Breath,* and excitedly explained, "I just started taking Bikram yoga two months ago, and love it."

I told him I took 6:00 a.m. Bikram yoga classes all through physical therapy graduate school. It was the only way I could guarantee getting my exercise. It was a lifesaver.

He asked, "What's your book about?"

I answered, "It's about knowing what you want in life and using your breath to get it."

He asked, "What do you mean by that?"

I responded, "We're often told meditation, exercise, and expressing our feelings are the keys to health and happiness. Those three things are actually acts of breathing. Meditation is minding our breath. Exercise demands we breathe more fully to fuel our working muscles. And, we express our feelings through our breathing: speak, cry, laugh, shriek, and so on."

Just then I felt really exhausted and thought, "I really need to meditate." That's when the guy in front of us shouted, "Would you guys shut up? I'm trying to sleep. You need to shut up." He punctuated his yelling with a scowl. I felt like crying and almost shut down to appease him, thinking that would stop his temper-tantrum. But then Rick politely asserted, "We have a right to talk. We're on a plane where passengers are permitted to talk to each other."

Rick lowered his voice, and continued asking me questions about yoga. He told me how much he missed his garden. Before he got divorced he grew vegetables in the house where his ex-wife and three kids now live. We talked about how much he wanted to garden with his kids. Get them outdoors, and away from their video games.

Then the wife of the man who snapped at us sneered at us. If looks could kill, she had already murdered us. She screamed, "My Mom just died. Shut up, you guys have to shut up." I felt utterly trapped and spiraled back to a time I felt trapped in our house. I was six years old and felt torn apart by having to take sides in a family feud. I thought, *That childhood situation perfectly matches this situation right now. I'm stuck on a plane where my need to meditate conflicts with Rick's need to talk and this couple demanding we shut up. Ironically this couple was the only ones yelling, and yet, they were telling us to be quiet.*

I felt incredibly conflicted. I did feel sorry for their loss, but was supremely pissed that they were holding us responsible for their feelings. Who the hell were they to censor us? Our talking wasn't the cause of their pain. A death in their family was the source. And Rick and I ending a heartfelt conversation wouldn't resurrect that family member.

As a child I held my breath to escape from unreasonable demands being asked of me, but it also made me lose touch with myself. At that moment, I exhaled long and slowly. I finally saw these competing needs were similar to my past life when I was eaten alive by rats. I knew the feeling oh too well. Now, on top of my feeling super unworthy of Tom Bird's praise, I had added the oh too familiar terror of being eaten alive by rats. I thought, *Shit! I really need to meditate.* I instinctively released another long slow exhale. I exhaled again and again.

Then I told Rick, "I got only two hours of sleep last night. My writing will provide a better explanation of what my book is about." I handed him my manuscript and told him to read these two letters, *Dramatize Your Breathing* and *The Beauty of Informal Meditation.*

While he was busy reading, I mediated and finally got centered. I realized I'm not serving anyone if I'm not truthful to myself. After meditating for five minutes, I flash-backed to reading Thomas Merton's *New Seeds of Contemplation* to you on your deathbed. That day I also shared with you one of my favorite Thomas Merton quotes. "The rush and pressure of modern life are a form, perhaps the most common form, of contemporary violence. To allow oneself to be carried away by a multitude of conflicting concerns, to surrender to too many demands, to commit oneself to too many projects, to want to help everyone in everything, is to succumb to the violence of our times."

You asked me why I loved that quote so much. I answered, "I'm a recovering people-pleaser. That quote reminds me to say, 'No' and set boundaries. It also cues me to maintain my boundaries by slowing down and minding my breath so I notice when someone has violated them. I can't believe Merton said that in the 1960s. What would he say about our even faster-paced lives now?"

On the plane, Merton's quote reminded me to never allow myself to be eaten alive by other people's demands. This situation required me to set my boundaries. And it's always hard for me to set boundaries when I don't feel worthy of setting limits. I also reflected on what it means to be compassionate. I thought about all the times I had thrown temper-tantrums and expected others to stop their lives because I didn't want to feel my feelings. I erroneously believed demanding others to change their behavior would change my feelings.

That's when I exhaled a blessing to the couple in front of us. I breathed in and out. With that deep breathing I gave myself full permission to set a boundary and continue my heartfelt conversation with Rick. I needed to talk instead of giving into a temper-tantrum. I exhaled fully. Inhaled fully. Exhaled fully. And, then in a low volume, I asked Rick what he thought of the letters. We spent the rest of the flight talking about how gardening is a form of informal meditation.

Love,
Natazha

From Invisible to Invincible   December 2016

Growing up, I played the role of the lost child. By holding my breath I became invisible to others and myself. I was afraid to express my true feelings or needs. 15 years ago I wrote this tale called "Hooray Soleil." It depicts my soul's desire for me to become invincible instead of invisible by setting boundaries through staying focused on my intentions rather than worry about pleasing others and appeasing bullies.

When I recently reread this story, I realized the Dalai Lama resembles Soleil. He's the perfect example of someone who went from being invisible to invincible. For centuries the secluded country of Tibet was isolated and invisible to the rest of the world. The Chinese bullied Tibet and forced the Dalai Lama to leave Tibet. Since then, the Dalai Lama has spoken on the world stage as an ambassador for meditation and Buddhism. His supreme boundaries make him invincible. Just like Soleil, he stays focused on his intention of staying connected to his breath and the present moment. He's never allowed Tibet's struggles with China to rob him of his serenity or feel ashamed. No matter what sticks or stones are thrown at the Dalai Lama, he remains calm and loving.

Dear Mom,

When I'm extremely clear about my intentions, I don't care what others think. Even better, I'm able to focus on my goals and manifest my heart's desire, just like Soleil in this story. When Soleil stops worrying about what the "bullies" will do to her, she focuses on what she wants and seamlessly sets a boundary. She also shines brightly for all to see.

Hooray Soleil!

Soleil is a stunning baby girl sun. Even as an infant, she knew how to shine brightly for all to see. Every day, her radiant sunlight allows her playmates, the plants and animals, to see where they are going and stay on their path. Soleil loves playing with her wildlife friends. She plays peek-a-boo by dodging in and out of the clouds. She tickles her pals with her warm, radiant sunbeams. Her sunshine feels really yummy on their backs and bellies. The plants perk up and grow faster whenever she blesses them with her sunshine. All her pals giggle whenever she sprays sunlight on the humans and changes their skin color.

When night falls, Soleil sleeps deeply. When Soleil awakes at sunrise, the plants and animals cheer, "Hooray Soleil! Hooray Soleil!"

She freely shares her gift of clear light, and sprinkles the oceans with streams of illuminated confetti and dancing sunbeams. With a twinkle in her eyes, she heats the earth to pop open plants. Her smile transforms rain into rainbows.

All is sunny and clear in her kingdom. Until suddenly two huge planets named Nasty and Bad Breath show up and scare Soleil. These planets are many times larger than Soleil and have sharp sticks, hard stones, and huge boulders protruding from them. Nasty and Bad Breath stand directly in front of Soleil and deliberately obstruct her view. She tries to peek around them, but they shift places to block her view. Soleil feels terrified and all alone when she can no longer see her playmates.

Nasty and Bad Breath call her names, "Little Miss Goody Two Shoes" and "Miss Silly Sunshine." Petrified these bullies *may* hurt her, Soleil runs away. Hiding behind some rain clouds, she sobs and sobs until she falls asleep. Nasty and Bad Breath are thrilled when Soleil stops shining. It becomes dark. And the plants and animals are afraid of the dark. Without her sunshine, the plants fade and droop. The animals can't see where they are going and get lost. They stub their toes and trip over tree roots. Everyone except Nasty and Bad Breath missed Soleil's sunshine.

Soleil feels awful seeing her friends in distress. She gets so upset she forgets all her fears and comes out of hiding. Radiating brighter than ever before, she shines from the North Pole to the South Pole and from the tops of the mountains to the bottoms of the oceans. Feeling love and compassion for her friends makes it easy for her to glow fiercely.

Her loving sunshine heals her friends. The plants perk up. The animals laugh and sing. Soleil smiles and shines more intensely when her friends look happy and healthy again. She sparkles more brightly and clearly than ever before.

When Nasty and Bad Breath see Soleil shining they yell, "How dare she feel good and shine?" They try to stop her by shouting, "Sugar Pie Sunshine" and "Miss Stupid Sunshine." Intent on helping her friends, Soleil ignores their name calling. She just keeps shining. "Hooray Soleil! Hooray Soleil!" her pals cheer.

Nasty and Bad Breath yell, "How dare the plants and animals cheer for Soleil?" They throw sticks at Soleil. She still stays focused on her friends. Soleil pays no attention to the sticks and lets them fly right past and through her clear sunlight. "Hooray Soleil! Hooray Soleil!" scream her friends.

For the first time ever, Nasty and Bad Breath are not getting their way. They want Soleil to stop shining right then and there. So they throw stones at her. Once again, Soleil intently concentrates on her playmates. And, the stones fly right through her bright light. "Hooray Soleil! Hooray Soleil!" boom the plants and animals.
"We'll teach that Miss Goody-two-shoes a lesson," shout Nasty and Bad Breath. "You asked for it Soleil." They throw huge boulders at her. Soleil doesn't even flinch. The boulders zoom right through her sphere of sunshine. "Hooray Soleil! Hooray Soleil!" scream the plants and animals.

Soleil's bright, clear light makes it perfectly clear that these two bullies are just big, fat cowards. Nasty and Bad Breath are completely exhausted after throwing sticks, stones, and boulders. These two scaredy-cats don't want anyone to see them weak and tired, so they fly away and are never seen again. As Nasty and Bad Breath speed away, the plants and animals hoot and holler, "HOORAY SOLEIL! HOORAY SOLEIL!"

Soleil smiles and beams with great pride as she lets out a gleeful giggle. She says to herself, "When sticks and stones are being thrown, I can shine intently from my throne." Once again, all is sunny and clear in Soleil's kingdom. The end.

Love,
Natazha

Tibetans taught me to be a Human Breathing　　　May 2017

I owe a huge debt to Tibet. Buddhist teachings, especially Tibetan teachings on breath and meditation, greatly influenced my thinking, and ultimately saved my life. Buddhism taught me that in order to be a whole human being I needed to be a human breathing. When I recently told my sister Noreen I had suffered from Dissociative Identity Disorder, she asked, "Do you ever worry about splitting again?" I answered, "No, because I breathe differently now. I no longer hold my breath to hold myself together. These days, I face a crisis by minding my breath rather than stop breathing. That's how I quit practicing the emotional numbing that fueled my Dissociative Identity Disorder."

I was first introduced to Tibet in 1988. I was walking along Shattuck Avenue to the Berkeley Psychic Institute (BPI) to my meditation class. A picture of the Dalai Lama's Potala Palace in Lhasa, the Dalai Lama's former home, mesmerized me. It was in the front window of a bookstore. I spent more than 10 minutes staring at this picture. I would have missed my meditation class had the storeowner not asked if she could help me. I've only seen the Dalai Lama speak once, and long to see Tibet. I almost went in 2012, but decided to visit Bhutan instead. The Chinese heavily occupy Tibet and I sensed I wouldn't see much of Tibetan culture anyway. Turns out I was right. While I was traveling in Bhutan all American visas to tour Tibet were cancelled and those American tourists were rerouted to Bhutan. I still visit an independent Tibet in my imagination. Try to honor this tiny country whenever possible.

Dear Mom,

It's been over a year since your death. I sense you now appreciate me identifying myself as Buddhist with a strong Irish Catholic accent. I hope you get a chuckle out of what I did today at my doctor's office. When asked to fill out a form about my ethnic background, I chose both Irish and Tibetan.

Mom, I hope you now understand Buddhism helped me honor my Catholic heritage; it never competed with it. Your favorite Christian mystic, Thomas Merton, said, "I see no contradiction between Buddhism and Christianity. I intend to become as good a Buddhist as I can." I also think Celtic spirituality, Christianity, and Buddhism grew from the same tree of love. Ultimately they all say the same thing. That's why the Dalai Lama and Thomas Merton were such good friends. Did you know the Dalai Lama considers Thomas Merton one of his spiritual teachers?

Buddhism taught me spirituality begins with the breath: to be a whole human being requires being a human breathing. Meditation unified my shattered soul and helped mediate a peace agreement between my sub-personalities. It invited all of me to participate through conscious breathing. My respiration offered a common ground for Bunny and Bernadette, a safe arena to resolve my internal conflicts and redeem myself. And, when I finally set boundaries in December 2016, I realized conscious breathing is essential for maintaining my boundaries as minding my breath tells me when my they've been violated.

I'm indebted to Buddhists, especially Tibetans, for inspiring me to heal through meditation and other breathing practices instead of overmedicating with drugs. That's why I'm so deeply disturbed by Tibet's current political situation. I see many parallels between Ireland and Tibet, and made a chart to illustrate those parallels.

Tibet	Ireland
Tiny, isolated mountain country	Tiny, isolated island nation
Spiritually oriented country	Spiritually oriented country In Middle Ages
Spirituality strongly influenced by Nature	Spirituality strongly influenced by Nature
Monks preserved mystical, sacred Buddhist traditions and scriptures	Monks preserved scriptures during the Dark Ages. Described in How The Irish Saved Civilization by Thomas Cahill
Dedicate merit of their meditation practice in a similar manner to making a blessing	Masters of making a blessing or a toast when drinking
Invaded by the Chinese	Invaded by Britain and many others
?????????????????	Won their Independence after 700 years

The comparison falls apart with Tibet still occupied by the Chinese. And, unlike the Irish Clans, the Dalai Lama has asked Tibetans not to kill (sacrifice) themselves for the cause of a Free Tibet. I do pray Tibet eventually gains their Independence, just as the Irish did. But, also I fear Tibet and its rich tradition of honoring the breath may perish with the Dalai Lama's death. I hope his last breath is not the last gasp of Tibetan civilization, but rather, the breath heard around the universe. And, Tibet is granted its independence, just as a meditation granted me my independence from trauma, grudges, and everything else that alienated me from the invisible joys of life that all too often go unnoticed in our hectic culture.

Two years before both you and Dad died, my gut sensed your deaths were on the horizon. The Dalai Lama has been like my Buddhist godfather, and I'm sensing his death is on the horizon. My experience of breathing more easily with you after your death offers me hope. I believe humanity, including the Chinese, may also breathe more easily with the Dalai Lama after he dies. That's how the Dalai Lama's spirit will positively influence humankind, and perhaps liberate Tibet.

Speaking of liberation, Mom, you liberated me from shame by using your mystic magic to keep me on track writing this book. To me, the Dalai Lama is the king of breathing and you're the queen of communicating through the breath, my Breathing Mama. Thanks for sharing your love and wisdom with me. I could never have written *Rescued by My Breath* without you.

Love,
Natazha

My Declaration of Integration Replaces
My Declaration of Independence   Nov 2016

Precious is my four-year-old self that experienced Uncle Mickey's sexual assault. She repeatedly vowed to never forgive my Mom. So I never expected this part of myself to reconcile with her. Writing this book blessed me in many ways, including Precious shocked me by forgiving my Mom. I felt something monumental shift inside of me as I wrote my letter to Uncle Mickey. A month later, Precious announced she wanted to hug my Mom, a clear sign she had forgiven her.

Dear Mom,

How I wish you were still alive so we could celebrate the miracle that happened this Thursday 11/10/16, nearly 30 years after I sent my brutally honest Declaration of Independence audiotape that left you feeling falsely accused of molesting me. I believe your mystic magic inspired this miracle. From the other side of the veil, you helped orchestrate my book writing with your special brand of "Mighty Mary Magic." Fifteen years ago, I failed to write my book on breathing. This time I stuck with it. I felt your presence energizing me every step of the way. Fueling me with determination and a sense of purpose when the going got rough. My book writing and meditation practice led up to today's miracle.

To understand this miracle, I first need to tell you about Precious. She's a part of me that vowed never to forgive you. She's my inner child ranging from four to six years old. During this time, our family life was particularly bleak. Almost everyone except Catholic Charities and Grandma Winnie had given up on us. All eight of us kids were terrified.

Precious couldn't bear witnessing her siblings' fit of rage against our circumstances. She couldn't bear the omnipresent threat of being put into foster care or the thought of never seeing you again. Every day for months, she'd ask, "When's Mommy coming home?" Grandma Winnie and Daddy would say, "Tomorrow." For nearly a year, tomorrow came and went, and you never came home. Precious learned not to trust or ask for help.

Precious reached the conclusion you were never coming back. She felt incredibly guilty believing you left because she'd done something wrong with Uncle Mickey. When you finally came home you were a different person. You smoked. Precious felt deeply betrayed. You weren't the Mommy she knew and loved. You were an imposter Mommy who demanded her loving Grandma Winnie to leave. Now, she had lost both her first mother and second mother. Precious felt so ashamed and hurt she vowed never to trust you again.

I call her Precious because she's the most vulnerable, loving, sweet, sensitive, and psychic part of me. Precious fits perfectly Dr. Elaine Aaron's description of a "highly sensitive" person. She feels very deeply, and is quite sensitive to energy and her environment. She led me to BPI, the Berkeley Psychic Institute. Her sensitivity was a supreme intelligence, psychic awareness, and instinctive knowing. Unfortunately, her sensitivity sometimes worked against her. She learned to hate it because being sensitive in her traumatic childhood environment was so painful. She was astutely aware of the dangers around her. I'm grateful she led me to BPI where I learned my sensitivity and psychic abilities were never the problem; the insanity of the situation was the problem.

In addition to not forgiving you, Precious became terrified of happiness and success. She thought no one would ever believe she was molested if I was successful. No one would understand how your institutionalization and mental illness made her feel terribly abused and neglected. I realized Precious was deliberately sabotaging my success because she didn't even want to risk the possibility of making you look good by succeeding. She feared you'd get the credit for her achievements and contentment. People would think Precious must have had a great mother to have turned out so well.

In many ways, Precious reminds me of Smokey, the misdirected part of me that insisted on smoking. Just like Smokey, Precious operated from a false pretense. Precious couldn't see you did love her and worked very hard to get out of Central Islip. You didn't protect her from Uncle Mickey because you didn't have the tools to protect yourself. And, just as I embraced Smokey and coached him to quit smoking, I needed to embrace and coach Precious to quit her addiction to shame and self-sabotage. She required my love and attention to feel safe to shine. I also needed to educate her that being happy was not proof she was never abused. It was proof she loved herself.

I worked with Precious in my morning meditation practice and psychotherapy where she showed up as intermittent left hip pain that had no apparent physical cause. I suspected this hip pain was Precious expressing her fear of success and shame. My experience with Smokey taught me that I needed to make Precious feel acknowledged and loved – all the things she didn't experience during your institutionalization.

I developed many ways to honor Precious. One way was breathing deeply into my belly with one hand on my stomach and the other on my heart. I deemed this breathing practice, "Breathing for Precious." About ten years ago I also declared October 4th as an official day to commemorate her pain. I chose October 4th because it's the Feast of Saint Francis, the day Grandma Winnie died, and near Yom Kippur, the Jewish Feast of Atonement. Each year I faithfully did a memorial service in honor of her pain, and reassured her I totally believed her story. Over the years, I also gently tried to educate her that me loving you, Mom, wasn't a betrayal of her. You always loved us, but you didn't have the tools to express that love and protect us. Precious wasn't receptive to that message. And, here's where the book writing came into play. I promised Precious I'd include the Uncle Mickey incident in our book. Despite being absolutely terrified to go public with that story, I wrote it down knowing Precious would sabotage writing this book if I didn't include it. And that paved the way for a supreme shift in Precious.

Today a miracle occurred. Precious forgave you, a month after I wrote my Uncle Mickey letter. Almost every morning, I lie to next Bob. We hug and breathe with each other. This morning, Bob was lying on his side with one leg bent on top of my tummy. He had one arm resting on my heart with my hand on top of that arm. Bob's other hand rested gently across my forehead. And my other hand was resting on my belly.

I felt warm, protected, and loved as I began my daily morning ritual of breathing deep into my belly to connect with Precious. I imagined myself rescuing Precious after Uncle Mickey attacked her. I saw her on the dining room table passed out. I came over and whispered, "I love you." I took Precious in my arms, and gently hugged her. I also imagined you coming up to us. Precious usually ignores you, but today she was completely different. Precious looked directly into my eyes, and said, "Mommy needs a hug too." I placed Precious in my lap and hugged her with one arm and used my other arm to hug you, Mom. Precious seemed very content with me hugging you, so I felt inspired to take it another step further. I gingerly placed Precious in your lap, Mom. And she hugged you while I hugged both of you from behind. Then, I placed Precious in my lap and had you hug both of us from behind. Precious fell asleep with a smile on her face when I had to end this visualization because I needed to go to work.

Mom, this miracle was reinforced when I attended my psychic meditation group this Sunday, November 13th. The session was about healing the Triad of the child (Precious), the adult (Me), and the parent (you). It reinforced Thursday morning's miraculous visualization with more visualization work that solidified the relationship between all three of us. I shared with my fellow psychics what happened last Thursday morning. I felt so healed by having others witness how Precious had forgiven you. It made Precious' invisible gift of forgiveness more real to me. I plan on continuing to celebrate October 4 in honor of Precious. Now it will be a tribute to her forgiving you and feeling safe to succeed and shine.

November 10 has become my day to celebrate my full integration. Precious was the last hold-out, the only sub-personality who refused to enjoy a fulfilling life. She was the last part of me stuck in the mid-1960s when my life was so desperate. Now she's happy and willing to enjoy success. And, that's a miracle. I never expected her to change her mind, but she did.

This time around it's not my "Declaration of Independence" but rather a "Declaration of Integration" that I'm sharing with you. After years of tuning into my breath instead of tuning out by holding my breath, I am able to process all my love and hate, shame and pride, sorrow and joy, courage and terror, and accept what happened. Forgive myself. Forgive you. Live in the present. Thanks for helping me reach this milestone.

I'm officially replacing my harsh, wildly raw Declaration of Independence audiotape with this Declaration of Integration letter. I noticed you kept my Declaration of Independence audiotape on your bedroom bureau for years, until 2013. You removed it after I helped you grieve Dad's death by staying with you for a week. I interpreted that as a sign you had officially forgiven me for sending that audiotape. I'm so grateful you forgave me when you felt falsely accused of molesting me. Now, I take my visualization of Precious forgiving you last Thursday, November 10, as a sign that I finally forgave you and Uncle Mickey and fully integrated. Integration is so much sweeter and more satisfying than Independence.

Love,
Natazha

Epilogue

These days I write to Precious instead of my Mom. I'm teaching her all about love so she feels safe to shine and quit her addiction to self-sabotage. She's slowly learning what makes love so special. The more love you give away, the more love you have.

I'm grateful I'm not educating Precious all by myself. Bob's devotion to me continues to enlighten her, and Lulu and E-Roy have entered our lives. When I heard of their Mom's suicide last October, my gut performed somersaults. I knew my friend's death would forever change the lives of her ten-year-old daughter, twelve-year-old son, and quadriplegic husband, but never realized how much it would impact Precious and me.

Back then, I felt unfit to help Lulu and E-Roy and asked my sister Gabrielle for help. She's a social worker who specializes in suicide prevention. I told her I cut Lulu's umbilical cord and enjoyed a special bond with her. I wanted to help both kids, but was afraid of E-Roy, who was infamous for throwing wild temper tantrums. I was scared I'd set poor boundaries and get so wrapped up in their woes that it would disrupt my book writing as well as the rest of my life. And I worried about not loving them enough and hurting them.

Gabrielle reassured me, "Natazha, you can only help these kids; you can't possibly hurt them any more than they already have been. Their Mom jumped off the Golden Gate Bridge. You can't top that. What they really need now is honesty, and you're incredibly honest. You're always willing to talk about the elephant in the room. Almost everyone's afraid to talk about the person who committed suicide. You can be that person who asks, 'Do you miss your Mom?' You can invite them to discuss her suicide, months and even years from now. And Natazha, you can set a boundary. Explain up front you can only be Lulu's big sister. You can't be a big brother to E-Roy."

Despite Gabrielle's pep talk, after attending their Mom's funeral in October, I never saw them in November. I inadvertently ran into them at a holiday gathering in December. In January I visited them in their cramped studio condo just around the corner from our home. The instant I entered their home I felt like I was drowning in a sea of unspoken sorrow. I stayed for only an hour and came home utterly exhausted, and napped for two hours. I waited a month to visit them again. That time I recovered with just a one-hour nap.

In March I began taking Lulu on excursions every other week. We wrote in journals, strolled all over the city, and chatted in my living room while drawing pictures. I told Lulu, "I saw you get born. Your Mom was so happy to see you. She absolutely loved you, but she had a big problem with loving herself."

Every time I dropped Lulu at her home, E-Roy would complain, "Why do you only take her? How come you never take me?"

I'd look him in the eye and say, "I'm a girl and can only be a Big Sister. I can't be your Big Brother. Ask your Dad to get you a Big Brother." Weeks went by and I continued taking only Lulu out, and answered E-Roy's protests by repeating, "Ask for a Big Brother."

When Easter rolled around, I told Lulu she could choose from these options: going to Golden Gate Park, the San Francisco Museum of Modern Art, or Mass at Saint Patrick's. Lulu loves the museum, so I was surprised when she picked Mass.

Easter was a wet, dreary day, and yet we enjoyed the mile walk to Saint Patrick's church. Mass was so crowded that at first we stood outside on the front steps of the church. We eventually made our way to the back of the church where I hugged Lulu from behind, the same way my Grandma Winnie held me as a little girl. Lulu melted in my arms. I ached as I sensed how much she needed my comfort and affection. Her quadriplegic Dad can't hug her and teachers these days don't dare touch their students.

As we inhaled and exhaled together I felt her grief more deeply and realized attending Mass was a special time she shared with her Mom, just as 5:00 pm weekday Mass was a special time with my Mom when I was her age. When it came time to receive communion Lulu turned around and whispered, "I really, really want to make my First Holy Communion." The way she said it made me weep. Most kids make this sacrament at seven years old, so at 10 years old Lulu had already waited three years. I suspected her Mom's mental illness had gotten in the way.

That night I asked Lulu's Dad, "Has Lulu ever told you she wants to receive her First Holy Communion?"

He replied, "She's wanted to do it for years. But her Mom and godmother let her down." In that moment, I had no idea how the hell I was going to make it happen, but I vowed to help Lulu make her First Holy Communion.

The next day, I asked one of my patients if she could help Lulu. She answered, "Yes, let me talk to Deacon Dan." A month later Deacon Dan agreed to give Lulu private lessons to receive both First Holy Communion and Confession.

When I phoned her Dad and told him about Deacon Dan, he insisted both Lulu and E-Roy make their First Holy Communion. I retorted, "I asked Deacon Dan to train only one child, not two. And why are you bringing up E-Roy now? I've never heard him express any interest in receiving communion. How do I know he really wants to do this?"

Her Dad firmly responded, "It's both kids, or no kids."

I hung up, pissed at him and determined to have only Lulu get trained. That night I stewed in my resentment. I imagined E-Roy wrecking the training by throwing temper tantrums and replayed the incidents in which one of my siblings misbehaved so badly everyone in our family lost a privilege. I thought about how Lulu would resent sharing my attention with E-Roy.

A few days later in my early-morning meditation, I breathed directly into my heart. I suddenly realized *E-Roy also lost his Mom and I deeply regretted repeatedly rejecting him in a time of need.*

The next day I apologized to him, "I'm so sorry, E-Roy. Both you and Lulu lost your Mom. It's true I can't be a Big Brother for you, but I can mother you. I feel awful about excluding you. I'm so glad you're joining us to receive First Holy Communion."

E-Roy graciously accepted my apology. He never held a grudge. The training went quite well. E-Roy asked lots of questions and enjoyed debating with Deacon Dan. They received their First Holy Communion on August 26, 2017. After the ceremony E-Roy asked to sign up for Confirmation classes.

Participating in their religious training enlightened me. It solidified the psychic shift that occurred when I wrote this book. I received many more epiphanies when we discussed the concept of original sin. It further clarified for me the interplay between breathing, shame, and maintaining boundaries.

Growing up, the concept of original sin was a source of shame. I learned I was born flawed by an indelible stain on my soul. Rabbi Harold Kushner helped me heal that shame by offering a different interpretation of original sin in his book, *How Good Do We Have to Be?* Kushner defines original sin as the belief that there isn't enough love to go around. And that belief leads to more sinning because we feel when someone else is loved he or she is stealing that love from us.

Lulu's and E-Roy's training made me realize I was wrong to assume Lulu would be jealous when E-Roy joined us. She was happy about it. I was also wrong to believe that I didn't possess enough love for both of them. I actually have limitless love, more than enough for the both of them. However, I do have limited time and energy. That's why I need to set boundaries on how I express my love.

Preparing them to receive First Holy Communion was a concrete task that cued me to set boundaries based around accomplishing that goal. I scheduled a weekly meeting for their religious training, served along with a meal. Their progress on this goal left me feeling that I had "loved them enough."

Kushner's perspective enabled me to better understand why Precious had hated my Mom so much. Why Precious erroneously believed my Mom never loved her and became afraid to shine. That's when I began writing letters to Precious to teach her *there's always enough love to go around. Love has no boundaries. However, we are human beings in a body limited by time and space, so how we express our love does require setting boundaries. And, we maintain our boundaries by minding our breath to notice when they've been violated.*

Dear Precious,

I'm so sorry you felt terrified and abandoned growing up. I now get it: you felt Mommy didn't have enough love for all her kids. You believed you had to compete for her love. Earn it. Be perfect by getting straight As. Be hardworking by doing the most household chores. Be her confidante by listening to her complain about Daddy.

Of course you were hurt and resentful when you got the best grades, did the most chores, and had listened to her complaints. And after doing all that, Mommy still didn't give you her attention. That must have been horribly painful for you. I hope you now see Mommy didn't hate you. She was just following a completely different set of rules, the rules of crisis management. She tended to the most needy, troubled kids and neglected the more self-sufficient and successful kids.

I now better understand why you were so afraid of success. On top of making Mommy look good, shining resulted in getting neglected. You got passed over for siblings in distress. What a double bind! You felt compelled to succeed to earn Mommy's love and yet punished for succeeding by getting ignored.

Oh, Precious, I so wish I could go back in time and hold you on my lap. Hug you tightly. Read out loud your favorite books.

Sing lullabies to you. Bake butter cookies with you. Stroll through the gardens at the Bayard Cutting Arboretum and smell the pretty flowers. Although I couldn't do it then, I imagine doing all those things with you now. I also breathe in your honor as much as possible.

Please know both Mommy and I have always loved you, but we messed up on expressing our love. I apologize for ignoring you for years. I'm sorry for all the times I tried to bully you into forgiving Mommy before you were ready to reconcile with her. I was being a big fat meanie to you.

Precious, I'm not betraying you when I love Uncle Mickey and Mommy. Because they're our ancestors, they are part of us. When I grieve for them, I'm grieving for you too. I'm very sad Uncle Mickey was so wounded that the only way he could express his pain was to molest his niece and grandniece. He couldn't express his suffering with his words or by attending therapy.

Mommy was so wounded 50 years ago she didn't defend you from him. You are absolutely right; it's unacceptable to not protect kids against pedophiles. But, please realize Mommy did change. She had the courage to stay in therapy where she learned to defend herself and children. She never stopped loving us, even when she expressed her love poorly. That includes neglecting you and not consoling you after Uncle Mickey attacked you. I hope you now believe Mommy did always love us and still loves us from afar.

I want to teach you, "There's always more than enough love." You don't have to earn my or Bob's love. When you're scared, we will love you. When you make mistakes, we will love you. We will always love you.

Here's one way Bob shows his love for us. Despite promising at least a thousand times to not leave the bedroom door open in the early morning, every once in awhile I leave that door ajar. Then the kitchen light wakes up Bob. He's forgiven me hundreds of times. I'll keep trying to close the door tightly. I'm not certain I'll succeed, but I am certain Bob will forgive me. It's one of the many ways he shows his boundless love for us.

I'm here for you, too. I love you through my breathing. I now hold you with my breath rather than hold my breath to ignore you. As you grew to trust me more, I felt more worthy of setting boundaries that keep love in and shame out. I vow to express my love for you as much as humanly possible so you feel safe to shine.

Love,
Natazha

Acknowledgements

I feel blessed for all the help I received writing this book. Thank you from the bottom of my heart and lungs to the countless people who supported my book writing.

- I never could have written this book without the love and support of my husband, Bob, along with the rest of my tribe and loved ones.
- Thank you Lisa Nichols and Reverend David McArthur for strongly encouraging me to attend Tom Bird's "How-to-Write-Your-Book-in-a-Weekend" retreat.
- I'm grateful for the great assistance and wisdom I received from Tom Bird and his crew: Sabrina Fritts, John Hodgkinson, Mary Stevenson, Denise Cassino, David Thalberg, and Bill Worth.
- Thank you Curt Fukada, Stephanie Hines, Igor Mitrovic, Auntie Pat, and Gail Pucci for your feedback on my first draft of this book.
- I so appreciate the folks at Choice Digital Marketing: Dusty Meehan, Megan Stauffer, and Christian Pederson. In addition to creating an awesome website and book cover, they held a vision of this book helping many people learn to rescue themselves with their breathing
- I feel honored to be part of the Dolphin Swimming and Rowing Club community. In my case it took a village of athletes to raise a writer.
- I'm grateful to my Monday night meditation group. They helped me explore how my breathing and boundaries interact as well as the works of Pema Chodron and Brené Brown.
- And of course, I want to thank my Mom. I breathe in honor of everyone who participated in my journey, especially my Mom.

Made in the USA
San Bernardino, CA
13 November 2017